Bidding
for the
General
Contractor

Paul J. Cook

Illustrations by
Carl W. Linde

©Copyright 1985

To obtain additional information concerning
Means products referenced in this manual please contact:

R. S. Means Company, Inc.
Construction Consultants & Publishers
100 Construction Plaza
Kingston, MA 02364
617-747-1270

Library of Congress Catalog Card Number Pending
ISBN: 0-911950-77-X

Preface

The hope of all bidders is to procure construction contracts. Since most contracts go to the lowest bidders, competition is keen. In the construction industry, *low bid* usually means *contract*. Observations of bid results provide statistical proof that low bids tend to be random among bidders, and this points to the probability that certain strategies can improve a bidder's chances of producing low bids.

Since bidding is an ongoing activity, a routine procedure makes the job easier, guards against slip-ups, relieves some of the stress, and delivers excellent bid packages on a continuing basis. The routine procedures described in this book are typical of well-organized bidders. Not much can be done to improve the method, but improvements in the skill of the bidder are possible through practice and hard work.

The degree of hard work invested in the bidding activity is a matter of company policy. One bidder may spare no effort in detailing and planning to minimize follow-up work, while another bidder may simplify the bidding work by leaving as many details as possible to later "field decisions." Both positions are arguable and defendable. Most bidding efforts fall between these extremes, depending on available time, bidding environment, personnel, and the need for work.

Competition can be fierce. The intensity of competition depends upon three factors: (1) the number of competing bidders, (2) the number and type of construction projects currently available, and (3) the economic conditions, both current and prospective. Fluctuations in the economy and the resulting behavior of competitors constitute the *environment* of the bidder.

In good economic times or bad, the company's need for work exerts more influence than most other factors on the quantity and quality of its bidding effort. The ideal of the bidder is to maintain a steady flow of new contracts in a quantity and dollar value never so low nor so high as to put the company at a disadvantage with the competition. This ideal is, of course, easier to write about than to accomplish, but it is theoretically possible and well worth the effort.

Table
of Contents

Part I
The Bidding
Procedure

Part II
Bidding
Techniques
and Strategies

Part III
Bidding A
Project

Part IV
Project
Management
(Bidding Follow-up)

Part V
Appendixes

Part 1
The Bidding Procedure

1.1
Introduction and Viewpoint

This book focuses on the process of bidding for the general construction (prime) contract. The related subjects of quantity surveying, cost estimating, project superintending, and construction company management are too extensive for inclusion in this book. Each of those departments of a construction organization deserves a separate volume.

To clarify the scope of this book, the focal point, and the parameters, Fig. 1.1a schematically portrays from beginning to end the organization of a construction project.

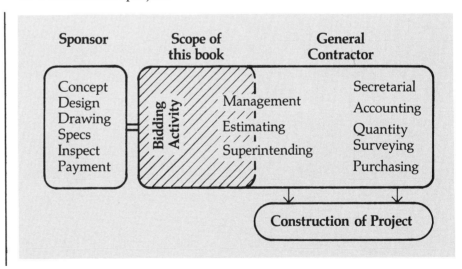

Figure 1.1a

To aid the visualization, let us divide the construction company into departments. The bidder's role is shown overlapping the adjacent activities of estimating, supervising, and business management.

The bidder attempts to select projects, to put together bids, and to procure contracts suitable to the needs of the company. In the process the bidder is personally involved in all departments and activities of the business. In the typical construction company, bidding is not a department; it is an *activity* in which all office personnel participate to various degrees, upon demand.

The term "bidder," as used throughout this book, means the person who has charge of the entire operation of a bid. The term may also occasionally refer to the company represented by that person. For the

meanings of other terms, see Appendix U.

Part I of this book outlines briefly the bidding procedures. Part II goes into greater depth, explaining strategies, techniques, principles, theories, and conditions that shape the bidding process. Part III presents an imaginary construction project and takes the reader step-by-step through the bidding. Part IV deals with project management (follow-up). Part V serves as an Appendix for reference data.

If it can be called a science at all, bidding is at best a theoretical science. It is a technology in that it uses techniques to simplify, to guard against errors, to improve speed and efficiency, and to produce relatively dependable levels of contractual agreements.

Bidding deals with a multiplicity of variables, i.e., the bidder makes a series of many choices. The bidder makes these choices guided by convention, experience, personal preferences and values.

The bidder's personal role in the company, whether owner, corporate officer, manager, or estimator, provides a viewpoint that produces a measurable effect upon the bid. The bidder's personality greatly affects the bid, by such traits as idealism, aggressiveness, or conservatism. These influences, however, tend to dissipate as a bidder accumulates experience. Any treatise on the subject of bidding must take into account the fact that many inexperienced bidders are active in the industry, learning the hard way and "winning" a great number of contracts at unnecessarily low prices. Evidence points to the probability that organizations can and often do fail because of poor bidding.

Figure 1.1b shows the complex relationship of the departments within a construction company, the projects in process of construction (A and B), and a new project in the process of bidding. The bidder (shaded area) receives a great volume of data for processing into the bid package for the project, depicted as C (see Sec. 1.2, the Bid Package).

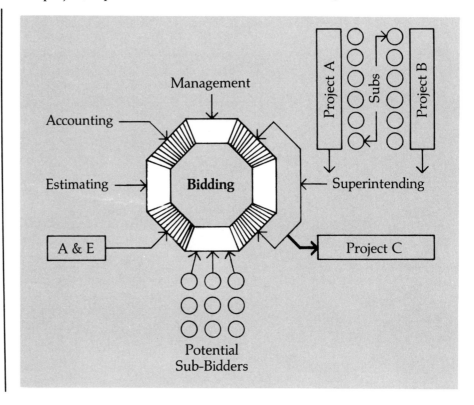

Figure 1.1b

The initial bid documents with drawings and specs are supplied by the A&E. Further communication between bidder and the A&E is minimal and formal, consisting of legal changes or clarifications to the bid documents by written addenda.

Within the construction company the bidder communicates with and draws from the various department's personnel the necessary data for the current bidding effort. The data flows almost entirely in one direction, i.e., to the bidder, who receives, analyzes, selects, and "puts the bid together."

Data, as well as assistance, is provided by interdepartmental cooperation in the bidding activity. The management, the accounting, the secretarial, the estimating, and the project supervisory staffs all contribute. Records from completed projects are also an excellent source of data. Projects currently in progress at this location (projects A and B) may supply data on labor costs, proven waste factors, and specific subcontractors' performances.

The proximity of subcontractors working on these projects makes them a convenient source of specialty information. The pool of subcontractors in the geographical area of the proposed project, C, although they have no current contract with the bidder's organization, are potential sub-bidders, analyzers of the project, and consultants to the bidders.

Since the term "bidder" personifies the construction company, we need a counterpart for the owner/A&E. Let us use the term "sponsor." The sponsor may be an individual, a partnership, a corporation, or a branch of government (federal, state, county, city). The term includes the architect, the engineer, and all other services that contribute to the creation of the bid documents.

1.2
The Bid Package

A construction bid is an *offer* to perform specific work and/or duties in return for a specified price. In this definition, "construction" means to assemble a variety of materials in order to bring about the physical reality of an architectural or engineering design. The "price" is usually an amount of money stipulated by the bidder in the bid proposal form. Since this amount is almost entirely compensation for the contractor's expenditures for labor, material, and equipment, the important figure is the small margin estimated for profit (see Sec. 1.10, Bond and Markup and Sec. 2.6, A Reasonable Profit).

A bid that meets the above definition in every respect is a *valid* bid, but not necessarily a *good* bid (see Sec. 2.8, A Good Bid).

The total bid package consists of two main parts: the sponsor's part and the bidder's part. The portion developed by the sponsor and given to the bidder is incomplete. It is the bidder's job to complete the package. Figure 1.2a itemizes a typical bid package.

Sponsor's Contributions

Drawings The graphic portrayal of the sponsor's concept, consisting of site location and improvement plans, architectural plans and details, structural plans and details, and mechanical and electrical plans and details.

Project manual The essential written information that cannot be effectively shown graphically and is complimentary to and inseparable from the drawings. The project manual should consist of:

1. Advertisement (invitation to bid)

Figure 1.2a

2. Requirements
    a. Instruction to bidders
    b. Bid forms
    c. Bond forms
    d. Experience qualification forms
    e. Contract form (agreement)
3. Standard clauses
    a. Labor laws
    b. Miscellaneous laws, rules, regulations
    c. Taxes, permits, licenses, inspections
4. General and special conditions
    a. Environmental protection
    b. Temporary facilities and utilities
5. Technical specifications pertaining to the various trades and sub-trades.

Bidder's Contributions

1. Bid bond
2. Experience qualification forms, filled in
3. Site investigation check sheet, filled in
4. Quantity survey sheets
5. Cost estimate price out sheets
6. Tentative progress schedule
7. All correspondence and telephone messages
8. All sub-bid quotations
9. Sub-bid analysis sheets
10. Bid spread sheet
11. Completed bid forms.

Figure 1.2a (cont.)

The bidder alone processes and retains the complete bid package. The estimates, cost sources, sub-bids, and bidding techniques are confidential. Each bidder begins with the same information (the sponsor's portion in Fig. 1.2a) and develops a complete bid package.

After distributing identical bid documents to the prospective bidders, the sponsor waits on the sidelines until all of the completed bid forms are returned. The sponsor may then accept one of them as the basis for a contract. (For a definition of "contract," see Part IV, Project Management.)

1.3 Ability, Motivation, and Objective

The essence of a *valid* bid, as defined in the preceding section, is the ability of the bidder (construction company) to fulfill the terms of the intended contract satisfactorily. A bidder whose ability is not known to a particular sponsor may be required to show proof of ability before submitting a bid. More often, a bidder may be required to fill in certain forms that are an integral part of the bid package (see Appendix C for example forms). These forms are designed to elicit facts to support the following qualifications.

Factual Information	Indicated Ability
Licenses	Professional
Credit	Financial
Contracts completed	Technical
Company officers	Managerial
Equipment	Physical
Bid bond (loosely implies all of the above)	

Except for the bid bond, a bidder is not always required to show proof of ability with every bid. Proof shown in the first bid to a particular

sponsor may serve for all subsequent bids. Some sponsors, assuming that the bid bond is tentative assurance of the bidder's ability, confine the consideration of further proof to the low bidder in post-bidding procedure.

The primary *motivation* of the bidder is the need for a job (contract). This may be an acute need, or merely a desire on the company's part to work up to its full current capacity (that is, the maximum volume of contracts the company can perform without having to increase its overhead). The degree of need is an important factor in the rating of a project for desirability (see Sec. 1.4, Analyzing a Project for Desirability).

Following are some specific motivations for getting a job:

1. When a bid invitation comes directly and personally from a sponsor's agent whose goodwill is desired. A doubtful alternative is "complimentary bidding."
2. When contracts are plentiful and there is little slack in the company's work capacity, a motivation may still exist for the following reasons:
   a. To keep from losing contact with market trends due to prolonged absence from bidding activity.
   b. To keep the active relationship with suppliers that is essential to a competitive position.
3. When an unusually desirable project becomes available. The bidder's *objective* is twofold: to procure a contract and to procure it at a profit, (see Sec. 2.6, A Reasonable Profit). Procurement alone is relatively easy. Procurement at a profit, however, becomes very difficult, (see Sec. 2.3, Probability of Low Bid).

The bidder's and the sponsor's motivations and objectives are related and complimentary:

Bidder Wants	Sponsors Wants
The contract	The lowest possible bid
Speedy completion	The earliest possible use
Cooperation and harmony	Compliance
Good profit	Quality work
Goodwill	Conscientious performance
Prompt payment	Follow-up corrections

In practice, most problems arise (1) from differing interpretations of drawings, specs, and quality standards, (2) from personality conflicts, and (3) from malfunctions in manufacturing schedules, material supply, and subcontractor performance.

Beyond the immediate objective, a bid leading to a contract, the bidder's long-range objective is a continuous procurement of well-spaced and profitable contracts resulting in steady company profit (see Sec. 2.6, A Reasonable Profit).

1.4 Analyzing a Project for Desirability

Assuming that the bidder has ability, motivation, and a clear objective, as described in the preceding section, the next step is to choose the best project on which to bid. The number of projects available is always limited, and the desirability of a project is a judgment that varies according to the differing viewpoint of each competing bidder. Bid dates (deadlines), dollar size, site locations, type of construction, and so on are conditions that affect the immediate choice. They continue to influence any deeper analysis that may follow.

Analysis of the project serves three purposes: (1) to reach a decision on whether or not to bid, (2) to determine the degree of effort and competitiveness to apply if the decision is affirmative, and (3) to establish the amount of the final markup for profit.

In reality, a bidder performs this analysis, referred to hereafter as a project's *d-rating*, or desirability rating, somewhat intuitively and with little conscious deliberation. A few typical conditions are:

1. Size (cost of the project in dollars)
2. Location of project (distance of the project from the home office)
3. Sponsor relation
4. Type of construction
5. Probable competitiveness
6. Labor market
7. Subcontractor market
8. Quality of drawings and specifications
9. Quality of supervision
10. Special risks
11. Completion time and penalty
12. Estimating and bidding time
13. Need for work
14. Other special advantages or disadvantages

If all these conditions were positive, the project would be highly desirable, the bidding competitive, and the markup minimal. If most of these conditions were negative, the project would be less desirable, the bidding conservative, and the markup maximum.

The markup (see Sec. 1.10, Bond and Markup) is a variable that helps to compensate for the strengths or weaknesses of a project, as summarized in its d-rating. For instance, Fig. 1.4a shows two projects of equal size with different d-ratings. The increased markup tends to make project A more desirable. And yet, if the theory expressed in Sec. 2.3 is correct, it should not seriously decrease competitiveness, since other bidders should also make similar compensations for the obvious differences.

	Basic Cost ($)	D-Rating	Markup (%)	Additional Cost ($)
Project A	4,200,000	78	* 10.2	428,400
Project B	4,200,000	88	* 9.0	378,000
		* Percentages taken from Fig. 2.6k		

Figure 1.4a

Figure 1.4b graphically portrays the principle.

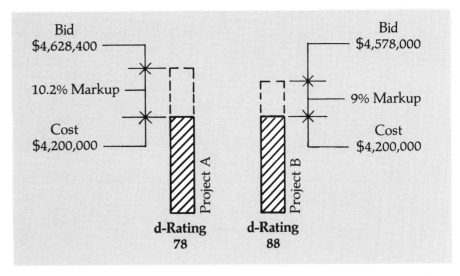

Figure 1.4b

If both projects were equal in d-ratings, the markups and bids would be equal. The d-rating works both ways, to raise or to lower a bid relative to some arbitrary average. It is thus a realistic aspect of good bidding practice.

Let us now examine each of the previously named conditions. We cannot expect them to be of equal weight, so there should be different rules for each. Let us reserve all numbers on the 0-100 scale below 30 and above 90 for very exceptional conditions, in order to give them additional impact in the final averaging.

1. *Size of project.* The ideal size is that which will fill up the company's unused bonding capacity (see Sec. 2.7, Bonding and the Reasons for Bonding Capacity). If, for instance, a company has a nominal bonding capacity of $20,000,000 and $12,000,000 of uncompleted work on hand, then an $8 million project would be an ideal size for bidding.

Let us rate projects for size between the two following extremes:

Ideal size	90
Smaller than ideal	50

2. *Location of project.* For the distance of the project from the home office, suggested values are:

Less than 5 miles	90
More than 30 miles	60

3. *Sponsor relations.* Experienced bidders know that the efficiency and cooperativeness of the sponsor's agents contribute to the desirability rating of a project and can influence the decision of the bidder on whether to bid or not. Suggested values are:

Known good relations	90
Unknown	70
Known poor relations	50

4. *Type of construction.* As a rule, a contractor is not equally experienced and capable in all types of construction, such as structural concrete, precast concrete, wood frame, steel frame, high-rise, or heavy engineering. The type of construction in which the company excels is the most desirable to a bidder and determines the rating between the following extremes:

Experienced in this type	90
Not experienced in this type	60

5. *Probable.* The bidder looks with less favor on those projects that attract a large number of bidders and excessive competition. This aspect of a project can carry a lot of weight, with values suggested as follows:

Light competition	90
Strong competition	60

6. *Labor market conditions.* Projects located in areas where there are an insufficient number of skilled workmen are of low desirability to bidders. Suggested values are:

Good quality and plentiful	90
Poor quality and few	60

7. *Subcontract market conditions.* The quantity and quality of available local subcontractors parallels that of workmen, and the suggested values are:

Good quality and plentiful	90
Poor quality and few	60

8. *Quality of drawings and specifications.* Quality is not a heavy factor, but it does affect the desirability of a project. Suggested values are:

Good quality	90
Poor quality	70

9. *Quality of supervision.* When the identity of the superintendent is known and of proven excellence, the project is more desirable to the bidder. An unknown superintendent, or one of mediocre ability, is a negative influence in the d-rating. The following values are suggested:

Known top quality	90
Unknown	80
Known mediocre quality	70

10. *Special risks.* Conditions such as solid rock, subsurface water, high altitude, extreme heat or cold, possibility of collapse, cave-in, etc., all affect the desirability rating. Depending on the degree of risk, values may be scaled between:

No known risk	90
Extreme risk	30

11. *Completion time and penalty.* When the time provided in the bid documents to complete the construction is extremely short and the penalty for delay is very high, the project loses desirability to the bidder. Values are:

Time sufficient and penalty low	90
Time sufficient and penalty high	60

12. *Estimating and bidding time.* If the bidder is not given sufficient time to put the bid together, a low level of desirability is assigned to the project. This condition might also exist because of the coincidence of two projects bidding on or near the same date. Values are:

Sufficient time to bid	90
Insufficient time to bid	50

13. *Need for work.* This condition could carry more weight than any of the others. If extreme, the bidder's need for work might reverse an otherwise unfavorable d-rating. Suggested values are:

Extreme need for work	100
Normal need	85
Very little need	50

14. *Other special advantages or disadvantages.* A bidder might have special incentives, positive or negative, such as the exclusive possession of a stockpile of materials. Or the bidder might have knowledge of a competitor's possession of such an advantage. The weight for this condition can vary considerably, but if there are no special advantages or disadvantages, an average value may be used, as follows:

Strong advantages	100
Average	80
Strong disadvantages	25

In a similar way, but with fewer facts, the bidder roughly analyzes the competition's probable degree of interest in the project. The result may cause a further final adjustment in the bidder's own evaluation.

Figure 1.4c is an example of a hypothetical project rated for desirability.

Figure 1.4c

1. Size of project in dollars	90
2. Location of project (distance from home office)	90
3. Owner, architect, inspector (sponsor) relations	80
4. Type of construction (experienced or not)	90
5. Competition	80
6. Labor market	75
7. Subcontractor market	80
8. Quality of drawings and specifications	85
9. Quality of supervision	90
10. Special risks	25
11. Completion time and liquidated damages	85
12. Time to estimate and bid	80
13. Need of a job (contract)	100
14. Other	85
	1,135

$$\frac{1,135}{14} = 81.07 \text{ average}$$

Two extremes are shown: special risk and need for work. These two exceptional conditions tend to balance one another and make the project of average desirability, according to the following scale:

Very desirable	85 to 90
Average	80 to 85
Undesirable	Below 80

Remember, a project may be made more desirable by an increase in the markup and by contingency allowances (see Sec. 2.19, Submitting the Bid).

1.5 Preliminary Steps in Bidding

Up to this point in the bidding process, we have that portion of the bid package provided by the sponsor. We have also given the project a d-rating. To complete the bid package, we should proceed as follows:

Step 1: Request a bid bond. The surety company that supplies bidders with construction bonds will need the following information:
  a. Project name, description, and name of sponsor
  b. The size of the project in dollars
  c. The bid date
  d. The completion time in calendar days

e. The rate to be assessed for liquidation damages
f. A report on the status of uncompleted work on hand

It is good practice to obtain a commitment from the surety as soon as possible, especially if the size of the project approaches the theoretical bonding capacity (see Sec. 2.7, Bonding and the Reasons for Bonding Capacity). A promise of bond from the surety clears the way for the huge investments in time, energy, and capital that go into the bidding.

Step 2: Take note of significant miscellaneous conditions. Check the time, cost, legal, and formal requirements in the bidding procedure and in the subsequent construction of the project. Typical miscellaneous conditions are:
   a. The bid schedule, whether in the form of a single lump sum or a breakdown of prices
   b. The exact time and place for the submission of the bid
   c. The identity and telephone number of the sponsor's representative to whom questions are to be directed
   d. The date and time of pre-bid conference, if any
   e. Special instruction regarding environmental protection
   f. The prevailing pay scales for workmen, including fringe benefits and subsistence
   g. Phasing of the construction work and the probability of overtime work
   h. Equal opportunity clauses
   i. Material testing, inspection, and quality control provisions
   j. Percentage of the work to be performed by the prime contractor (not sublet)

Step 3: Advertise as a prospective bidder. Placing the bidder's company name on published lists of prospective bidders is the best way to contact the unknown prospective sub-bidders, material suppliers, and manufacturers. The bidder should inspect the published list of prospective bidders to ensure that the company is in fact properly identified, with the correct address and phone number. Errors in this regard can block the flow of essential sub-bids, and thus be fatal to successful bidding.

Step 4: Research the cost of materials. Search for sources and prices of critical, scarce, or hard to get materials, equipment, and subcontract items. This effort may require correspondence, phone calls, and personal contacts.

These activities absorb the full time span from receipt of the sponsor's bid package to the bid deadline. Therefore, it is a good idea to start immediately! Early discussions with special suppliers provide an opportunity to clarify potential problems, such as compliance with the specs, delivery schedules, taxes, and inclusions and exclusions (see Sec. 2.13, Researching for Sub-Bid Coverage).

Step 5: Inspect the jobsite. Since the bidder's main activity is the compiling of sub-bids, it is advisable to investigate the jobsite in order to establish a factual basis for analysis and discussion with the sub-bidders. Some typical site conditions to look for are:
   a. Structures to be removed or protected
   b. Paving, curbs, and fences to be removed
   c. Trees, brush, grass, and weeds to be removed
   d. Accessibility to the jobsite
   e. Working, storage, and parking space
   f. Earth borrow and disposal areas
   g. Sources of power and water
   h. Soil conditions (hardness, etc.)

i. Water conditions, both surface and underground

For more discussion of these factors, see Sec. 2.11, Jobsite Investigations.

Step 6: Research prospective sub-bidders. The purpose here is to determine the reliability and competitiveness of subs and suppliers (see Sec. 2.13, Researching for Sub-Bid Coverage). A second purpose is to alert interested subs in major trades to begin work, as the time to prepare estimates and bids is limited. A later, more intensive inquiry should be made a few days before the bid deadline to check with undecided subs.

1.6 Reviewing the Estimate

After completing the preliminary steps discussed in the previous section, the project is given to the estimating department to perform the quantity surveying and pricing out of labor, materials, and equipment. For a complete presentation of this work the reader is referred to the book, *Estimating For the General Contractor*, by this author and published by R.S. Means Company, Inc.

The bidder consults regularly with the estimating staff so that problems may be resolved and decisions made promptly. The estimating work is confined to those trades that the company performs directly and does not sublet. The only exceptions to this rule are certain strategic reasons (see Sec. 2.14, Budgets, Plug-in Figures, and Allowances).

To be competitive, the estimator's work should be as objective as possible in order to provide a sound foundation for the bid. The estimated cost of the general contractor's own work may be a minor part of the total bid amount, but its accuracy is vital to the success or failure of the bid, as well as to profit or loss.

In Fig. 1.6a, Chart A is an example of a typical building project composed of only 20% prime contractor work and 70% subcontractor work. Chart B is an example of a project composed of 60% prime contractor and 25% subcontractor work. Chart C is an example of a project composed entirely of subcontractor work ("brokered"). The risk of financial loss increases proportionately with the percentage of prime contractual work and justifies a compensation in the amount of the markup, as shown in the three charts. An excessively large percentage of prime contract work, as in chart B, is an example of "special risk," as described in Sec. 1.4, Analyzing a Project for Desirability. Consequently, the bidder strives to maximize the subletting of portions of the project.

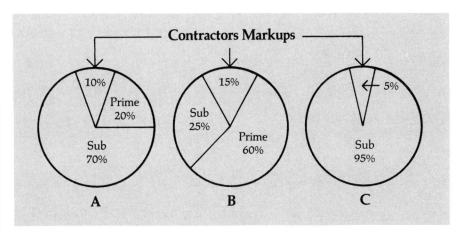

Figure 1.6a

From the bidder's viewpoint, a completely subcontracted project, as in Chart C, is theoretically most desirable. Items affecting the decision of whether or not to subcontract include:

1. One or more trades may be highly specialized and outside the scope of the prime contractor's ability or legal qualifications.
2. Subletting may be more economical, due to specialist's efficiency.
3. In general the goodwill of subcontractors is preserved by the practice of subletting to them rather than competing with them.
4. The contract documents may limit the bidder to a specific percentage of subcontract work to prevent "brokering" of the project, which sponsors tend to regard as a weakening of prime contractor responsibility.

The exact determination of the prime/sub ratio cannot be made at the beginning of the bidding procedure. A judgment of the ratio is made during the composition of the estimate summary sheet. (Fig. 1.6b is an example of a summarized project manual.) A summary sheet is the basic tool in the estimating and bidding procedures and serves the following purposes:

1. Provided in Figure 1.6b is a breakdown of the project into trades and elements according to the way they will probably be quoted by subs and suppliers. For convenience, and to help define the scopes of sub-bids, the specification section numbers are referenced in the extreme left column. It is expected, ideally, that subs will cover an entire section—no more, no less. Exceptions to this rule are provided for in the bid spread sheet (see Sec. 1.7, The Bid Spread Sheet).
2. Identification of the scope of work under alternative bids and the trades affected.
3. A preliminary decision regarding:
   a. Trades and work items to be figured in detail by the estimator
   b. Portions of the project to be budgeted as alternative to sub-bids
   c. Trades and items that will be left entirely to sub-bidders

Figure 1.6b is a form custom-made by the bidder, in cooperation with the estimating department, for a particular project. A standard from is used by some bidders for convenience and efficiency. (Two standard forms by R.S. Means Company are provided in Appendix F.)

ESTIMATE SUMMARY SHEET

Project __Science Lab__   Bid Date __9/18/84__

Location __Long Beach, CA__   Calendar Days to Complete __600__

Spec. Section		Base Bid	Alt. No. 1	Alt. No. 2	Distribution
01100	General conditions	X	—	—	Ⓔ
02050	Demolition	X	Add	—	Ⓔ,ⒷS
02200	Earthwork	X	Add	—	ⒷS
02400	Asphalt concrete paving	X	Add	—	S
02450	Chain link fence	X	Add	—	S
02480	Irrigation & landscaping	—	X	—	S
03100	Cast-in-place concrete	X	Add	—	Ⓔ
03200	Reinforcing steel	X	Add	—	S
04200	Masonry	X	Add	—	S
05100	Structural & misc. metal	X	Add	—	Ⓔ,ⒸS
06100	Carpentry & millwork	X	—	—	Ⓔ,S
07100	Roofing & roof insulation	X	—	—	S
07200	Wall & ceiling insulation	X	—	—	S
07600	Sheet metal work	X	Add	—	S
07900	Caulking & sealants	X	—	—	ⒷS
08100	Finish hardware	X	—	—	ⒺS
08200	Metal doors & frames	X	—	—	ⒺS
08500	Metal windows & glazing	X	—	—	S
08700	Steel overhead doors	X	—	—	S
09100	Painting & wall covering	X	Add	—	S
09200	Ceramic tile	—	—	Add	S
09300	Lathing & plastering	X	—	—	S
09400	Metal framing & gyp. bd.	X	—	—	S
09500	Resilient flooring	X	—	Deduct	S
09600	Carpeting	—	—	Add	S
09700	Acoustical tile	X	—	—	S
09800	Glazed wall coating	X	—	Deduct	S
10100	Toilet partitions	X	—	—	S
10200	Building specialties	X	—	—	ⒺS
10300	Portable partitions	X	—	—	S
11100	Adjustable loading ramp	X	—	—	S
11600	Dental casework & equip.	X	—	—	ⒸS
12100	Fixed theater seats	X	—	—	S
13100	Radiation protection	X	—	—	ⒸS
13200	Walk-in refrigerator	X	—	—	S
13300	Integrated ceiling	X	—	—	S
14200	Hydraulic elevator	X	—	—	S
15000	Mechanical	X	—	Add	ⒸS
16000	Electrical	X	—	Deduct	ⒸS

X = basic prices; **Add** or **Deduct** = dollar amounts to be added or taken away from the basic prices for work under the alternative bids; Ⓔ = items to be figured by the estimator; Ⓑ = items to be budgeted; S = items or trades to be quoted by subs;

Ⓒ = critical items or trades that will receive special personal attention from the bidder.

Figure 1.6b

Section 1.1, Introduction and Viewpoint, depicts in Figs. 1.1a and 1.1b the participation of all permanent employees of the company in the bidding activity. Duties and responsibilities are delegated through the estimate summary sheet. The example in Fig. 1.6b separates as follows:

Portion of Project	Delegated To
To be accurately estimated: Trade or work items marked Ⓔ in the right-hand column; general conditions; selected portions of demolition; concrete work; installation of miscellaneous metal; carpentry; installation of millwork; installation of finish hardware; installation of metal door and frames; installation of building specialties	Estimator
To be budgeted for comparison to sub-bids: Trades or work items marked Ⓑ in the right-hand column; portion of demolition; earthmoving; caulking and sealants	Estimator
To be routinely investigated by mail or telephone for probability of sub-bids: All trades marked S in the right-hand column (see Sec. 2.13, Researching Sub-Bid Coverage.)	Secretary, clerk, and/or estimating assistant
To be investigated in depth: Special trades marked Ⓒ in the right-hand column that are vital to the success of the bid, but that cannot be investigated routinely by the office personnel	The bidder, personally

The bidder decides which trades are critical and complex, requiring personal communication with the probable sub-bidders. With the guidance of the summary sheet, all portions of the project are pursued for cost values, prices, and sub-bids.

Let us now focus on the bidder's participation in the estimating work. The bidder is very often the chief estimator and supervises as well as performs the actual estimating work. The in-depth knowledge of the project, gained from many hours of work on the drawings and specs, makes the estimator a natural candidate for the job. But an estimator may not be an ideal candidate. One disadvantage is that the estimator's concentration on technical details continues unbroken to the bid deadline. Bidding deals with the business side of construction work and calls for traits of personality and temperament not always possessed by the more technically oriented estimator.

A bidder who is not an expert estimator needs to be well informed about unit costs in order to review the estimator's work. The responsibility here is not to correct the estimate, but to adjust, adapt, and incorporate it into the bid package. Figure 1.6c is an example of a concrete estimate prepared by the estimator and reviewed by the bidder. Certain items are changed without obliterating the estimator's original figures. It is the bidder's prerogative to apply judgment values conducive to a *successful* bid. Note, however, that some unit prices are actually raised, as it is also the bidder's responsibility to produce a bid that will be rewarded by a *profitable* contract. As some of the prices are pressed downward, it becomes increasingly important that all other prices be accurate.

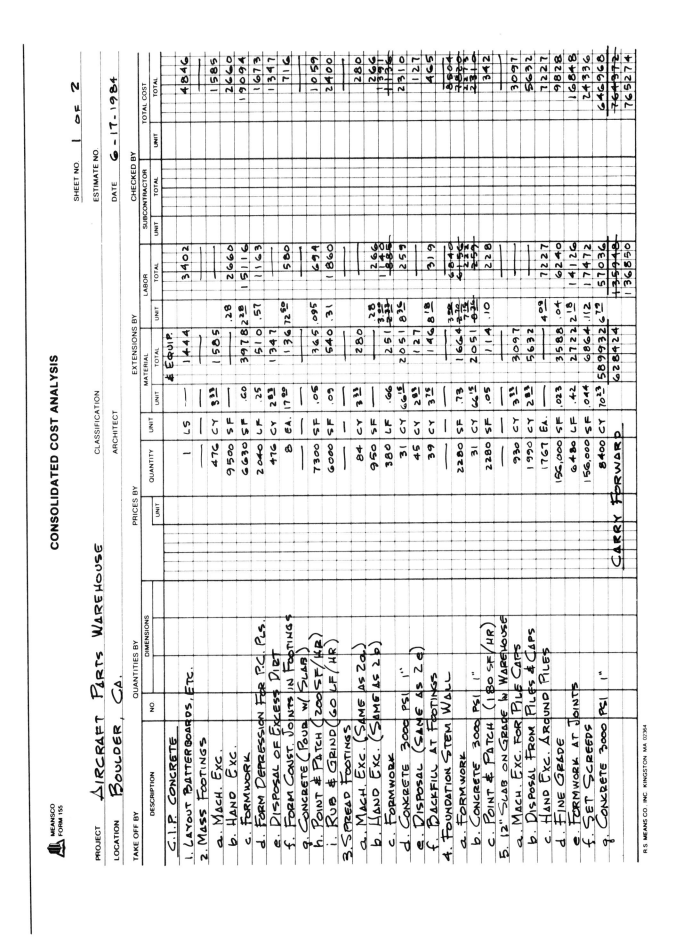

Figure 1.6c

CONSOLIDATED COST ANALYSIS

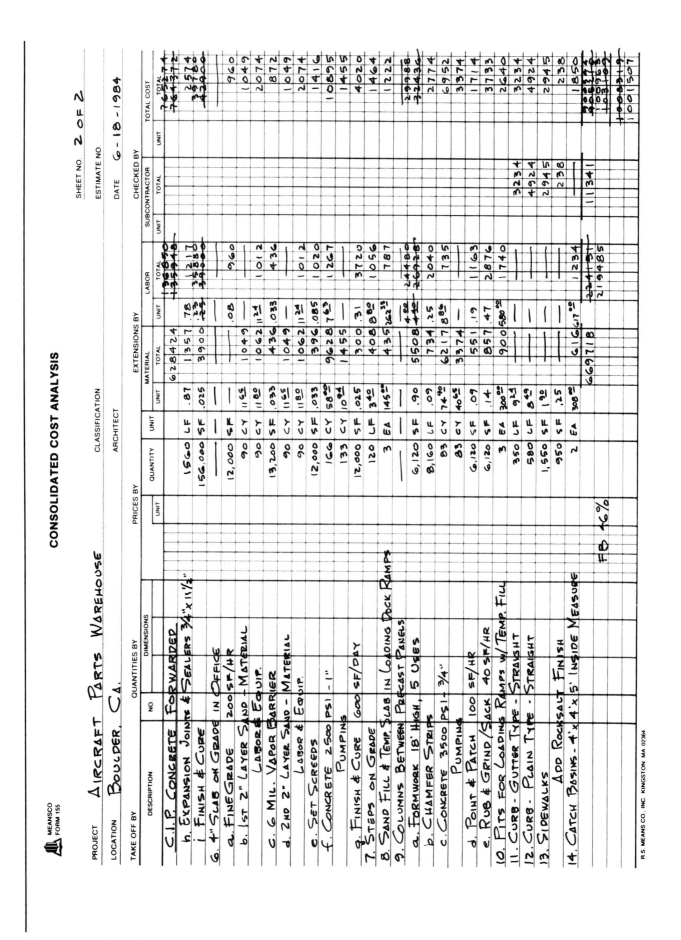

Figure 1.6c (cont.)

Assuming that the estimate was made by an experienced estimator, the bidder does not make trivial changes. Numerous small increases and decreases tend to average out and leave the final sum unaltered. A few large changes can significantly alter the final sum, as those shown in Fig. 1.6c.

The bidder's sources of cost information are:

1. Records from completed projects (see Sec. 2.21, Follow-up Work). The estimator uses the records objectively; the bidder may exercise a broader, a more speculative, or even a more cautious interpretation.
2. Reference books, such as *Building Construction Cost Data*, by R.S. Means Co., Inc., revised and updated annually (Appendix I).
3. Consultants, such as estimators, project superintendents, subcontractors, engineers, and material suppliers.
4. A personal reservoir of cost data accumulated through wide experience in bidding.

The actual unit costs used by the bidder are usually a compromise between the various data. These cost judgment decisions are based on the special conditions of the current project and its d-rating. From the same set of data, a bidder will choose different unit prices in the bidding of different projects. Figure 1.6d is an example of labor unit prices from various sources for the bidder's consideration in reviewing the estimate in Fig. 1.6c. The circled unit costs are the bidder's selections.

Figure 1.6d

	Line Items in Figure 1.6c	Estimator's Figures	Cost Records	Reference Books A	B	Consultant Suggestion	Bidder's Valuation
3c.	Form footing sides (sf)	2.33	2.21	2.80	3.26	—	(3.00)
3f.	Backfill footings (cy)	(8.18)	8.59	9.00	7.77	—	8.00
4a.	Form foundation walls (sf)	2.70	2.56	2.97	2.83	(3.00)	2.75
4b.	Place conc. in found. (cy)	8.36	(7.15)	9.03	8.78	—	8.50
5d.	Fine grade for slab (sf)	(.04)	.03	.034	.045	—	.035
5i.	Finish & cure slab (sf)	.25	.26	.33	(.23)	—	.22
6e.	Set screeds (sf)	(.085)	.07	.095	.077	—	.09
9a.	Column forms (sf)	4.40	3.90	3.82	3.74	(4.00)	5.00

As a rule, neither the lowest nor the highest unit prices are chosen from the various data groups. Preference is given to the estimator's figures, since they already reflect some consideration of the unique conditions of the current project.

Some guidelines for reviewing estimates are as follows:

1. Give special attention to large quantities and high price items which, by small changes in unit prices, can produce significant effects in the bid amount.
2. Look for extremes, such as small quantity items with small unit prices and large quantity items with large unit prices. Because of mobilization costs, unit prices *decrease* as quantities increase.
3. Give priority to labor unit costs, as they are more dependent on judgment than are material costs. When checking a line item of labor, convert the unit price to man-hours, days, weeks, and/or months; convert them again to crew-hours, then visualize and judge the adequacy. Any resulting change in the unit price can then be calculated, as in the following example:

1/2" plywood roof sheathing, 16,000 sf @ $.20 = $3,200

If a crew consists of two carpenters and one laborer at a total hourly rate of $51.00, then

$3,200/51 = 62.75 crew-hours

and

16,000/62.75 = 254.98 sf/crew-hour
Thus,

254.98/32 = 7.97 sheets of 4' x 8' plywood per crew-hour

Finally, because it is a three man crew,

7.97/3 = 2.66 sheets per man per hour

Reduced thus to one-man hourly production, an item of work comes within the range of a bidder's visual powers. In this example, the bidder is satisfied that the estimated unit cost of $.20/sf is in accordance with what a workman can and probably will do.

In some cases, such as drilling holes, installing hardware, and setting anchor bolts, one-man hourly production may still be beyond the bidder's visual powers. The work should then be reduced further to minutes, or fractions of an hour. For example,

Drill 1" x 6" holes in concrete, 480 ea. @ $2.50 = $1,200

At the pay rate of $16.00/hr, how many holes would be drilled per hour? How many minutes per hole?

Answer: 16/$2.50 = 6.4 holes per hour; 60/6.4 = 9.38 minutes each

With the estimated production reduced to this elementary level, the bidder is able to conclude that the unit price is optimistic. Provision is needed for layout, time to move equipment from place to place, possible repairs, re-drilling, and rest periods. A revision would be as follows:

Decrease production to 15 minutes per hole (4 holes per hour), and the unit price becomes 16/4 $4.00 each. The change in the estimate is:

Drill 1" x 6" holes in concrete, 480 ea. @ $4.00 = $1,920

4. Note that when estimated labor production is changed, any associated equipment cost will probably require a proportionate change.
5. Attempt to adjust material unit costs by close study of waste allowances, reuses (as in form lumber), and salvage value. It is hoped that we can obtain lower quotations from suppliers, alternative grades and kinds of materials, and so forth.
6. Visualize methods and sequences of construction to improve and replace those assumed by the estimator.

Reviewing of estimates is performed by the bidder in consultation with the estimator. The bidder needs current data on labor rates, labor production, material costs, equipment rental rates, and equipment

production. Examples of such data are given in Part V of this book as follows.

Appendix J   Payroll Taxes and Fringe Benefits

Appendix K   Labor Crew-Hour Costs

Appendix L   Typical Labor Production and Unit Costs

Appendix M   Equipment Production and Rental Rates

Appendix N   Typical Material Prices

Appendix O   Labor Cost Function

1.7 The Bid Spread Sheet

Bidders differ in the format they use for tabulating the estimates and sub-bids, marking up, and summarizing to arrive at the final bid amounts. One rule common to all bidders is the use of a sheet large enough to show all the figures "spread out." The format suggested in this book is detailed in Sec. 2.12, The Bid Spread Sheet, and used later in Part III, "Bidding a Project." Figure 1.7a is a simplified example reduced greatly in size.

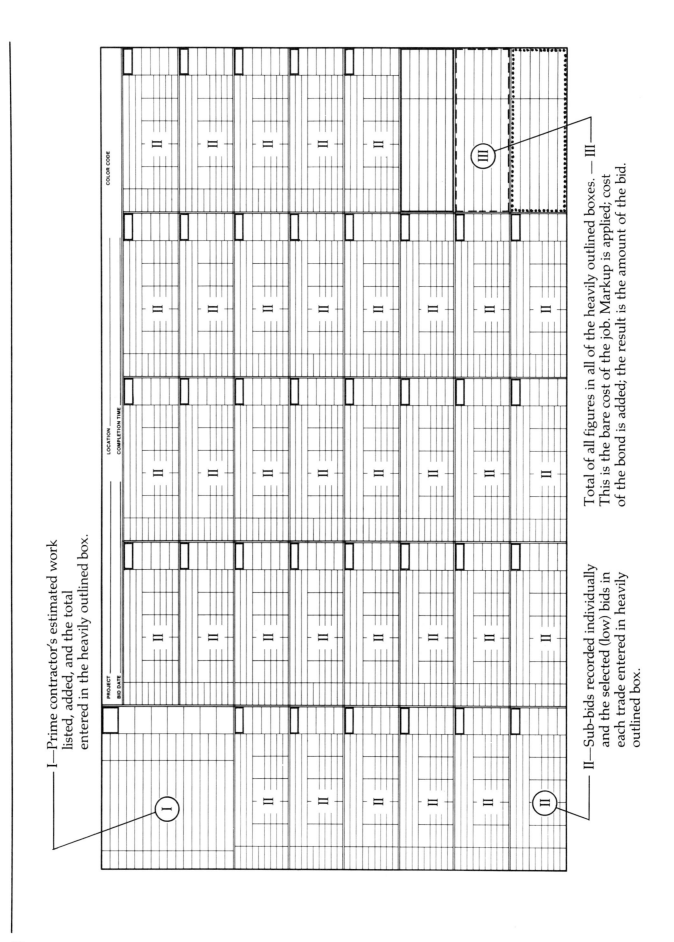

I—Prime contractor's estimated work listed, added, and the total entered in the heavily outlined box.

II—Sub-bids recorded individually and the selected (low) bids in each trade entered in heavily outlined box.

Total of all figures in all of the heavily outlined boxes. — III This is the bare cost of the job. Markup is applied; cost of the bond is added; the result is the amount of the bid.

Figure 1.7a

20

I. Upper left-hand corner. Items estimated by the bidder, to be provided by the prime contractor and not sublet, such as:
   a. Surveying
   b. General conditions (field overhead)
   c. Concrete and structural excavation work
   d. Carpentry work
   e. Caulking and sealing
   f. Installing miscellaneous metal
II. Main body of the sheet. Subcontract items, extended individually, such as:
   a. Demolition
   b. Earthwork
   c. Other trades, as shown in Fig. 1.6b
III. Lower right-hand corner. Total cost of project and markup; the amount of the bid.

1.8 Researching for Sub-Bids

It is important to know *who* will be bidding and what trades each sub will cover. The bidder desires and needs the following information:

1. A *complete* list of prospective sub-bidders and suppliers.
2. *All* the sub-bid and supplier quotations as early as possible.
3. The most *complete* coverage possible by each bidder of the respective trade or work item.

Some of the methods a bidder uses to realize the above aims include:

1. Obtaining from the sponsor a list of "plan holders" (those people who have been issued bid documents). Not all plan holders will produce bids, but the list is a time-saving tool and a good way to start the research.
2. Mailing out letters or post cards to subs, suppliers, and manufacturers who:
   a. Are named in the drawings and specs
   b. Specialize in certain materials or skills
   c. Have bid with you on similar construction in the past
   d. Have been recommended
   e. Are not local or in your "stable" to get unbiased comparisons
3. Using a personally compiled roster (see Sec. 2.13, Research for Sub-Bid Coverage), telephone all subs who have previously shown interest in bidding projects of the same type and size.
4. Realizing from the feedback, as generated by the above research techniques, the weak areas of prospective sub-bid coverage. Then, concentrate on strengthening the weak areas. In the event that one or more trades may not be adequately covered, make a *budget* as a possible alternative (see Sec. 2.14, Budgets, Plug-in Figures, and Allowances).

1.9 The Bid Assembly

Because the majority of sub-bids are received in haste, some only minutes before the bid deadline, careful preparation is necessary in order to:

1. Receive *all* of the sub-bids.
2. Avoid errors in understanding and recording the sub-bids.
3. Obtain all of the specifics in the sub-bids, such as point of delivery, taxes, inclusions, exclusions, and other qualifications.
4. Compare and analyze the sub-bids.
5. Select the best (not necessarily the lowest) sub-bids in each trade.
6. File for quick reference all sub-bids and prices.

7. Summarize and double-check the additions in the bid spread sheet to determine the total cost of the project.
8. Determine the markup and the cost of performance bond.
9. Fill in the bid form, including alternative bids and names of proposed subcontractors (if required).
10. Deliver the bid to the sponsor.

For a thorough presentation of the final three or four hours of the bidding process, see Sec. 2.18, Putting the Bid Together.

1.10
Bond and Markup

The cost of bonding is a *true* project cost, and since it is predicated on the total cost, it is calculated last. For instance, if the cost of a bond is .6% and a project cost estimate is $5,000,000, then

$$\$5,000,000 \times .6\% = \$30,000$$

and

$$
\begin{array}{r}
\$5,000,000 \\
+ \quad 30,000 \\
\hline
\$5,030,000 \text{ total cost}
\end{array}
$$

The markup consists of two parts: (1) the contractor's general business overhead, and (2) the contractor's profit. These may be added to the estimated bare cost of the project in two separate amounts or one combined figure.

The overhead is not a true project cost; it is the construction company's cost to operate as a business, prorated to each bid. For instance, if the company's overhead cost is $200,000 per year and the expected gross contracts (sales) are $10,000,000, then the overhead is

$$\$200,000/\$10,000,000 = .02, \text{ or 2\% of total business.}$$

Profit markup on a bid is a variable, dependent on the market (competition). Within the limits imposed by competition and the d-value of a job there are certain value guidelines that help the bidder to decide on an appropriate markup profit.

Another time-saving method is to combine overhead, profit, and bond in one markup, as follows:

Overhead	2.0%		
Profit	7.0%	Project cost	$5,000,000
Bond	.6%	Plus 9.6%	480,000
Total	9.6%	Bid amount	$5,480,000

Efficient as this method is, some bidders avoid using it because the true amount of profit is not evident and the markup looks deceptively high. Also, it produces a lower bid total, as the overhead and profit are calculated from a cost which does not include the cost of the bond.

The markup procedure is further rationalized and explained in Sec. 2.6, A Reasonable Profit.

1.11
Submit the Bid

For the typical bid, the place and time for delivery is fixed and inflexible. The bidder decides and arranges beforehand the manner of delivery, which may be one of the following:

1. Hand carry from the bidder's office to the point of reception.
2. Telephone the bid amount to a representative who is located near the point of reception.
3. Telegraph or mail.

The bid form, which was partially filled in earlier, is completed, signed, and sealed in a properly addressed envelope.

To be fair to all bidders, the sponsor (particularly of public projects) refuses to accept bids delivered late, even by a few seconds. A late bid may contain competitive advantages denied to the prompt bidders. On the other hand, bids delivered only a few minutes early may fail to benefit from late, low sub-bids. Of the three methods named above, number 2 provides the maximum time for putting the bid together and for checking all of the figures. This method of delivery is discussed fully in Sec. 2.19, Submitting the Bid.

1.12 Follow-up

Since the bidder is usually a construction company executive, that person's involvement in a successful bid continues well into the construction work. Intimate knowledge of the project is indispensable to the immediate paper work that follows award of a contract. The follow-up work includes these details:

1. Outline to company management staff the best (not necessarily lowest) sub-bidders and material suppliers.
2. Draft (rough) all subcontracts and purchase orders.
3. Prepare, or participate in, the drawing of a construction progress schedule.
4. Prepare progress payment schedules.
5. Transmit information and instructions to the project superintendent.
6. Prepare a format for maintaining actual cost records.

Follow-up work is discussed in detail in Sec. 2.21 Follow-up Work, and in Part IV, Project Management.

Part II
Bidding Techniques and Strategies

2.1 Introduction

Part I gave the reader a general overview of the bidding procedure as it is practiced in a typical general contractor's office of medium size. Part II goes deeper into customary methods for controlling the bidding activity to produce a steady flow of bids on projects in the types, sizes, and numbers as nearly suited to the company's needs as possible.

The goal is always to produce *good* bids which at the same time have excellent prospects of being low bids. Techniques and strategies include insight into the reading of drawings and specifications, correct analysis of the competition and other d-rating factors, good judgment in short term and long term ethical considerations, methods for selecting minimum markups, and systems for screening out the best (not necessarily lowest) sub-bids in the last few critical moments before the bid deadline.

2.2 Reading the Drawings and Specifications

The bidder, the quantity surveyor and the estimator have special interests and responsibilities. Each of them must study the drawings and specs in his own personal way. The bidder reads them in a broad, overall, but shallower way than the other specialists. The bidder's responsibility is to see that all parts of the project are covered in the bid, but the finer details are left to the estimators, subcontractors, and others. In fact, the bidder is more of a business manager than a technician, delegating the work to be done (see Sec. 1.6, Reviewing the Estimate). Although number "crunching" by the bidder is unavoidable, his work consists mostly of strategic discriminations in the realm of people and their various proposals.

The bidder looks for ambiguities, omissions, contradictions, and other potential problems in the drawings and specs in order to submit a good bid. Should ambiguities, etc. be discovered, the bidder faces decisions that may include requesting clarification from the A&E. Some cases may be minor; others may be serious enough to cause postponement of the bidding, or severe enough to suggest abandonment of the project (see Sec. 1.4, Analyzing a Project for Desirability).

As the basic drawings and specs pass from hand to hand, sub-bidders and suppliers should promptly sound their questions and comments to the prime bidder. Sub-bidders, when uncertain of the ambiguities in their own sections of the drawings and specs, often wait until the bid deadline to communicate with the bidder. Consequently, many of the problems they introduce must be dealt with hastily (see Sec. 2.18, Putting the Bid Together). To avoid this risk, a bidder develops a unique way of reading to discover potential problems as early as possible.

The bidder begins reading with the need to rate the project for desirability. He reads with more depth to prepare the bid spread sheet (see Sec. 1.7, The Bid Spread Sheet). As questions are brought to the bidder's attention by subs and others, the bidder concentrates more upon details, words, and phrasing.

It is probable that the bidder becomes as knowledgeable of the project overall as the architect, engineer, draftsman, or any other person connected with it. Generally, the designer illustrates and describes what is wanted, and the bidder figures out how to construct the project. The bidder is able, through subletting, to delegate many of the how-to details, but some of them remain in the domain of the prime contractor and are the bidder's personal responsibility (see Sec. 1.6, Reviewing the Estimate).

While delegating the responsibility for in-depth reading to subs and others, the bidder acquires the information needed to assemble a *good* bid (see Sec. 2.8, A Good Bid). As projects vary in scope, no complete checklist is possible. Following are some examples of information gained through studying drawings, reading specs, and communicating with subs:

- Bid deadline, date, and hour and place that bids are to be delivered
- Approximate cost range (preliminary estimate)
- Bid schedule (alternative bids)
- Bonding requirements
- Wage determinations (pay scales)
- Union rules, jurisdictions, and fringe benefits
- Statement of bidder's qualifications
- Contractor's license requirements
- Materials testing requirements
- Special equipment requiring long lead times
- Special inspection requirements
- Environmental protection requirements
- Special taxes and insurances
- Protection of existing structures
- Availability and cost of utility services
- Pedestrian safety (lights, barricades, flagmen)
- Progress chart requirements
- Percentage of work to be performed by the prime contractor (not sublet)
- Construction warranties
- Quality control provisions

- Security requirements
- Acceptable substitute materials

The bidder, as well as the estimator, will need to be familiar with the main structural features of the project. Typical examples are:

1. The Jobsite
   a. Size and shape of the site
   b. Terrain—slopes, canyons, etc.
   c. The extent and nature of necessary clearing
   d. The type of soil
   e. Probable underground conditions such as water and rock
2. Structural
   a. Type of footings—spread type, grade beams, piers, pilings
   b. Excavation and backfilling conditions, need of shoring
   c. Special reinforcing steel design features, such as doweling, welding, supporting, and grout
   d. Unusual concrete forming requirements
   e. Above ground construction—type of construction, concrete beams and columns, concrete slab, concrete block, structural steel, etc.
   f. Suspended floors and roof construction—steel decking, concrete fill, cast-in-place concrete slabs, joist and pan slabs, precast slabs, etc.
3. Architectural
   a. Exterior materials and finishes
   b. Interior finishes—walls, floors and ceiling
   c. Partitions and doors
   d. Cabinetry and millwork
   e. Color schedules
4. Mechanical and electrical
   a. Exterior overhead and underground
   b. Main features of piping, wiring, equipment, and fixtures
   c. Installations that pose construction scheduling and coordination difficulties

The bidder first scans the plans and specs for significant features of the project. From long practice, he becomes very skillful at comprehending the scope of the project and its main points very swiftly.

2.3 Probability of Low Bid and Receipt of Contract

Contracts usually go to the lowest qualified bidder, a practice which fosters indifference to the relative abilities of the bidders. This is true to a lesser degree in the use of "select bid lists" by some private sponsors. Private sponsors usually reserve the right to waive low bids and to award the contract to the bidders in whom they have the greatest confidence. Realizing that a sponsor may invoke this right, bidders often resort to competitive strategies in their pursuit of reasonably profitable contracts.

Bidding Strategies

1. Choose types of projects in which the bidder's company has demonstrated competency. The advantages include:
   a. Attraction of the sponsor's approval in the event that alternative to the low bidder is being sought.
   b. Competency through practice and experience which tends to push construction costs down to improve the chance of a low bid.

c. Competitive prices from subs and suppliers who, based upon their knowledge of the bidder's competency, feel they must "back the probable winner."

The focus here is the production of a successful bid; the question of widening the company's competence through diversification is an entirely different subject. Some degree of diversification takes place automatically, as all projects differ.

2. Improve and use effectively knowledge of competitor's strengths and weaknesses. This information can be used as a guide for:
   a. Choice of projects to bid
   b. How competitively to bid
      (i) How much markup to apply to the bare cost
      (ii) How much risk to take (for instance, in questionable subs)

This knowledge comes with continual bidding practice and provides a useful appraisal of the probable competitiveness of the prospective bidders on any project. As an example, imagine the following list of bidders (Fig. 2.3a).

Bidder	Appraisal	Rank
I.N. Valid Const. Co.	An out-of-town company that may not receive the best local prices	+5
Claw Hammer Company	Many contracts on hand; no great need for new work	+4
Pen N. Ink Engineering	Not experienced in this type of construction	+3
Taciturn Builders	A mechanical contractor not experienced in prime bidding	+2
Likable Const. Co.	Reputed to be a consistent conservative bidder	+1
Your Own Company	Competitive	0
Will Bid & Sons Bldr.	Very competitive in this type of construction	−1
Minimodel Concepts	Known to be in great need of new contracts	−2

Figure 2.3a

The rank is a judgment of each bidders' probable position in the final bid results, relative to your own company.

Appraisals such as those in Fig. 2.3a are only educated guesses; in this example, one may draw the following conclusions:

1. Only two of the eight bidders (Will Bid & Sons and Minimodel Concepts) are judged likely to be more competitive than our own company.
2. These are not bad odds. A normally competitive approach may be sufficient. Many variables could cause both Will Bid and Minimodel to bid higher than we expect.
3. We should reserve our most strenuous efforts to be competitive for situations in which the odds are much worse than the appraisal shown in Fig. 2.3a; otherwise, we may be trapped into leaving too much on the table.

Bidders are prone to overestimate the importance of the competitive effort and to forget that it is only one of many variables affecting the final bid result. Using the guidelines in Sec. 1.4, Analyzing a Project for Desirability, the situation appraised in Fig. 2.3a would be considered

relatively light competition that deserves a weight of about 85.

All of the data regarding competition is general and circumstantial; some is rumor, some is self-evident, but much of it is based on fact. Here are some examples of data:

1. Why a competitor may not be competitive:
    a. Could possibly withdraw due to overloaded bid schedule (company is listed on many projects).
    b. May not be able to furnish a bond (the project is larger than the bidder's historical range).
    c. Is not experienced in this type of construction.
    d. Is currently unpopular with subs and suppliers (may not receive important low prices).
    e. May be overly cautious due to recent bad experience with a project similar to the present one.
    f. Maintains a high overhead.
    g. Is known to be a typically conservative bidder.
2. Why a competitor's bid may be unpredictable:
    a. Is known to be erratic (often high or low, but never consistent among the bidders).
    b. Is completely unknown to the bidder and cannot be evaluated.
    c. All data are neutral (no apparent advantages or disadvantages).
3. Why a competitor may be competitive:
    a. Is known to be very low in work and needs new contracts greatly.
    b. Is known to be highly competent in this type of construction.
    c. Does specialty work, in addition to the usual prime contractor trades, that other bidders customarily sublet (mechanical, for instance).
    d. Is already on the jobsite doing work under another contract similar to this project, and thus has the advantages of mobilization, materials, subcontractors, and inside information not easily available to other bidders.
    e. Owns special equipment that other bidders can obtain only by renting at presumably high rental rates.
    f. Is known to be inexperienced in this type of construction (inexperience can cause either high or low bidding).
    g. Is aggressive and tends to overestimate ability to perform.
    h. Operates with very low overhead, great energy, and volume (many contracts and low markups).

In analyzing the competition, those who cannot be ranked, as in group 2 above, may be given zero ranking, equivalent to our own company, and contribute no positive or negative weight in a scale such as Fig. 2.3a. For instance, if three of eight prospective bidders were unpredictable, the desirability rating of the project could be calculated as if there were only five bidders.

3. Favor projects with the least number of bidders. There may be exceptions to this rule. For instance, it might be better to bid a project having, say, eight relaxed bidders than a project with three extremely eager competitors.

If all bidders were equal in all respects and perfectly consistent in their bidding, the probability of being the low bidder on any project would be "one" in the number of bidders (if seven bidders, the probability would be 1 in 7). We are interested here in the low bid, but the mathematical principle would be the same regarding all other positions—second, third, fourth, and so on. This rule is mentioned here because it will be

shown later that, because many competitors are not consistent bidders, a very consistent bidder will tend to fall below the midpoint in the range of bids (see Sec. 2.8, A Good Bid).

4. *Choose those projects that have the highest profit potential relative to completion time.* For example, in Fig. 2.3b project Y is preferable to project X.

Project	Potential Profit, $	Completion Time
X	180,000	18 months
Y	150,000	12 months

Figure 2.3b

Although this choice might not increase the probability of a low bid, it will increase the potential for total profit within a year. Project Y, being completed sooner than project X, creates a faster return on the investment dollar, reduces the percentage of fixed overhead per contract dollar, releases potential bonding capacity sooner, and makes available supervisory personnel for new projects.

5. *Bid as many well-selected projects as possible.* Naturally, bidding an increased number of projects increases the probability of winning more low bids.

In reality, low bids do not occur with absolute mathematical predictability. Figure 2.3c shows an example of low bid expectations, versus actual low bids, assuming an average number of 9 bidders on all 27 projects.

Number of Projects	Low Bids (Expected)	Low Bids (Actual)
1	(1 in 9)	
2		
3		Low
4		
5		Low
6		
7		
8		
9	Low	
10		
11		
12		
13		
14		
15		
16		
17		
18	Low	
19		
20		
21		
22		
23		
24		Low
25		
26		
27	Low	

Figure 2.3c

The ratios of actual low bids in Fig. 2.3c may be read in this order of occurrence:

1 in 3
2 in 5
3 in 24 (or 1 in 8)

Ratios such as these have much greater significance when taken from the tabulation of a large number of bids. If the list in Fig. 2.3c were extended to 200, a considerable gap could occur between any two low bids without appreciably effecting the overall ratio. The main value of these ratios to the bidder lies in their significance to the competitiveness of the bidder's own company. Figure 2.3d shows how a bidder might rate his own company.

Figure 2.3d

Bidder's Self-Rating
(Assume an average of 8 bidders per job)

If bidder's ratio is:

1 in 10: should be *seriously concerned* (not competitive)
1 in 8: should not be complacent
1 in 6: should be pleased, but cautious
1 in 4: should be *seriously concerned* (too competitive)

Fig 2.3d shows how there is cause for concern when a bidder's actual "batting average" approaches either extreme—not competitive, or too competitive. Observe that the bidder is pleased only if the ratio is slightly *less* than the theoretical norm. This may be regarded as a healthy level of competitiveness.

Luck has a bearing on the awarding of contracts. It favors those bidders who develop skill in all particulars of the bidding profession. Bidders must rely on luck in those areas over which they have little or no control. For example:

The availability of numerous desirable projects on which to bid.
The strengths and weaknesses of the competition, and the number of qualified bidders vying for the contract.
The providential ways in which a bidder avoids unforeseen hazards and errors of judgment in bidding.
The availability of competent and competitive subcontractors.

In Fig. 2.3e, assuming that both bidders are equally worthy, the simple assumption is that bidder X is "unlucky" and that bidder Y is "lucky."

Figure 2.3e

Bid Results

Bidder X	$3,211,800
Bidder Y	$3,211,550

As a sequel to the example in Fig. 2.3e, luck may show a later reversal when X and Y both discover a huge mistake, such as the bid of a subcontractor who is unable to perform as promised. In this case, it is Y who is unlucky.

A final conclusion is: Any assessment of luck made before the completion of construction work and the final cost accounting would be premature.

2.4 Ethical Considerations

Of all the phases in a construction project, perhaps the bidding phase is the most vulnerable to ethical questions. It is open to the outside world's zealous competition and the resulting, often ruthless strategies that seem to "go with the territory." Let us confine this discussion of ethics to the bidding activity alone, without making moralistic judgments.

Ethics is another name for *fair play*, the control of one's conduct to avoid any form of injury to other contestants. A bidder must examine and evaluate every scrap of incoming information, but is unable always to recognize an unethical situation on sight. The question of propriety is one of several questions the bidder automatically asks of every source of every quotation, and assumes in the absence of evidence to the contrary that the situation *is* ethical and the proposal is made in good faith. Daily experience and observation reinforce that being ethical is the rule in bidding—being unethical, the exception.

Exception though it may be, unethical behavior deserves discussion in any complete study of the bidding process. Most situations in bidding are opportunistic rather than outright unethical, because the searching, seizing, and using of opportunities toward successful bids is "the name of the game." Conflict occurs at a hard-to-define line between *legitimate* and *non-legitimate* opportunism. The following is a list of examples:

1. Presumably legitimate opportunities:
   a. Holding an exclusive low quotation—one not available to competitors (obtained without disclosing other sub-bids).
   b. Services of expert consultant, not available to other bidders.
   c. Possession of special equipment not available to other bidders.
   d. Possession of superior specialized skill in one or more critical trades.
   e. Exploratory investigations, such as earth borings, made at the bidder's own expense.
2. Clearly non-legitimate opportunities:
   a. Having inside information, not available to other bidders, on the exact amount of the sponsor's preliminary estimate and budget.
   b. Accepting and using a sub-bid that appears too low (perhaps in error) relative to other bids without asking confirmation from the sub-bidder.
   c. Asking a sub-bidder for a special price, lower than the sub's quotation to other bidders.
   d. Accepting a sub-bid that arrives after the bid deadline.
   e. Using a low bid obtained by "peddling" the amounts of other sub-bidders.
   f. Permitting a sub-bidder to raise his previously too-low bid to just under the next lowest bid.
   g. Dispensing any information at all that would give one sub-bidder an advantage over another.

When a question of legitimacy arises relative to a proposal, the bidder has three options:

1. Discard the proposal
2. Accept and use it (incorporate it into the bid)
3. Use a modified amount

Except to the purist, there are no pat rules; each case is decided on its own merits. To discard an opportunity off-hand could amount to failure in the competition. Some bidders are of the firm belief that their competitors are actively exercising non-legitimate strategies. A realist

views the subject of ethics, within limits, as necessary roughhousing at the goal line. The limits are mostly self-policed by the demands of "good business," as each bidder conceives it. A bidder cannot exceed certain limits without paying penalties in the forms of litigation and loss of reputation, with consequent financial loss.

Faced with the necessity to be competitive, the bidder has two options regarding ethics: (1) the short view, with its rewards and penalties, and (2) the long view, with its rewards and penalties. The short view is the expedient or opportunistic action most likely to bring success in the bidding of the present project. The long view is the possibility of greater profit in the future through the maintenance of the goodwill of a majority of the members of the entire construction industry. There is a financial risk in both views.

2.5 Competition and the Bidder's Need for Work

Occasionally a bidder may bid a job in a relaxed manner. But the more that work is needed and the more desirable the particular job, the greater the effort to push down all incoming prices. In that direction there are acceptable legitimate ways, legitimate but unacceptable ways, and non-legitimate ways.

Before considering these ways, let us note again that the bidder's goal is not merely to be low bidder, but to procure the contract at a profit (see Sec. 1.3, Ability, Motivation, and Objective). The fact is, no competitor wants to lose money. This means that they all have their own internal restraints. The advantages shift back and forth between bidders from bid to bid, so it is possible for you to be low bidder periodically without leaving too much on the table. Competent bidding techniques can be depended upon to produce a fair share of low bids at levels not unnecessarily low or unprofitable (see Sec. 2.3, Probability of Low Bid and Receipt of Contract).

A valuable lesson from hindsight is this. A series of low bids prove, as a rule, that when you have the advantages to produce a low bid, these advantages can cause your bid to be too low. Consequently, in the competitive scramble for contracts, a certain conservatism may be in order, based on a realistic assessment of your chances.

Good bidding techniques alone may not be enough. It is important that a competent construction company exist to back up the bidder. The bidder must also possess certain mental, temperamental, and personality traits for consistent, repeated performance. Lowering of a bid puts a strain on the construction organization and challenges its capabilities. The bidder's self-confidence and confidence in the company are called upon increasingly as competition tightens.

Figure 2.5a illustrates the progressively risky measures in the direction of competitiveness. Level A represents a noncompetitive, but otherwise *good* bid (see Sec. 2.8, A Good Bid). The level may be lowered to B by certain acceptable, legitimate cuts, such as:

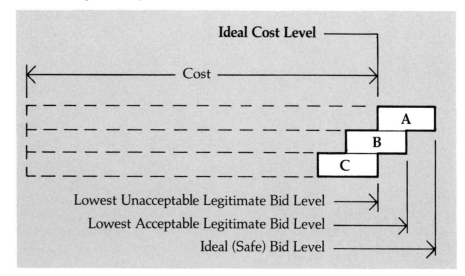

Figure 2.5a

1. Removing slack and tightening up all figures
2. Devising more economical methods of performing the construction work
3. Finding sources of more competitive material and equipment prices
4. Substituting "or equal" materials
5. Planning tight completion schedules in order to reduce general conditions costs
6. Applying the lowest possible markup

The level may be pushed down further, to C, by measures which, although both legal and ethical, may not be wise in a business sense. Examples of such *unacceptable, legitimate* cuts are:

1. Scheduling an unrealistically short time to complete construction.
2. Taking calculated risks or gambles on unproven methods of construction.
3. Using overly optimistic estimates of both labor and equipment production.
4. Taking a chance on cutting quality material and workmanship.
5. Taking a chance on an incompetent or insolvent sub.
6. Applying insufficient markup.

Bidders unconcerned with possible long term damages to their business reputations might also attempt to lower the bid by questionable methods. For example:

1. Any of the legitimate methods listed above, carried to reckless extremes.
2. Any of the unethical strategies as defined in Sec. 2.4, Ethical Considerations.

In Fig. 2.5a, a *good* bid would fall between levels A and B. Note that as the bid level is pushed downward, the bare cost level, by calculated risk, is also reduced; level C is below the cost level of A, but level B is safely above the cost of level A.

Section 1.4, Analyzing a Project for Desirability, shows several conditions influencing the choice of a project, the intensity of

competition, and the amount of markup. *Need for work*, as a rule, forces bids downward more than any other factor. It contributes most to the spread that is often seen in bid results, and is the main deterrent to the interested bidder whose workload is at or near capacity. There is no motivation to bid successfully against "hungry" competitors. Yet as the workload steadily declines and the need for new work grows, a bidder may continue to bid in a selective and relaxed manner, responding to projects having higher d-ratings.

The loaded-to-capacity situation is rare and of short duration, as is the opposite, no work at all. The typical situation of an active bidder is between those two extremes.

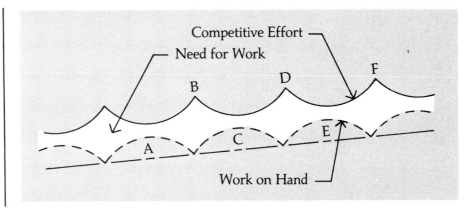

Figure 2.5b

In Fig. 2.5b the dashed line represents the volume of work on hand, peaking at A, C, and E. The solid line represents fluctuations of bidding intensity, peaking at the points of least work on hand: B, D, and F. The dash-dot-dash line represents a gradual growth in company assets due to successful bidding and profiting. As soon as new work is obtained competitive effort relaxes. The space between the solid and dashed lines represents the varying need for work.

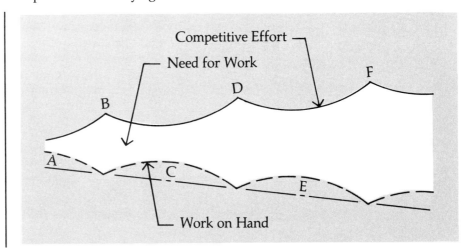

Figure 2.5c

Figure 2.5c shows what would happen if bidding were not continuously successful. The growth curve slants downward; the peaks of the competitive effort curve increase in height; the need for work becomes acute. Desperation bidding (below the B level in Fig. 2.5a) takes place.

Because of the extremely low bidding, work on hand increases again, but because it is low-profit work, the growth line cannot rise above horizontal, as in Fig. 2.5d. Need for work continues to be great, but until contracts are obtained that produce profit, the growth line will not resume the healthy, upward (positive) slope, as shown in Fig. 2.5b.

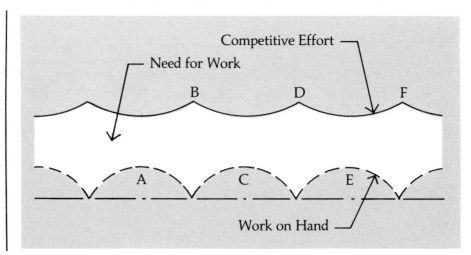

Figure 2.5d

2.6
A Reasonable Profit

An exorbitant profit is hardly relevant for discussion here, because competition precludes it. Probably no one would begrudge a bidder a "reasonable" profit. But what is reasonable?

Let us begin the answer as follows: A company could show a profit on each of its contracts and still decline in net worth. That would indicate an unreasonably low profit. To a bidder, therefore, a "reasonable" profit would be that percentage which, relating to an overall policy of marking up bids, contributes to growth in company assets as much as competition permits.

The problem of how much to mark up the bare cost of a project for profit is a difficult one because it is unknown how many contracts a bidder will procure over a given period. The amount of markup is one of the *estimated* items in a bid package. Figure 2.6a illustrates the way an estimated annual profit may be distributed between contracts.

Distribution of Estimated Annual Profit

Desired annual profit, say, $250,000

Assume competition permits 5% markup

Gross annual contracts required $\dfrac{\$250,000}{.05} = \$5,000,000$

If actual annual contracts total up to:	The markup must be:
$ 3,000,000	8.33%
$ 4,000,000	6.25%
$ 5,000,000	5.00%
$ 7,000,000	3.60%
$10,000,000	2.50%

Figure 2.6a

The amount of desired annual profit can be approximated from data such as:

1. Company history and growth curve.
2. Limits permitted by bonding company or bonding capacity (see Sec. 2.7, Bonding and Bonding Capacity).
3. The capacity of the present construction organization to perform work without increasing the overhead.

As we shall see, the desired profit is tempered by certain hard realities, such as intensity of competition and the type of projects available, so that the actual percentage of markup used is a compromise and varies from bid to bid (see Sec. 1.4, Analyzing a Project for Desirability).

There is an optimum markup for each project, depending on its size and its d-rating, as will be shown later in this section. The bidder is forced to pursue projects of various size to maintain the volume of work necessary to pay for overhead and produce a healthy growth of the company. The bidder must count on the success of future bids, as illustrated in Fig. 2.6b, where A is the present project and B,C,D, E, and F are hypothetical future bids.

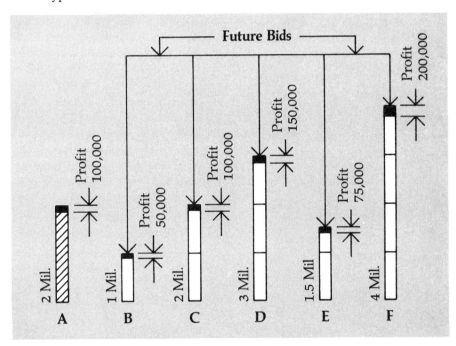

Figure 2.6b

If the bidder could predict the number of future projects the company will win, and select them in an ideal range of sizes, it would be possible to apply approximately the same percentage of markup to each project, as in Fig. 2.6b, where 5% is used across-the-board. The desired annual profit (minimum) of $250,000 could be realized in several combinations, as follows:

Projects	Total Expected Profit ($)
A + B + C	250,000
A + D	250,000
C + D	250,000
B + F	250,000

The bidder who follows a plan projected a year or more into the future should do better than the bidder who has no plan at all. Long term plans for procurement of contracts should be flexible, allowing for times when actual performance falls below expectations. When a company

procures a continuous flow of new, well-spaced, reasonably profitable contracts, times of low performance are balanced off by those times when performance exceeds the plan. Fig. 2.6c shows the peaks and valleys experienced in a hypothetical company's growth line. In this example, the spacing of and the profit from construction jobs cause the growth curve to rise or fall in consecutive years, but the average may be a gentle rise over all.

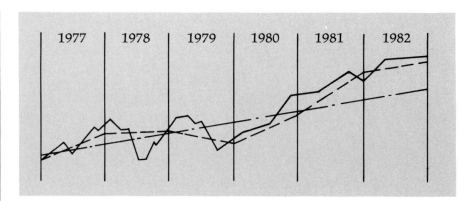

Figure 2.6c

The peaks and valleys resemble the crests and troughs in ocean waves; a contracting business "rides the waves." The overhead cost, when it exceeds the profit, forms the down-slope; a new source of profit (contract) forms the up-slope, as depicted in Fig. 2.6d.

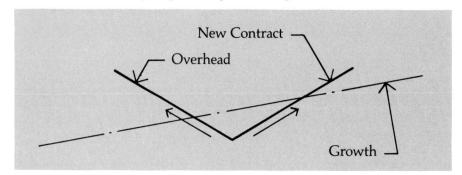

Figure 2.6d

If not enough profitable work is obtained to cover the contractor's overhead costs, overhead dominates profit. We thus produce a downslope, as in Fig. 2.6e.

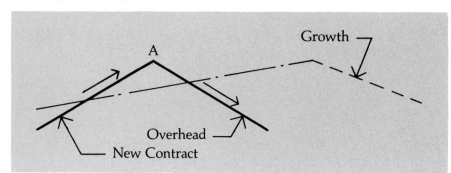

Figure 2.6e

If a new profit-bearing contract is not procured quickly, the growth line (G) tends to slope downward under the influence of overhead (o) as shown in Figure 2.6f.

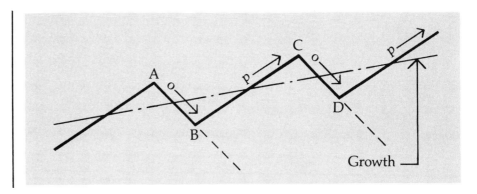

Figure 2.6f

If all else is constant, the tilt of the growth line is dependent on the constant flow of profitable contracts. A series of profitable contracts obtained too far apart in time may fail to offset overhead's steady erosion of assets, as depicted in Fig. 2.6g.

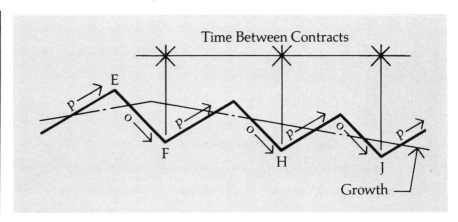

Figure 2.6g

Spacing is an important factor in the need for work; a new contract is not only needed, but is needed *now*! With growth curves descending, insolvency becomes a threat for all and a reality for some unless recovery is rapid. The greatest threat to a construction bidder is not the competition, but economic recession, which reduces normal competition to "survival of the fittest."

The need to space new jobs may be so great that it can pressure a bidder into making unrealistically low bids, defended by any of the following reasons:

1. The wish to retain competent crews and supervisory personnel
2. A strategic move to open the way to bid advantage or negotiation of some other, more profitable job
3. The honor and prestige of constructing a significant, publicized project
4. The hope that good management, change orders, or luck might produce a pickup
5. To pay the overhead

Before leaving this topic, let us consider some of the criticisms of bidding at cost (buying a job).

1. If practiced widely by bidders it would be ruinous to the construction industry.
2. It increases the risk of loss, which is present in even a potentially profitable job. A reasonable markup does two things at the same time. It increases the probability of profit and provides a contingency (see Sec. 2.14, Budgets, Plug-in Figures, and Allowances).

3. Due to the tightness of income from a nonprofit contract, payments to subs and suppliers may be delayed, causing loss of goodwill or credit, which would be detrimental to the bidding of future, profitable jobs.
4. Nonprofit performance discourages bonding companies from increasing the bidder's bonding capacity.
5. It uses bonding capacity that could otherwise be available for other, more profitable jobs.

The contractor's markup, as defined here, is an amount conveniently shown as a percentage of the total bare cost. It combines the contractor's overhead cost for doing business and an allowance for profit. Let us consider overhead first, and then profit.

A bidder must not overload each bid with the contractor's total annual overhead cost. The amount of overhead incorporated into each bid should be only the amount the company spends during the project's construction. Usually, a contractor has work under construction that is paying a portion of the overhead; therefore, a new project must carry only a *prorated* share.

In Fig. 2.6h the overhead for project BC may be calculated as follows:

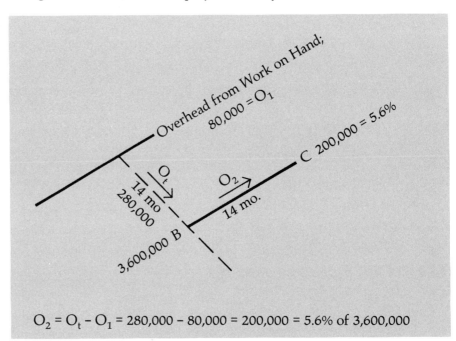

$$O_2 = O_t - O_1 = 280,000 - 80,000 = 200,000 = 5.6\% \text{ of } 3,600,000$$

Figure 2.6h

If the overhead is $240,000 per year ($20,000 per month), the work on hand is paying an overhead share of $80,000, the size of project is $3,600,000, and the completion time is 14 months, then, the overhead markup is

$$\frac{14 \text{ months} \times \$20,000 - \$80,000}{\$3,600,000} = .056 = 5.6\%$$

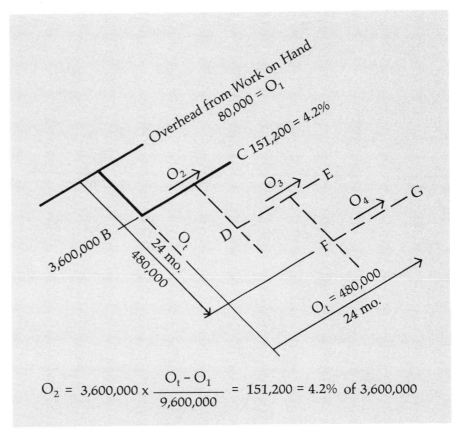

$$O_2 = 3{,}600{,}000 \times \frac{O_t - O_1}{9{,}600{,}000} = 151{,}200 = 4.2\% \text{ of } 3{,}600{,}000$$

Figure 2.6i

This example is based on the pessimistic possibility that no other contracts will be procured in the next 14-month period. The point was made in Fig. 2.6b that competition between bidders forces a more optimistic view, a calculated risk that additional contracts will be procured, thus justifying a reduction in the prorated share of overhead. Figure 2.6i shows a bid schedule planned to spread the overhead between work on hand (WOH), present project in process of bidding (BC), and two theoretical future projects, (DE) and (FG). The spacing is assumed to be:

	Size	Procurement	Completion	Extension
BC	3,600,000	now	14 mo.	14 mo.
DE	1,500,000	6 mo.	12 mo.	4 mo.
FG	4,500,000	8 mo.	16 mo.	6 mo.
	$9,600,000			24 mo.

That is:

$$\frac{24 \text{ months} \times \$20{,}000 - \$80{,}000}{\$9{,}600{,}000} = .042 = 4.2\%$$

to be applied to the present bid BC. Figure 2.6i does not indicate a specific overhead for future projects, DE and FG, because their individual cases will be reconsidered when they are bid. We are interested now in an amount to incorporate into the current bid. Because the success of future bids calls for more guesswork, based upon past bidding results, it is practical to set a standard percentage for overhead: 4% will be used hereafter as a constant in the markups for overhead. The total markup will be composed as in Fig. 2.6j.

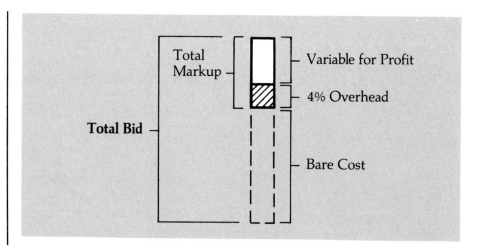

Figure 2.6j

A bidder should construct and periodically revise a graph for finding the markup to suit each bid. The following graph, Fig. 2.6k, is intended only as an example.

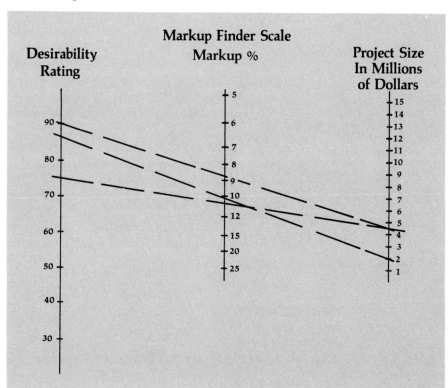

Figure 2.6k

Its construction is based on the following assumptions:

1. That 4% is included as a constant for overhead.
2. That the gross annual volume of construction work by the bidder's company, as limited by bonding and organizational capacity, is $15,000,000.
3. That the goal for gross profit is $600,000.

Consistent with the foregoing conditions, the average markup would be:

Overhead, constant 4%
Profit $ 600,000 .... 4%
                                             ——
Total $15,000,000 .... 8%

The goal of $15,000,000 for our company is possible, but it is not likely to be achieved every year. The average markup of 8% would not be suitable to every project. Each project is rated for desirability (see Sec. 1.4, Analyzing a Project for Desirability). Fig. 2.6k simplifies the process of selecting suitable markups. If desirability were not considered at all, markup percentage would still vary with the size of a project. If size were not considered, markup would vary with its desirability rating. This markup finder scale coordinates both variables. For the purpose of demonstrating the use of Fig. 2.6k, the following three examples are given:

> *Example 1:* Project size $2,000,000
> Desirability rating 87
> Markup found in Fig. 2.6k = 10%
> (Composed of 4% overhead + 6% profit)

> *Example 2:* Project size $4,500,000
> Desirability rating 90
> Markup found in Fig. 2.6k = 8.7%
> (Composed of 4% overhead + 4.7% profit)

> *Example 3:* Project size $4,500,000
> Desirability rating 75
> Markup found in Fig. 2.6k = 10.4%
> (Composed of 4% overhead + 6.4% profit)

Summary

The procedure illustrated in Fig. 2.6k provides a working guideline for determining the reasonable markup that may be assigned to a bid. Yet the skill of calculating reasonable project markups can never depend solely on a fixed mathematical formula. The bidder should also bear in mind a number of variables that strongly determine whether or not a bid will be competitive.

As well as judging the size and desirability of a project, the bidder must give his attention to economic circumstances, the number and quality of competitors, and the need for construction work in that area. All of these conditions act to force prices up or down, dictating the percentage of profit that can be called "reasonable" for a given project. If a company is to compete, the figures the bidder quotes must be in tune with current market conditions.

The knowledgeable bidder is also willing to risk lower markups in times of need, staking his decision on the hope of recovery and on confidence in the company's chances of procuring profitable future contracts.

In all, ability to determine appropriate markups calls not only for thorough analysis of the work proposed, but sensitivity to shifting economic conditions and needs within the construction industry.

2.7 Bonding and the Reasons for Bonding Capacity

The requirement that contractors provide performance and payment bonds started as a protection for the owner, but side benefits fell to the bidder, including the following:

1. The competition is improved through the screening out by bonding companies of substandard bidders.
2. A "safety valve" is imposed on a bidder, thus limiting and controlling the rate of contract acquisition and company financial commitments.
3. The credibility of a bidder is heightened in the view of sponsors by the endorsement of a reputable bonding company.

A common cause of contractor bankruptcy is the over-extension of financial and physical resources. When a bidder does not observe and stay within the limits of the company's resources, the bonding company imposes a ceiling. This basically good restriction can be a problem to a bidder whose bonding capacity (ceiling) is barely sufficient to cover the needed volume of work.

It is desirable for a bidder to have bonding capacity in excess of what is needed to meet growth ideals. The means of achieving such a happy state are in the province of company management, and not directly relevant to the subject of this book. The bidder has four main concerns regarding bonding:

1. Being aware of the amount of available bonding capacity in order to plan the number and size of projects for immediate estimating and bidding.
2. Making the best possible use of surplus bonding capacity.
3. Applying for and obtaining the bonds promptly as needed.
4. Calculating and including the cost (premium) of the bond in the bid (see Fig. 2.7a).

Data for Computing Cost of Bond		
Estimated Cost of Project		Multiply By
From	To	
0	1,000,000	.0075
1,000,000	1,500,000	.0063
1,500,000	2,000,000	.0060
2,000,000	2,500,000	.0058
2,500,000	3,000,000	.0056
3,000,000	4,000,000	.0055
4,000,000	5,000,000	.0052
5,000,000	6,000,000	.0050
6,000,000	7,000,000	.0048
7,000,000	9,000,000	.0047
9,000,000	11,000,000	.0046
11,000,000	and over	.0045

Figure 2.7a

The bidder stays aware of available bonding capacity by contacting the surety agent regularly and by keeping track of work on hand. Bonding capacity is always a rough figure subject to several variables that include company assets, organization, history, level of work on hand, personal relationships between bidder and bonding agent, personal indemnifications by company officers, and characteristics of the current project under consideration. A simple example is as follows: Suppose that bonding capacity is $12,000,000 and work on hand (uncompleted) is $8,000,000, then available bonding capacity is $12,000,000 – $8,000,000 = $4,000,000. The latter figure is the maximum size of any project, or combination of projects, for which the bidder may expect to receive bonding.

To make the best possible use of the bonding capacity and to improve credit with the surety companies, the bidder must make every effort to:

1. Select a type of construction in which the company has proved its competency.
2. Select projects with minimal risk, such as those composed of a high percentage of subtrades relative to prime contractor work.

3. Require major subcontractors to furnish bonds, thus reducing risk to the prime bidder.
4. Select projects with relatively short completion times in order to increase capital turnover and to show more immediate financial growth.

In cases of growth-line decline, or stagnation, as illustrated in Figs. 2.5c and 2.5d, the reluctance of bonding companies to provide bonds is understandable. Upward financial mobility is a major consideration in winning a surety's confidence. In a sense, the surety "bets" on the bidder, so long as projections predict a winner. Stagnation and decline of the growth curve occur periodically in all construction companies, but are serious only if company assets are meager and/or stagnation continues for a long time.

Once a company establishes a relationship with a bonding agency, applying for and obtaining the bid bond is a simple routine, outlined in Sec. 1.5, Preliminary Steps in Bidding. The cost of the bond varies with the bidder/surety relationship. The simplest method is a straight percentage (such as 1%) of the total amount of the marked up bid. But for the established medium size contractor, a rate based on project size is not uncommon. Figure 2.7a is a typical table of such variable rates that will be used in the bidding example given in Part III.

Section 1.10 shows how the bond premium may be placed as the very last item in the bid compilation, following the contractor's markup, or placed among the cost items before the final markup.

2.8 A Good Bid

The immediate goal of a bidder is to bid as low as possible. More generally, the goal is to produce a *good* bid, whether it is the low one or not. To define a *good* bid, let us first consider the ideal bid. The ideal bid may be described as a take-it-or-leave-it bid, at a "fair" level to the sponsor, but with no calculated risk to the bidder. Ideal bids are occasionally offered by bidders, but they are exceptional. The real world's best version of the ideal bid is the *good* bid.

Some bidders may argue that a bid cannot be *good* unless it is the low bid; the more thoughtful bidders would say that the real quality of a bid can be known only after completion of the construction. Both views are extreme; the first is hasty, and the second assumes that the bidder has no faith in his ability to perform. Let us now attempt to define a good bid, as follows:

1. The appearance of a bid relative to the other bids is only a clue to its quality. It is possible that a bid that appears low and out-of-line could be a *good* bid, but usually a *good* bid has a respectable appearance. It is hoped it will achieve the dual goals of the bidder, namely, that it be closely competitive and that it be positioned in the lower half of all the bids. If it *is* the low bid, it should be close to the next lowest bid. A large gap between the lowest bid and the next lowest bid informs the bidder (assuming no errors) of a failure to recognize certain bidding advantages which he held over competitors.
2. Without regard to appearance, a *good* bid has the following qualities:
   a. Reputable and dependable subcontractors
   b. Complete coverage (no omitted items)
   c. Accurate quantities and price-outs
   d. Realistic completion time allowances
   e. Practical methods planned for problem items

f. Appropriate markup
g. Properly executed bid forms with bond, alternative bids, acknowledgement of addenda, etc.

By repeated submission of *good* bids, the probability of low bidding is increased because of definite improvements in bidding skills.

A hypothetical comparison of the breakdown of competitor's bids might appear as in Fig. 2.8a. Each bid contains some components (trades) that are higher in price than the competitor's counterparts.

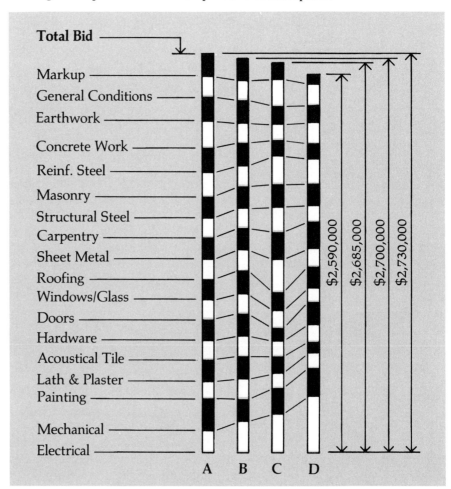

Figure 2.8a

They tend to average out so that the total bid amounts are close together. However, bidder D appears to be exceptionally lower in the total amount. Is it a good bid? Even if no other fault can be found, bidder D has not made a good bid because too much was "left on the table." That is, there is too large a difference in dollars between the low bid and the next lowest bid. The bidder's aim is to produce a low, but not *too* low bid.

2.9 Construction Progress Schedules

The progress schedules discussed in this section are of three kinds:

1. The time in calendar days to estimate and put the bid together.
2. A simple bar graph of the time in months for completion of construction as a basis for estimating the general conditions (see Sec. 2.15, Reviewing General Conditions).
3. The real schedule for controlling the actual time of construction in the field.

In many cases of bidding, one or more of these schedules are not necessary; however, they can be valuable any time the bidder chooses to use them. Let us examine them in the order given.

The schedule of time to estimate and to put the bid together is described in the book, *Estimating for the General Contractor*, by this author, and published by R.S. Means Co., Inc. Three graphs and examples are reproduced here from that book. The reader should keep in mind that estimators and bidders can vary widely in speed and efficiency, so that the periods of time given in these graphs should be taken as averages.

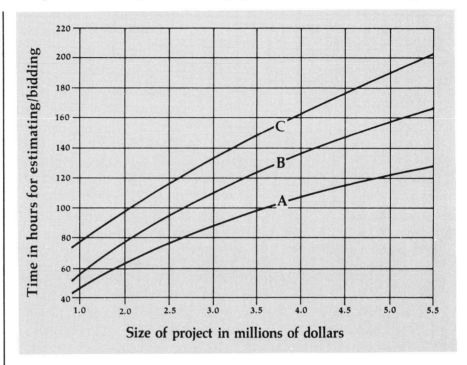

Figure 2.9a

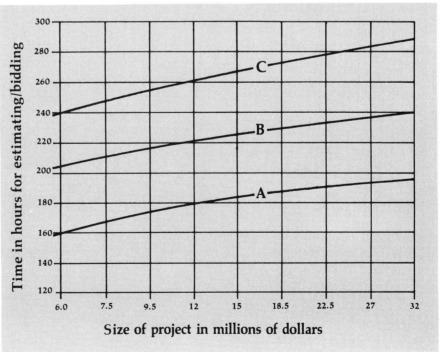

Figure 2.9b

From Figs. 2.9a and 2.9b the bidder is able to approximate the number of calendar days required from receipt of the sponsor's bid package to the date of the established bid deadline. This enables him to decide if there is enough time to accomplish the work concurrent with other projects already in the process of bidding. To use the graphs, the bidder must make a value judgment, i.e., choose the curve most suitable to the current project, or decide to interpolate between, over, or under the curves as drawn. The curves represent the following:

Curve A: simple projects (warehouses, factories, etc.)

Curve B: projects of medium complexity and cost (schools, offices, shops, etc.)

Curve C: complex projects (hospitals, restaurants, engineering facilities, etc.)

The hours shown vertically at the left margin are *net* working hours; therefore, adjustments for interruptions must be made when converting hours to calendar days. Weekend days, holidays, and other nonworking days may be added to the total estimated bidding time.

Example 1: A project is advertised in the cost range of 2-3 million dollars. The estimator judges the complexity as halfway between B and C. From the graph the time to estimate and bid would be:

$$\frac{90 + 122}{2 \times 4} = 26 \ 1/2 \text{ days}$$

Figuring 4 net working hours per day, add 6 days for three intervening weekends and round upward for a total of 33 calendar days.

Example 2: The preliminary estimate for a project of classification A is 5 million dollars. The estimating and bidding hours from the graph are 120 (4 net hrs/day):

Working days are: 120/4 = 30
Calendar days (4 weekends): 30 + 8 = 38

Example 3: A project more complex than C and expected to cost about 3 million dollars may, from the graph, require 160 hours to estimate and bid (4 net hrs/day):

Working days are: 160/4 = 40
Calendar days (5 weekends + 2 holidays): 40 + 12 = 52

Note that in all three examples the time could be reduced by increasing the average number of daily working hours.

To aid in estimating and bidding, a simple bar graph can be valuable. Figure 2.9c, borrowed from *Estimating for the General Contractor*, is an example of such a bar graph. Each important segment (trade) is given a calendar period, and most of the time periods overlap so that the total time to complete the construction is *net*. Without the use of a graph such as this, project completion time would be only a rough guess. The bar graph approach is better than a rough guess; if constructed with great care, it could serve as an effective construction progress schedule in the field. This type of graph will be mentioned again in Part IV, Project Management, and in Part III, Bidding a Project.

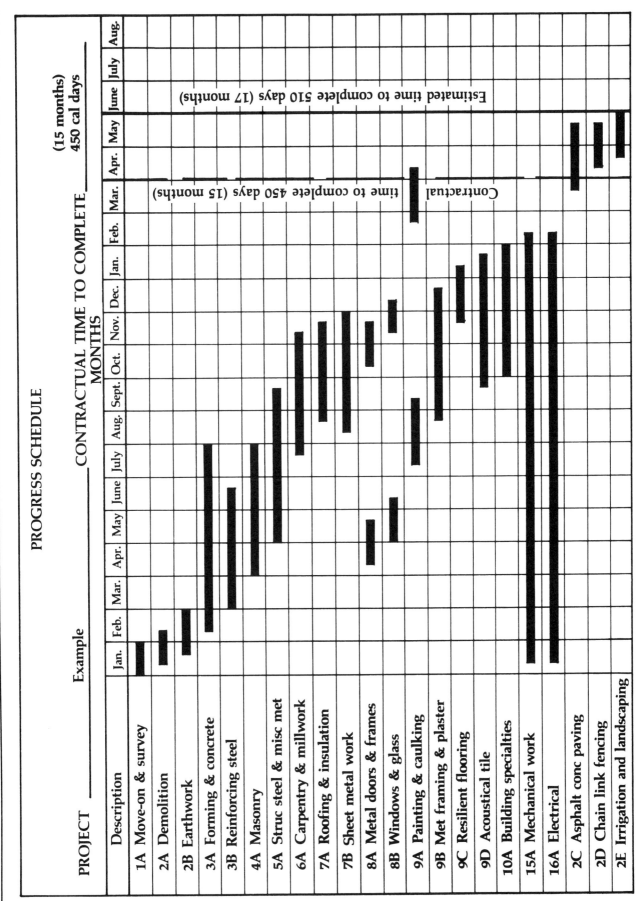

Figure 2.9c

49

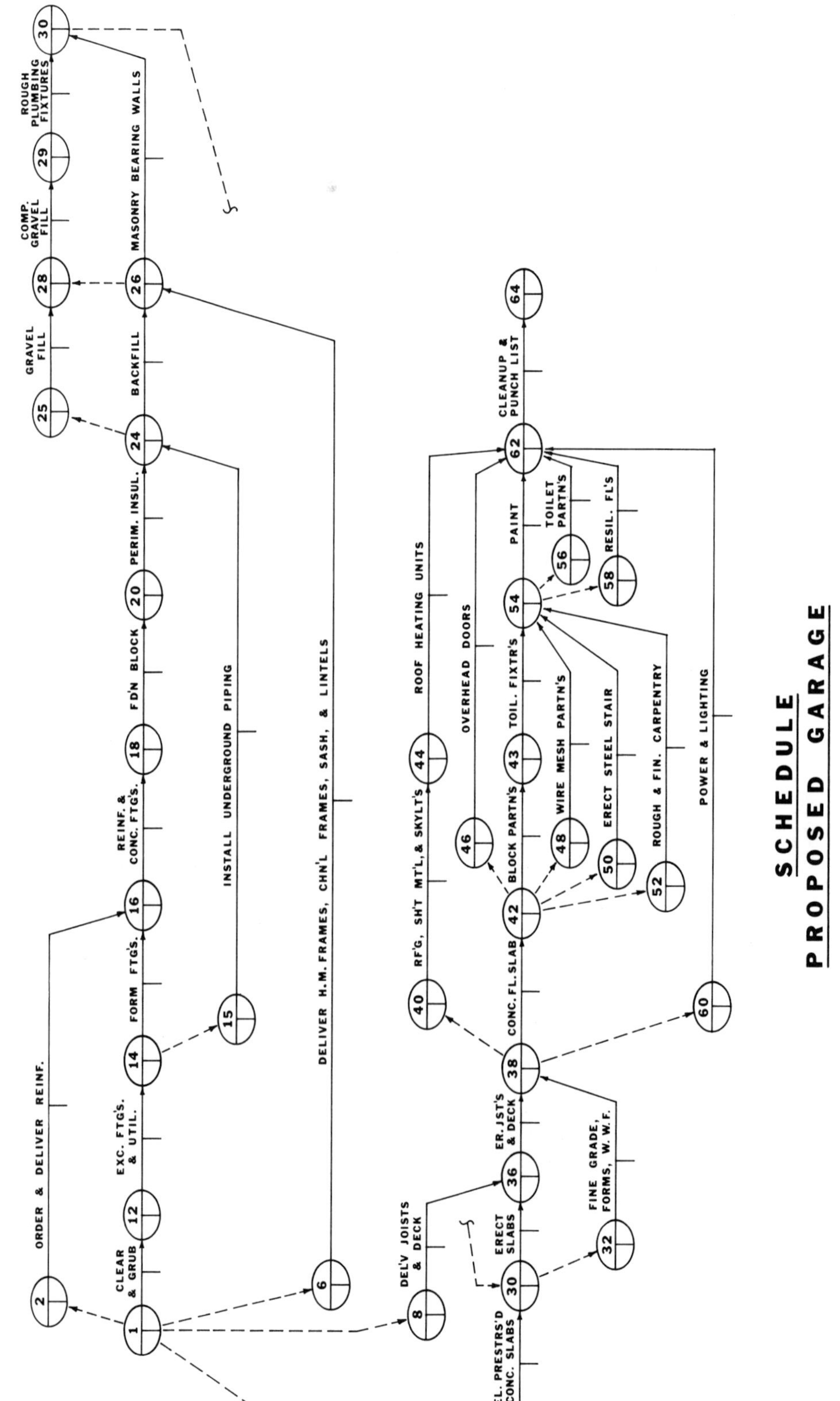
SCHEDULE
PROPOSED GARAGE
ORDER & DELIVER REINF.
CLEAR & GRUB
EXC. FTG'S. & UTIL.
FORM FTG'S.
REINF. & CONC. FTG'S.
FD'N BLOCK
PERIM. INSUL.
BACKFILL
MASONRY BEARING WALLS
GRAVEL FILL
COMP. GRAVEL FILL
ROUGH PLUMBING FIXTURES
INSTALL UNDERGROUND PIPING
DELIVER H.M. FRAMES, CHN'L FRAMES, SASH, & LINTELS
DEL'V JOISTS & DECK
DEL. PRESTRS'D CONC. SLABS
ERECT SLABS
ER. JST'S & DECK
FINE GRADE, FORMS, W. W. F.
CONC. FL. SLAB
RF'G, SH'T MT'L, & SKYLT'S
ROOF HEATING UNITS
OVERHEAD DOORS
BLOCK PARTN'S
TOIL. FIXTR'S
WIRE MESH PARTN'S
ERECT STEEL STAIR
ROUGH & FIN. CARPENTRY
POWER & LIGHTING
PAINT
TOILET PARTN'S
RESIL. FL'S
CLEANUP & PUNCH LIST
1
2
6
8
10
12
14
15
16
18
20
24
25
26
28
29
30
30
32
36
38
40
42
43
44
46
48
50
52
54
56
58
60
62
64

Figure 2.9d

Complex projects may require better scheduling methods than the bar graph. A network scheduling system, for example, CPM (critical path method), is perhaps the best means available to contractors. It has become a service offered competitively by specialist engineers. For this reason, busy bidders rarely construct these sophisticated schedules themselves, even if they possess the skill.

When bidding a project, the bidder chooses a scheduling method, if one is not specified, and either estimates its cost or selects a sub-bid for this service. The reader who wishes to understand and become proficient in network scheduling is referred to *Means Scheduling Manual*, by F. William Horsley, published by R.S. Means Co., Inc.

Figure 2.9d, borrowed from the above mentioned book, is a simple illustration of the method. But more important to the reader at this point are the suggested cost values in Fig. 2.9e for complete, computerized, and monthly updated network schedules proportioned to various sizes of projects. These prices are only representative, and their main value is for checking the validity of sub-bids, or for budgeting in lieu of sub-bids. This type of schedule will be discussed in greater detail in Part IV, Project Management.

Progress Network Schedule Costs Including Monthly Updates

Multiply the total amount of the anticipated bid by:

Size of Project (in Dollars)	A (Simple Project)	B (Medium Complex)	C (Complex Project)
1 to 2 million	.0030	.0040	.0050
2 to 4 million	.0015	.0020	.0025
4 to 6 million	.0010	.0015	.0020
6 to 10 million	.0008	.0012	.0015

Figure 2.9e

2.10 General Bidding Strategies

The bidder wants to produce the low bid, to win the contract, and to take responsibility for the construction. Success in these aims requires that he take a long view of the project as well as tending to the immediate concerns of drawing up a competitive bid.

Inexperienced bidders often neglect the long view, choosing to "get the contract first and worry about details later." To an extent, this is necessary; some details of a project cannot be planned in advance, and must be left to "field decisions."

Expert bidders, however, try to incorporate as much long-run planning as possible into the early stages of the bidding process. After studying each project, the seasoned bidder knows which details will be best served by long-run strategies and where the short view may be more effective.

Bidders rarely get to choose all the strategies they will press into service. More often, they act as the needs of the individual project dictate. Some long and short views compare favorably to one another. Others differ greatly and call for a clear-cut choice on the part of the bidder. Some typical examples are as follows:

Short-Run Strategies

1. Approach the bidding work with a positive attitude. Expect to produce the successful bid. A negative expectation tends to be self-fulfilling.

2. Avoid commitments to subcontractors and suppliers. Be prepared to use estimates and budgets when they are lower than sub-bids.
3. Take chances by using low bids from subs whose competency and/or solvency is in doubt.
5. Plan to produce an acceptable standard of quality.
6. Choose the literal interpretations of items and details in the drawings and specs (assuming they are lower in cost).
7. When options are offered in the specs, take the least expensive.
8. Plan to provide the minimum in general conditions, such as cleanup, barricades, field office, supervision, etc.
9. Break down subcontract and material items into as many small portions as will bring forth lower prices, even though this may cause administrative problems in the future.
10. Leave as many items as possible open to negotiation with the sponsor and with subcontractors.
11. Count heavily on company *esprit de corps* to make a profit from a tightly bid contract.
12. Plan to conduct the construction of the project on a strictly legal basis with all parties concerned; disregard any bad or "goodwill" consequences.

Long-Term Strategies

1. Favor sub-bids that include *all* of the items related to their trades in order to (a) have fewer subcontracts to supervise, coordinate, and manage, (b) reduce the risk of errors of omission, and (c) reduce the probability of disputes. This is the reverse of a short-run strategy.
2. Obtain as many sub-bids as possible, make fair selections, and commit as soon as possible after the bid deadline. Avoid making sub-bidders wait for information and decisions. A dependency relationship to subs is better in the long run, contrary to the short view.
3. Firm up as many items as possible with sponsor and subs, and avoid future negotiations (the reverse of the short-run strategy).
4. Base the bid on realistic expectations of the performances of administrators, supervisors, workmen, and subcontractors.
5. Take pride in the appearance of the project while in process of construction, as well as in the completed product.
6. Strive, within practical limits, to secure the goodwill of sponsors and subs.

The bidding of a typical project includes many choices of strategies, and a combination of long and short-run views.

2.11 Jobsite Investigations

The bidder has a unique viewpoint that differs from the viewpoints of estimators, superintendents, subcontractors, sponsors, and others. The same as the general contractor's overall viewpoint, the bidder's view encompasses the following:

1. The visible jobsite
2. The invisible jobsite (underground, etc.)
3. The drawings and specs
4. Adjacent properties
5. Persons on or near the site
6. Agencies, authorities, public works

All answers and information will be sorted and analyzed and may require further research by questioning the A&E and by consulting

with specialists, experts, and professional people. A proper site investigation accomplishes:

1. A complete comparison of the drawings and specs to the facts, as witnessed at the site.
2. The acquisition of information additional to, or differing from, that presented in the drawings and specs.
3. A space and dimension realization that might not easily be imagined from the scaled drawings.
4. The acquisition of knowledge to be passed along to others, such as subcontractors.
5. The development of confidence in the resulting estimated costs and sub-bids pertaining to the site work.

Site Investigation Check Sheet

Project _____ Bid Date _____

Location _____ A&E _____

1. Distance from home office _____
2. Subsistence for workmen required? yes _____ no _____
3. Railroad spur available? _____ How near? _____
4. Working room: none _____ little _____ ample _____
5. Equipment rental available? _____ how near? _____
6. Labor available? _____ quantity? _____ skill? _____
7. Subcontractors available? _____
8. Source of water _____
9. Source of power _____ telephone _____
10. Need fences, barricades, lights, flagmen? _____
11. Soil conditions _____ hardness _____ wetness _____
12. Extent of clearing, grubbing and tree protection _____
13. Location of disposal area _____ fees _____
14. Source of import fill material _____
15. Security requirements _____
16. Source of concrete, lumber, etc. _____
17. Remarks _____
_____
_____
_____
_____

Investigation made by _____ Date _____

Figure 2.11a

A check sheet such as in Fig. 2.11a is useful in making a thorough, one-trip investigation. It serves two other purposes: (1) as a proxy investigation by someone other than the bidder, when that is necessary, and (2) as a permanent document, of potential legal value, that is made part of the bid package (see Sec. 1.2, The Bid Package). The check sheet may be designed by the bidders to their own liking, or it may be a

standard form such as Means' Job Site Analysis Sheet, shown in Appendix P. Figure 2.11a contains typical items for investigation, explained as follows:

1. *Distance of project from home office* is important for two reasons: (1) the direct cost of travel for manager, superintendent, workmen, and equipment, and (2) construction quality and cost control. Another important distance consideration is within and around the job site itself. Large sites may require vehicles to haul men and materials, and they may also be a cause of reduced daily productivity.

2. *Subsistence for workmen* (compensation for travel costs, food, and accommodations) must be provided in certain cases; the bidder must determine (a) if the project site lies within a subsistence zone, (b) the particular trades that must be compensated, and (c) the per diem rate per person.

3. *Availability of railroad spur* also means any conditions for the delivery of large-quantity or massive manufactured items by means other than rail.

4. *Working room* for job office, storage sheds, the activities of prefabricating, subcontractor materials storage, and parking of vehicles and machinery is essential. The bidder seeks the answers to such questions as:
   a. What portion of the site is available for a temporary staging ground?
   b. Is the area adequate in size and shape?
   c. Does the working area require clearing, grading, drainage, or other preparation? If so, does it require restoration when the project is completed?

5. *The availability of construction equipment* is an important question when a project is located a great distance from a commercial center. In that case, not only would the "move on" and "move off" be costly, but the rental rates would probably be higher than average.

6. *Availability of labor,* particularly skilled workmen, can be a valid question when the project is remote from large cities and/or if the work is highly specialized.

7. *Availability of subcontractors* is a question applicable to projects isolated from centers of construction activity, particularly when work is plentiful in those centers.

8. *Sources of water,* if indicated on the drawings, should be confirmed. Look for valves and fire hydrants, or wells, and note the distance required for temporary piping to convenient points on the site. Consider the need for pumps, water storage tanks, and/or the need for hauling water by tanker truck from specific off-site locations.

9. *Sources of power* and the availability of voltage should be identified. If power source is a great distance from the construction site, consider the alternative of portable generators.

10. *Fences and traffic control* may range from none required, through moderate need, to extensive need. Judge the need for all direct and indirect traffic control, including barricades, lights, signs, signals, flagmen, detours, bridges, pedestrian walks, and canopies.

11.-12. *Soil conditions and clearing* as indicated in the drawings and specs may require further investigation. Typical of the facts and characteristics to be looked for are as follows:
   a. Soil type for ease of excavation
   b. Soil quality for compactness as fill

   c. Presence of rock requiring blasting
   d. Presence of underground or surface water requiring pumping or draining
   e. Extent of grass, weeds, brush, etc. requiring stripping
   f. Quantity of existing topsoil available for reuse.

This information may be obtained by one or a combination of the following methods:
   a. Simple observation of the visible surface
   b. Examination of eroded slopes and recent man-made excavations
   c. Inquiry of local people who may have first-hand knowledge of the soil
   d. Performance of minor excavations by means of hand tools
   e. Exploratory excavating or drilling by means of mechanically powered equipment
   f. Employment of a soils engineering consultant

13. *Location of dump or disposal area* is sometimes indicated on the site drawings, but even when it is thus shown, a visit is recommended to learn the exact distance of travel, cycle time, the nature of roads, the capacity of the dump, the type of material accepted, the requirements regarding compacting and grading, and the fees. When a disposal area is not indicated on the drawings, an attempt should be made to find one. Sometimes more than one dump site is necessary to dispose of different materials—earth, rubble, trash, toxic materials, etc. When it is impossible to determine exact locations of dump sites, minimum distance information is helpful, such as "disposal to 7 miles, minimum; level, paved roads; moderate traffic."

14. *Sources of borrow fill material* should be investigated for distance, cycle time, probable type of equipment required for loading and hauling, sufficiency of the quantity of material available, and so forth.

15. *Security* may be an important need in some cases, demanding consideration of fencing, guards, guard dogs, watchmen, patrol service, special insurance, etc. An alternative is a rough estimate, or allowance, to replace items vulnerable to theft and vandalism.

16. *Sources of construction materials* may be an important determination for remotely located projects, or for unfamiliar neighborhoods. Regarding miscellaneous supplies, two main sources are needed: (a) a convenient over-the-counter supplier for items such as hardware, and (b) a supplier of bulk materials such as lumber, plywood, and plumbing. The source of basic structural materials such as sand, gravel, and transit mixed concrete is of primary importance, since if none is available within a practical distance, a portable batching plant might be a feasible alternative. In addition to source, firm quotations for significant materials are desirable for incorporation into the bid.

17. *Remarks* include all relevant information not covered in the preceding 16 items. Examples are:
   a. Obstacles not shown on the drawings
   b. The need of temporary access roads
   c. Hazardous conditions
   d. Special climatic or other environmental conditions

Site investigations are often a group participation consisting of the bidder, estimator, assistants, and major subcontractor's representatives. Group investigations can result in a valuable exchange of viewpoints.

Figure 2.11b illustrates a method of supporting the drawings for reference while conducting a project investigation. Clamped to a tripod-

supported board, the drawings are easily turned, measured, marked, secured against blowing by wind, kept clean, and transported. They are thus available for inspection by everyone in the site investigation party. The information gathered from the site investigation influences all subdivisions of the bid, but is most significant in recording and pricing the general conditions (see Sec. 2.15, Reviewing General Conditions).

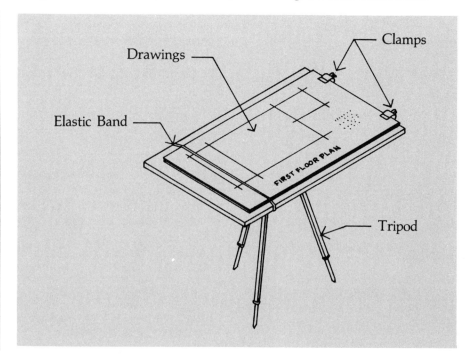

Figure 2.11b

2.12 The Bid Spread Sheet

It is possible to itemize all of the estimates and sub-bids on a standard (letter or legal) size sheet of paper, but that method is not conducive to teamwork, or to the complicated comparisons of sub-bids that take place on bid day. Of the various methods used by different bidders to put the bid together, the spread sheet is one of the most successful.

The central problem, as the deadline approaches, is the great volume of work that must be done in a short time and in a small space. It is a consequence of the competitive bidding system and its need for absolute deadlines. Figure 2.12a dramatizes how the bidder is suddenly deluged with a hundred or more sub-bids. Each line represents a single subcontractor or supplier who has days or weeks to prepare his quotation, but gives the prime bidder only a few hours, or more typically a few minutes, to put the entire bid together.

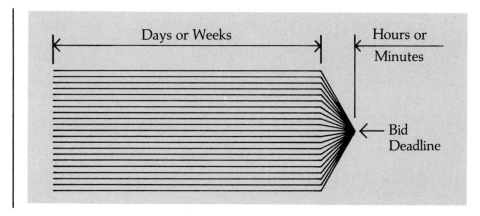

Figure 2.12a

This short period is the *critical moment* in the bidding process. It is the moment when great winning or losing price combinations and risk-laden decision are made, and the time when irreparable mistakes are most likely to occur. Preparation for this moment is the main activity of the bidder from the first receipt of the sponsor's bid package. Heightening the suspense for all participants is the double-edged risk of losing the contract to a lower bidder, or risking commitment to an unprofitable contract.

Of the many activities that occur on bid day, this section focuses on the main tool—the bid spread sheet—for putting the bid together. In a single comprehensive package this sheet serves the needs shown in Table 2.12a.

Table 2.12a

Need	Provision
1. Accessibility to all members of the bidding team.	Sheet, as large as necessary, spread out on a standing-height table and approachable from at least three sides (see Appendix T, Bidding Room Arrangement).
2. Visibility; quick and easy focus on the trades as they are randomly tabulated, compared, reviewed, and selected.	Make the headings large, bold print and list them in a logical sequence, such as alphabetical or by spec section numbers.
3. To minimize last minute work and related chance of error by completing as many items as possible as early as possible.	Isolate the prime bidder's previously estimated trades in the upper-left block of the spread sheet. These are completed items not to be confused with the uncompleted sorting of sub-bids.
4. To recognize the differences in scope and coverage between sub-bids; to compare, select, and record for future proof.	Use columns to differentiate sub-bids, so that the best combinations may be identified.
5. A sharp separation of the best price in each trade from all the working figures in order to avoid confusion in the final summary.	Make a heavily framed box, adjacent to each sub-trade grouping, in which to enter the final price.
6. A system for differentiating the base bid and alternative bid figures.	Use a system of color coding the framed-in pricing boxes.
7. To isolate the final figures for the base bid and alternative bids for study, adjustment, and markup.	Place in lower right-hand corner of the spread sheet a large, color-coded box to match the smaller boxes for individual trades.

1100	GENERAL CONDITIONS	250,792	1,533,092
2050	DEMO. FOR REMODELING	68,400	
3100	C.I.P. CONCRETE	972,560	
5100	INSTALL MISC. METAL	33,000	
6100	CARPENTRY - ROUGH	109,950	
	CARPENTRY - FINISH	81,790	
7900	CAULKING & SEALANTS	36,600	

05100 STRUCTURAL & MISC. METAL

	STRUC.	MISC.		

08700 STEEL OVERHEAD DOORS

06100 MILLWORK

	DOOR LOUVERS	LAM. PLASTIC		
BUDGET	1,200	12,000		
JOINTSR	No	No		

09100 PAINTING & WALL COVERI[NG]

	PAINTING	WALL COVER	ALT. 1

01050 DEMOLITION — 442,500

02200 EARTHWORK — 112,500

	DEMO	EARTH WORK		ALT. 1	
HEADACHE	175,000	No		42,000	
DOZERS	No	267,500		70,500	
DO-ALL	500,000	YES		130,300	

07100 ROOFING & ROOF INSULATION

	ROOFING	INSUL.		

09200 CERAMIC TILE

	LATH & SCRATCH		ALT. 2
BUDGET	1,800		

02400 ASPHALT CONC. PAVING

	A.C. PAVING	HEADERS	STRIPING	ALT. 1	

07200 WALL & CEILING INSULATION

09300 LATHING & PLASTERING

02450 CHAIN LINK FENCE

				ALT. 1	

07600 SHEET METAL

		WALL LOUVERS		ALT. 1	

09400 METAL FRAMING & GYP. BO[ARD]

	METAL FRAMING	GYP. BOARD	

02480 IRRIGATION & LANDSCAPING

	IRRIG.	LAND- SCAPE			

08100 FINISH HARDWARE

09500 RESILIENT FLOORING

09600 CARPETING

	RESIL. FLOOR	CARPET	ALT. 2
BUDGET		19,000	

03200 REINFORCING STEEL

		HOISTING	WELDING	ALT. 1	
BUDGET					

08200 METAL DOORS & FRAMES

09700 ACOUSTIC TILE

	ACOUSTIC TILE	SUSP. CLG.	

04200 MASONRY

		RE-BAR	SHORING 2,800	ALT. 1	
BUDGET					

08500 METAL WINDOWS & GLAZING

	WINDOWS	GLAZING	SLIDE. DOORS	

09800 GLAZED WALL COATING

			ALT. 2

Figure 2.12b

LOCATION ___Long Beach, Calif.___

COMPLETION TIME ___600 Cal. Days___

COLOR CODE
{ BASE BID ——————
{ ALT. 1 — — — —
{ ALT. 2 ooooooooooooo

| ...ERHEAD DOORS | | | 10100 | TOILET PARTITIONS | | | 13300 | INTEGRATED CEILING | | |

| ...& WALL COVERING | | | 10201 | BUILDING SPECIALTIES | | | 14200 | HYDRAULIC ELEVATOR | | |

...TING | WALL COVER | ALT. 1

| ...TILE | | | 10300 | PORTABLE PARTITIONS | | | 15000 | MECHANICAL | | |

...& | ...TCH | ...00 | ALT. 2 | | ALT. 2

| ...& PLASTERING | | | 11100 | ADJUSTABLE LOADING RAMP | | | 16000 | ELECTRICAL | | |

ALT. 2

| ...MING & GYP. BOARD | | | 11600 | DENTAL CASEWORK & EQUIP. | | |

...AL | GYP. ...ING | BOARD

| ...T FLOORING | | | 12100 | FIXED THEATER SEATS | | |

...IL. | CARPET | ALT. 2
...OR | 19,000

BASE BID | COST
| MARK-UP
| SUBTOTAL
| BOND COST
| ADJUSTMENT
| TOTAL

| ...TILE | | | 13100 | RADIATION PROTECTION | | |

...STIC | SUSP. ...F | CLG.

ALT. 1 | COST
| MARK-UP
| SUBTOTAL
| BOND COST
| ADJUSTMENT
| TOTAL

| ...WALL COATING | | | 13200 | WALK-IN REFRIGERATOR | | |

ALT. 2

ALT. 2 | COST
| MARK-UP
| SUBTOTAL
| BOND COST
| ADJUSTMENT
| TOTAL

Figure 2.12b (cont.)

Figure 2.12b is an example of a spread sheet in the first stage of preparation. Using the data from the estimate summary sheet in Fig. 1.6b, each trade or trade grouping is given a block for tabulating and comparing sub-bids.

The large block in the upper-left corner is filled in with the bidder's own prices, produced by the company's estimating department. These prices are shown as completed, added, and entered in the heavily framed code box. Of course, these may be subject to revisions, but for general practical purposes, this huge portion of the bid can be set aside while the bidder concentrates on sub-bids for other trades.

A few sub-bids received early are recorded to show the reader how the spread sheet is used for tabulating, comparing, combining, and selecting. In this example the combination of Headacheball ($175,000 for demolition) and Dozer, Inc. ($267,500 for earthwork) is lower than Do-All's all-inclusive bid of $500,000. Headache's and Dozer's combined bid for Alternative 1 is also lower than Do-All's bid.

The blocks in the lower-right corner of the sheet are filled in and ready for the final totals and markups. All the figures in the solid outlined boxes will be added to arrive at the bare cost of the base bid; the net total of the figures in the boxes outlined with dashes will produce the cost of Alternative 1; and the net total of the figures in the boxes outlined with circles will produce the cost of Alternative 2.

The purpose in this section is to show how the sheet is started. In Sec. 2.18, Putting the Bid Together, this sheet will be completed.

The use of the spread sheet will again be demonstrated in Part III, Bidding a Project.

2.13 Researching for Sub-Bid Coverage

For convenience, the term "sub-bid," as used here, includes quotations of all kinds—material, equipment, services, manufactured items, and off-site and on-site fabrication. It is better to rely on voluntary sub-bids, if all categories are covered, than to solicit bids from subs who may lack interest. There may be exceptions to this rule, as noted below.

It is possible to bid well-publicized projects without deliberately contacting a single sub. This can be done by advertising as a prospective bidder, and then simply waiting for the phone to ring and the mail to arrive. At the other extreme, a bidder might initiate an aggressive inquiry/solicitation process such that every possible sub-bidder is contacted, leaving few surprises on bid day. The degree of effort put forth by the bidder depends on the following.

1. *Company philosophy and policy.* One company's practice may be to contact a minimum of selected subs, while another company's habit is routinely to phone and/or write to every sub on an extensive roster.

2. *The nature and location of the project.* The number and type of subtrades is a guide to the appropriate investigative effort. A project located outside the bidder's familiar locale requires greater effort, since it is possible that out-of-town bidders may experience price discrimination from local subs.

3. *Publicity of the project.* A private, non-competitive, negotiated project, or a select-bid-list project, requires the bidder's initiative in obtaining sub-bid coverage. On the other hand, a public (government) project is usually widely advertised. Many subs thus obtain documents directly from the sponsor and prepare bids entirely on their own initiative.

4. *Cost estimating and budgeting ability of the bidder.* A bidder who lacks knowledge or confidence to calculate the values of sub-trades will more actively solicit sub-bids.

5. *Volume of bidding work.* Bidders who bid few and large projects only may have time to research sub-bid coverage thoroughly. Bidders who bid many relatively small projects may not have time to do more than minimum research.

6. *Special features of the project.* Lower response of sub-bids occurs when:
   a. For strategic purposes, the bidder prefers not to advertise as a prospective bidder.
   b. A project consists of one or a few major sub-trades, and the bidder knows beforehand the identity of the qualified sub-bidders.

Whatever the response of sub-bidders, a systematic method is desirable, beginning with a roster of currently active subcontractors similar to the example in Fig. 2.13a. Regular use of the roster keeps it current, with names and phone numbers constantly revised. Since this roster is used almost entirely in direct telephoning, mailing addresses may be omitted. For inquiry by mail, a second roster may be kept, complete with addresses. When there is sufficient time, written communication is especially desired. To save long-distance phone costs, inquiries by mail may be justified. In this section, we will focus on the more usual person-to-person approach.

The "call sheet," as the roster is sometimes called, classifies subcontractors by trades. Knowing the names of persons, who can make direct "yes" and "no" responses saves call-back time. Portions of the telephone inquiries can be delegated by the bidder to others. Routine trades requiring no discussion may be delegated to assistants.

Since the call sheet is a standard form for use in the bidding of all jobs, it contains the names of subcontractors whose trades are not involved in every project. Therefore, in using it the bidder designates by check marks certain subs to be called who seem the most suitable and the most likely to be interested, for the following reasons:

   1. Their trades are involved in the project.
   2. They are known to be professional and dependable.
   3. They are known to be competitive.
   4. They tend to specialize in the particular type of construction represented by the current project (commercial, institutional, military, etc.).
   5. There are few subs in their specialty.
   6. They are presently doing similar work under another contract.

Ideally, a series of three calls should be made: (1) at the beginning, to register the reactions of the subs, (2) again, near the midpoint in the bidding process, to check those subs whose first responses were indefinite; and (3) just before the deadline, to inquire of any remaining nonresponsive subs.

The purpose of such an exhaustive research is the assurance of receiving all sub-bids available—all that the competing prime bidders, too, will have. (This is somewhat like having knowledge of the other "card player's hand.") There is no perfect assurance, however, because:

   1. Subs whose responses were positive may still fail to bid.
   2. Subs do not always bid the same amount to all prime bidders.
   3. Unknown (such as out-of-town) subs may offer surprise bids.
   4. Subs do not all bid to all prime bidders.

Example
Sub-bid Call Sheet
(One of Several Sheets)

Trade	Person	Phone Number	Response
Demolition			
Headacheball	Carson	290-3546	yes
Crusher Spec.	Tillford	987-1543	no
Do-all Demo	Ed S.	102-3945	maybe
Level Bros.	Tim Level	787-8787	no
Earthwork			
Heaping Load	Bob Ricks	456-7676	?
Dozers Inc.	Joe Snow	666-7890	yes
Grubbing Co.	McKay	432-0987	no
Fencing			
Obstacles, Inc.	Jean	798-1110	maybe
Partitioners	Moody	756-7772	yes
Stop-all	Greg J.	889-9898	?
Masonry			
Histackers	Davis	254-1727	yes
Block & Sons	Jim Block	714-9295	yes
Moneyline	Conrad	344-8484	no
Struc. & Misc. Steel			
Ringer Steel Co.	J. Ringer	678-1222	yes
L.T. Pizza Iron	R. Burr	554-4123	yes
Rusty Fabricators	Sandy	765-7020	maybe
Reinforcing Steel			
Fast Benders	Presley	987-7544	yes
Stout Steel	Jim Stout	447-2322	?
Better Rebar	Alan	124-9033	yes
Millwork			
Joint Splicer Ind.	Rudy Redwood	557-7000	yes
Miter Square Fac.	Doris	457-6606	yes
Fancy Casework	Mac	447-4477	no
Mechanical			
Plumco	Jack Evans	798-3446	yes
Low Temp	George	889-6720	maybe
Comfort Co.	A. Choo	456-4567	?
U.G. Spec	Gopher	102-4205	yes

Figure 2.13a

Figure 2.13a shows a system of symbols for recording the calls and responses. Secondary, but important, information results from these inquiries, for instance:

1. Insights into the attitudes, advantages, and disadvantages held by competing prime contractors from knowledge passed through subs.
2. Knowledge of new prospective prime bidders, or of those withdrawing from the contest.
3. Risk or problem areas in the project, as discovered by subs.
4. Knowledge of items that subs might exclude from their work, requiring further research or budgeting work by the bidder.

Names of positive responding subs may be entered on the spread sheet, Fig. 2.12b, to provide a concept of the probable sub-bid coverage and to save time in the crucial moments of the bid assembly.

2.14 Budgets, Plug-In Figures, and Allowances

As the bid deadline nears, assessment of the bid coverage strengths and weaknesses becomes apparent. Some of the trades promise complete and competitive coverage; some only moderate and relaxed bidding; a few trades are uncertain as to coverage and correctness of bid prices.

Exclusive reliance on sub-bids might produce an out-of-control prime bid—one that is too high or too low and contains some last-minute wild guesses for items not covered. To avoid this, the bidder prepares rough estimates or budgets of the trades that are expected to be weak in sub-bid coverage. This activity might continue through to the deadline, as the need arises. For instance, the promise of a dependable bid on a trade or portion of a trade might vanish at the last moment, thus requiring a hasty calculation for a plug-in figure or allowance.

True estimates for these exclusions are preferred, but they are seldom possible for two reasons: (1) the bidder's lack of expert knowledge of the trade, and (2) shortage of time. Estimating is usually done in haste, thereby delivering a varied range of dependability. For example:

1. *The budget* takes the form of an estimate, with quantities and unit prices, but it falls short of the accuracy and dependability of a true estimate. When the bidder has reference to unit cost information, budgets can be dependable enough to serve as a basis for later negotiation of subcontracts. Figure 2.14a is an example of an asphaltic concrete paving budget made with reference to *Building Construction Cost Data*, published by R.S. Means Co., Inc.

Prepare and roll subgrade	7,130 sy @ $ .65 =	$ 4,635
6" base course	7,000 sy @ 2.27 =	15,890
3" a.c. paving	7,000 sy @ 5.60 =	39,200
1½" a.c. topping on exist. paving	2,000 sy @ 2.87 =	5,740
¾" sand finish course	9,000 sy @ 1.48 =	13,320
2" a.c. sidewalk	130 sy @ 3.84 =	499
	Total	$79,284

Figure 2.14a

2. *A plug-in figure* is a very briefly computed budget. If cost information or time to estimate is not available, a quick approximation of value may be made by a few overall quantities and all-inclusive unit prices. Figure 2.14b shows the same asphaltic concrete work given in Fig. 2.14a, but calculated more briefly and with unit prices rounded out.

3" a.c. on 6" base course	7,000 sy @ $10.00 =	$70,000
2" a.c. sidewalk (no base)	130 sy @ 4.00 =	520
1½" a.c. topping on exist. paving	2,000 sy @ 5.00 =	10,000
	Total	$80,520

Figure 2.14b

3. *An allowance* is simply a lump sum "thrown in," with less mathematical support. This recourse may be the only one available at the last moment, as in the event of no sub-bids, and is to be avoided if at all possible. Figure 2.14c shows an allowance for the example of asphaltic concrete paving work that was calculated with slightly more detail in

Figs. 2.14a and 2.14b. Here, it is lumped together in one quantity and one unit price, both rounded off.

Figure 2.14c

a.c. paving, all kinds	9,200 sy @ $9.00 = $82,800

An *ideal* bid is composed entirely of estimates and firm sub-bids. Budgets, plug-in figures, and allowances are used only as temporary aids in the bidding process; it is intended that they be replaced with sub-bids before the deadline.

A *typical* bid falls short of the ideal and contains a few budgets, plug-in figures, and allowances. Within reason, these need not be critical to the outcome of the bidding. In Part III, Bidding a Project, these temporary expedients are fully demonstrated.

Looking back, we can see that budgets, plug-in figures, and allowances are only names for different degrees of accuracy in the estimate, as can be visualized in Fig. 2.14d. These shade together with no distinguishable points of division.

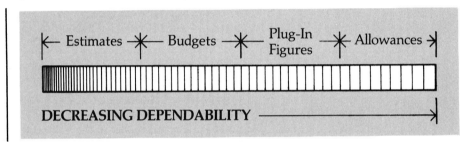

Figure 2.14d

2.15 Reviewing the General Conditions

In Sec. 1.6, Reviewing the Estimate, portions of a project to be performed by the bidder's own company (prime contractor) were reviewed by the bidder after estimates were made by the estimating department. The estimated cost of general conditions deserves special attention because it involves judgment and experience in the cost records of many completed projects.

A check list is a valuable tool for reviewing General Conditions. The following Check List is borrowed from *Estimating for the General Contractor* (see Sec. 2.9). Items with check marks refer to the estimate reviewed and adjusted in Fig. 2.15a.

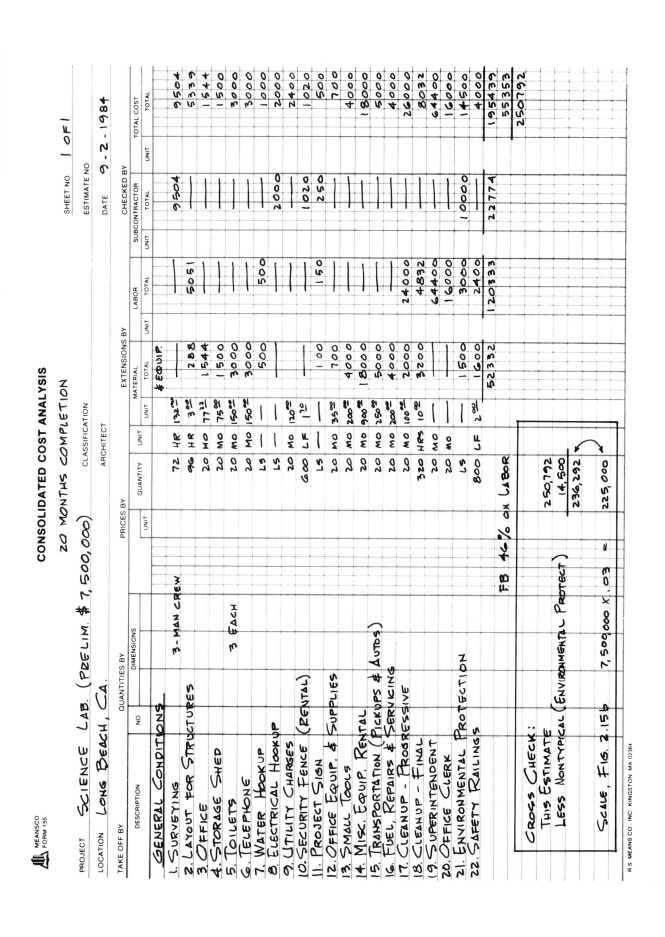

Figure 2.15a

General Conditions Check List

✔ Surveying
✔ Layout for structures
✔ Office (contractor's)
   Office (inspector's)
✔ Storage shed
✔ Toilets
✔ Telephone
✔ Water hookup
✔ Water monthly charges
✔ Electric power pole and service
✔ Electric power monthly charges
✔ Security-yard fence and gates
✔ Signs (project and safety)
   Temporary closures, doors, and windows
✔ Office equipment, supplies, and printing
✔ Small tool purchase, sharpening, and depreciation
✔ Miscellaneous equipment rental
✔ Oil, fuel, tires, repairs, and servicing
✔ Pickup trucks and transportation
   First-aid and fire equipment
   Dust and noise control
✔ Cleanup (progressive)
✔ Cleanup (final)
   Window and fixture cleaning
✔ Superintendent
   Travel (administrative staff)
   Travel (workmen)
   Subsistence
   Freight costs to jobsite
   Generator for electric power
   Barricades and canopies
   Scaffolding
   Lights, flagmen, and bridges over ditches
   Sewer and water connection fees
   Building and plan-checking fees and permits
   Engineer's and professional fees
   Progress schedules and CPM network analysis
   Special insurance and taxes
   Equipment and purchasing
   Ferry or bridge tolls
   Shoring of trench or pit sides
   Dewatering
   Premium for hot- or cold-weather work
   Premium for unskilled labor
   Temporary access roads and detours
   Overtime work
   Extra drawings and specs not supplied by A&E
   Photographs
   Underpinning and protecting adjacent property
   Watchman
✔ Office clerk and time clerk
   Project manager
   Extra foreman
   Special hoisting, elevators, and towers
✔ Environmental protection
✔ Safety provisions, railings, etc.

Installation of owner-furnished materials or equipment
Locating, protection, and repairing underground utilities

Even a rough idea of the general conditions cost of a project is useful for cross checking. Because the size of a project and the time to complete construction determine the cost of general conditions, a formula is possible. Figure 2.15b is an example of a scale used to find the approximate cost of general conditions. It should not be used as a substitute for a carefully detailed estimate. An estimate should be made first, and then cross-checked by drawing a straight line between the completion time on the vertical scale and the project size on the vertical scale. Now locate the point on this line which coincides with the project size on the horizontal scale. The decimal at the intersection, multiplied by the project size, gives an approximate cost for General Conditions.

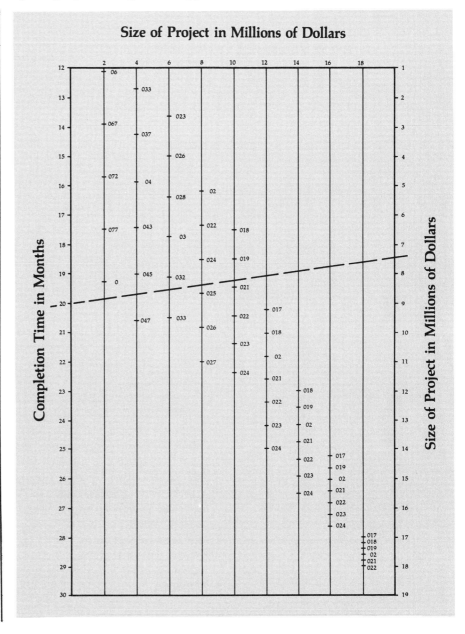

Figure 2.15b

In this example, multiply .03 x $7,500,000 = $225,000. This is 5% lower than the detailed breakdown in Fig. 2.15a of $236,292. If the bidder is satisfied with the total revised estimated cost ($250,792 in this

example), then the figure is printed in its proper place in the upper-left corner block of the spread sheet, as shown in Fig. 2.12b.

2.16 Guarding Against Errors

The terms "error" and "mistake" are here used interchangeably. The four main types are:

1. Mistakes of judgment
2. Errors of omission
3. Mistakes of arithmetic
4. Slips

Mistakes of judgment are perhaps the most serious because they are the least correctable. The bidder is held accountable for judgment, but is forgiven the "human" errors of omission, arithmetic, and slips, which have a better chance of correction before the bid deadline.

Whereas omissions, arithmetic, and slips have to do with the mechanics of bidding, judgment deals with choices, opinions, values, decisions, methodology, imagination, and so forth. Those portions of a project that depend on judgment are almost exclusively the personal responsibility of the bidder, and judgment errors are not as likely to be discovered by checkers as the other three types of errors.

The following are two examples of judgment errors and ways to avoid them:

1. Choosing a project. It can happen that no fault lies in the estimating or bidding work, but that a project was unsuitable for this contractor. To avoid this error, invest time in the analysis of a project as described in Sec. 1.4, Analyzing a Project for Desirability.
2. Evaluating the construction completion time. If the time is greatly over or underestimated, the cost differential can be significant. To avoid this, invest sufficient effort to construct a realistic progress schedule similar to the example in Sec. 2.9, Construction Progress Schedules. Such a schedule need not be more detailed for bidding.

Errors of omission are avoided by the use of check lists and by the use of routine methods or reading the drawings and specs (see Sec. 2.2, Reading the Drawings and Specifications). Routine methods are habits developed from experience in bidding. For instance,

1. Use a systematic procedure in summarizing the drawings and specs to avoid omitting entire trades.
2. Use the bid spread sheet for separating and comparing sub-bids (see Secs. 1.7 and 2.12) to avoid omitting portions of trades and borderline items easily overlooked by everyone.
3. Fill in all spaces on columnar sheets with *something*, if only dashes, for no-cost or plug-in figures. Should an omission occur, any amount plugged in for an item is better than no amount at all.
4. Use check lists, such as the following, to avoid omitting small items:
   a. Estimate summary sheet, Fig. 1.6b
   b. The bid spread sheet, Figs. 1.7a and 2.12b
   c. Site investigation check sheet, Fig. 2.11a
   d. General conditions check list, Sec. 2.15

Mistakes of arithmetic can be avoided by having someone other than the original estimator check all extensions conscientiously.

It is a good habit for the bidder routinely to "eyeball" all figures for approximate correctness. It is a good idea to check extensions, quantities, and unit prices. All large numbers, whether they are quantities, unit prices, or extensions, should be examined. Examples of

errors are shown in Fig. 2.16a, including for contrast a small error of the kind that might not catch the attention of any but a trained eye.

Example	Quantity	Unit Price	Extension	Error
1	16,000 sf	$ .25	400	$ 3,600 low
2	60 hrs	161.00	966	8,694 low
3	360 cy	9.10	32,760	29,484 high
4	125 sf	2.92	240	125 low
			Net Error	$17,065 high

Figure 2.16a

In Example 1, the bidder's attention is caught by the large quantity; the error is obvious, since .25 = 1/4, and one-fourth of 16,000 is 4,000. In Example 2, the unit price is relatively high. Rough mental arithmetic produces: 60 x 160 = 9,600, indicating a decimal point error. Example 3 shows an extension disproportionately large for the small quantity and unit price. Mental arithmetic would produce: 9 x 360 = 3,240 as the approximately correct figure. Example 4 contains an arithmetic error that would probably escape the bidder's notice, since all figures are small, and the error is a round figure.

While errors on the low side could mean financial loss, errors on the high side could mean loss of the bid. All of the methods named above guard against both low and high errors. The two main causes of low cost errors are faulty quantities and omissions; the two main causes of high cost errors are faulty quantities and double-coverage of certain items. Methods for guarding against these errors are discussed in Sec. 2.17, Preparing to Bid, and in Sec. 2.18, Putting the Bid Together.

Slips is a general category for all errors that cannot be clearly classified as judgment, omission, or arithmetic. It includes combinations of those three, as well as transpositions, misquoting, mishearing, mismeasuring, misreading, misnoting, and forgetting. Most of these are avoided by well-designed estimating and bidding forms, by developed skill in estimating and bidding techniques, and by careful cross-checking.

The best guard against errors is the bidder's in-depth knowledge of the project. A person who steps in to supervise the bidding at an advanced stage is at a disadvantage in recognizing errors. That person has to make broad assumptions and accept figures at their face value. This need to know the project in depth is the reason that the bidder is often the original estimator.

A knowledge of the various material quantities in the project and the unit prices is valuable in the recognition of sub-bid errors. Plug-in figures made in advance by the bidder or estimator make it possible to recognize the following type of error:

Timber piling (sub-bid received) $110,000

Bidder's previous plug-in-figure $225,000
(225 ea. @ $1,000)

In response to questioning, the sub reveals an error in estimated quantities.

Even without knowledge of quantities and unit prices, the bidder is often able to recognize potential errors by comparison of sub-bids. When two or more sub-bids are within close range, and another bid is out of proportion, the bidder is justified (although not necessarily

obligated) in checking the latter for error. For instance, suppose the following electrical bids are received:

Bid A: $398,000
Bid B: $405,000
Bid C: $389,000
Bid D: $260,000

In this instance, the bidder has no knowledge of the quantities or unit prices and can only reason that sub-bid D probably contains a gross error. Section 2.18, Putting the Bid Together, provides other instances of this, along with procedures for resolving such problems.

2.17 Preparing to Bid

In order to minimize the work on bid day and to use the limited time to best advantage, everything that is possible should be completed the day before. Preparations typically include the actions as shown in Figure 2.17a and 2.17b.

Joint Splicer Industries
101 Woodwork Drive
Arcadia, CA

To: Your Company   Sept. 15, 1984

Regarding: Science Lab, Long Beach, CA

We propose to furnish all millwork and cabinets in accordance with section ___06100___ of the drawings and specifications, except items listed below under "exclusions," for the lump sum price of _____
(price to follow)

Exclusions: Metal doors and frames
                 Metal louvers and glass in doors
                 Hardware, except for cabinets
                 Laminated plastic
                 Installation

Addenda Acknowledged: #1,2 & 3   Terms: Standard
Conditions: FOB jobsite, sales tax included

Joint Splicer Industries

By *Rudy Redwood, Mgr.*

Figure 2.17a

1. Analyze all flyers (mailed-in proposals) and record the information on the bid spread sheet. (Figure 2.17a is an example of a flyer.) Only pieces that will be phoned in on bid day remain to be considered. Figure 2.17b is an example of the bid spread sheet at the intermediate stage of the bidding procedure.
2. Contact all prospective sub-bidders whose intentions are still in doubt. Try to determine:
   a. Whether or not they will bid. This completes the inquiries started earlier (see Sec. 2.13, Researching for Sub-Coverage).
   b. The particular items they will bid, and items they will exclude.
   c. Their viewpoints on particular technical or business questions, such as quantities, unit prices, methods of construction, hoisting, scaffolding, and so forth.
3. Review all bidding documents, such as bid forms, bid bond, and instructions regarding the formalities (such as time and place of the bid opening, addressed and sealed envelope, etc.).
4. Study any and all addenda and incorporate them into the bid.
5. Make up any budgets, plug-in figures, or allowances that are needed.
6. Enter all completed estimates in the prime bidder's block (upper-left corner of the spread sheet, Fig. 2.17b). Do not total the estimates, since there may be cause for revisions.
7. Make up special sub-bid comparison sheets when more space is needed than is provided on the spread sheet. See Fig. 2.17c for an example.
8. Make a rough total of the project costs, if enough figures are available. It may be useful to do so because a knowledge of the approximate amount of the bid is a basis for deciding the markup and avoiding a last-minute snap decision.
9. Review and adjust the earlier evaluation of desirability rating (see Sec. 1.4, Analyzing a Project for Desirability) and, based on the rough total costs of the project and the markup finder scale (Fig. 2.6k), decide on a markup to be used. Even this markup is tentative because facts appearing up to the bid deadline may alter the desirability rating. If they do, a final adjustment to the selected markup is quickly accomplished.

				1,533,092	PROJECT	SCIENCE LAB.				LOCATIO
1100	GENERAL CONDITIONS		250,792		BID DATE	SEPT. 18, 1984				COMPLE
2050	DEMO. FOR REMODELING		68,400							
3100	C.I.P. CONCRETE		972,560							
5100	INSTALL MISC. METAL		33,000							
6100	CARPENTRY - ROUGH		109,950							
	CARPENTRY - FINISH		81,790							
7900	CAULKING & SEALANTS		36,600							

05100 STRUCTURAL & MISC. METAL

	STRUC.	MISC.	ALT. 1
RINGER			
PIZZA			

08700 STEEL OVERHEAD DOORS

	DOORS	INSTALL
BUDGET	No	20,000
OVER DR.		YES

06100 MILLWORK

	DOOR LOUVERS	LAM. PLASTIC
BUDGET	1,200	12,000
JOINTSR.	No	No
MITER SQ.	No	No

09100 PAINTING & WALL COVERI

	PAINTING	WALL COVER	ALT. 1

01050	DEMOLITION			442,500
02200	EARTHWORK			112,500

	DEMO	EARTH WORK		ALT. 1
HEADACHE	175,000	No		42,000
DOZERS	No	267,500		70,500
DO-ALL	500,000	YES		130,300

07100 ROOFING & ROOF INSULATION

	ROOFING	INSUL.
TOPPERS		
NO-LEAK		

09200 CERAMIC TILE

	LATH & SCRATCH	ALT. 2
BUDGET	1,800	

02400 ASPHALT CONC. PAVING

	A.C. PAVING	HEADERS	STRIPING	ALT. 1
BUDGET	79,284	YES	1,750	6,800
BLAZERS		YES	No	

07200 WALL & CEILING INSULATION

	WALLS	CEILINGS
BATCO	45,000	21,400

09300 LATHING & PLASTERING

02450 CHAIN LINK FENCE

	FENCE		ALT. 1
PARTITIONERS	22,100		1,100

07600 SHEET METAL

	WALL LOUVERS		ALT. 1
BUDGET	3,700		
LEADERS			

09400 METAL FRAMING & GYP. BO

	METAL FRAMING	GYP. BOARD
WALLERS		No
GYPERS		

02480 IRRIGATION & LANDSCAPING

	IRRIG.	LAND-SCAPE
GREEN I.		No
BEAN S.	No	

08100 FINISH HARDWARE

	HARDWARE
BUDGET	22,000

09500 RESILIENT FLOORING

09600 CARPETING

	RESIL. FLOOR	CARPET	ALT. 2
BUDGET		19,000	
UNDER FT.		No	
RECARP	No	21,200	
FLOORER			

03200 REINFORCING STEEL

	HOISTING	WELDING	ALT. 1
BUDGET			
FAST B.			
BETTER R.			

08200 METAL DOORS & FRAMES

	DOORS	FRAMES
SLAMMER	37,480	YES
ACCESS		YES

09700 ACOUSTIC TILE

	ACOUSTIC TILE	SUSP. CLG.
TILESPEC		

04200 MASONRY

	RE-BAR	SHORING 2,800	ALT. 1
BUDGET		2,800	
HIGH ST.			
BROCKSON			

08500 METAL WINDOWS & GLAZING

	WINDOWS	GLAZING	SLIDE. DOORS
SLIDERS	No	No	18,500

09800 GLAZED WALL COATING

		ALT. 2

Figure 2.17b

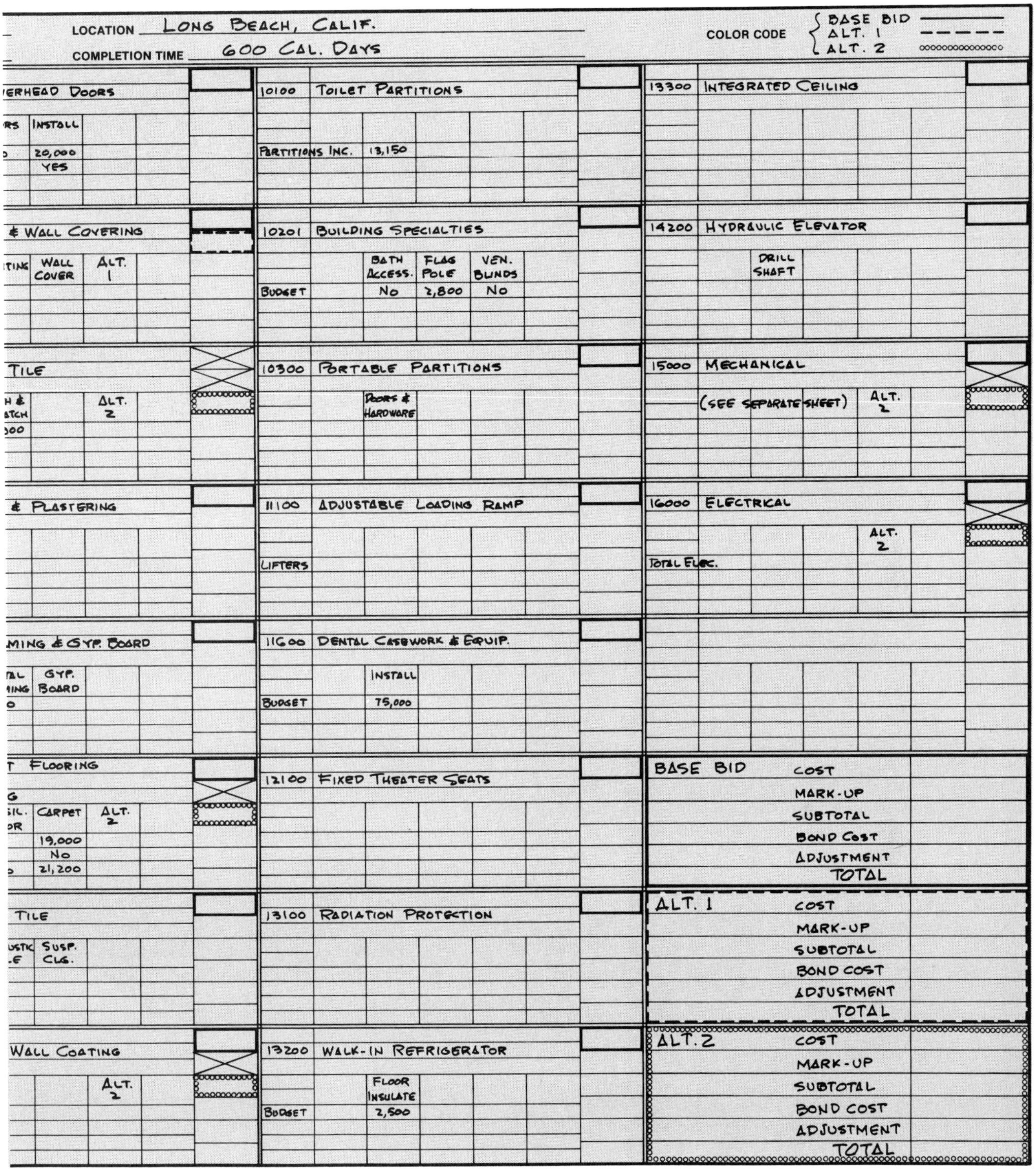

LOCATION LONG BEACH, CALIF.
COMPLETION TIME 600 CAL. DAYS
COLOR CODE: BASE BID; ALT. 1; ALT. 2

...ERHEAD DOORS
...RS | INSTALL
... | 20,000
| YES

... & WALL COVERING
...TING | WALL COVER | ALT. 1

TILE
...H & ...ATCH | ALT. 2
...300

... & PLASTERING

...MING & GYP. BOARD
...AL ...MING | GYP. BOARD
...O

...T FLOORING
...G
...SIL. ...OR | CARPET | ALT. 2
| 19,000
| NO
... | 21,200

... TILE
...USTIC ...E | SUSP. CLG.

... WALL COATING
ALT. 2

10100 TOILET PARTITIONS
PARTITIONS INC. | 13,150

10201 BUILDING SPECIALTIES
| BATH ACCESS. | FLAG POLE | VEN. BLINDS
BUDGET | NO | 2,800 | NO

10300 PORTABLE PARTITIONS
DOORS & HARDWARE

11100 ADJUSTABLE LOADING RAMP
LIFTERS

11600 DENTAL CASEWORK & EQUIP.
| INSTALL
BUDGET | 75,000

12100 FIXED THEATER SEATS

13100 RADIATION PROTECTION

13200 WALK-IN REFRIGERATOR
| FLOOR INSULATE
BUDGET | 2,500

13300 INTEGRATED CEILING

14200 HYDRAULIC ELEVATOR
DRILL SHAFT

15000 MECHANICAL
(SEE SEPARATE SHEET) | ALT. 2

16000 ELECTRICAL
ALT. 2
TOTAL ELEC.

BASE BID: COST; MARK-UP; SUBTOTAL; BOND COST; ADJUSTMENT; TOTAL

ALT. 1: COST; MARK-UP; SUBTOTAL; BOND COST; ADJUSTMENT; TOTAL

ALT. 2: COST; MARK-UP; SUBTOTAL; BOND COST; ADJUSTMENT; TOTAL

Figure 2.17b (cont.)

			Section 1500 — Mechanical Work			
	Sewer	Water	Plumbing	Air Cond.	Heating	Total
Budget		$290,000			$175,000	
Plumco	no	no	yes	no	no	
U.G. Spec.	yes	no	no	no	no	
Comfort Co.	no	no	no	yes	incl.	
Low temp	yes	incl.	no	yes	no	
Allco	yes	incl.	incl.	incl.	incl.	

Figure 2.17c

In Fig. 2.17b the spread sheet, which was started in Fig. 2.12b, is further developed with information from flyers and a few early sub-bids. All of the known prospective subs are named in their appropriate blocks. Information is arranged in a manner to simplify the comparisons that will later be made in haste.

Since sub-bids are often incomplete, they require additions or subtractions in order to make coverage equal. The dollar differences then become apparent. Budgets, plug-in figures, and allowances are useful and sometimes necessary to complete the comparisons. Figure 2.17c demonstrates in detail a typical assortment of proposed bids for the mechanical trades. A "yes" indicates portion subs will bid; a "no" indicates item subs will not bid; an "incl." means that the item will be included in the sub-bid and will not be quoted separately.

The bidder has computed budget figures for exterior water ($290,000) and heating ($175,000) and placed these figures on a color-shaded line to distinguish them from firm bids. The combinations shown in Fig. 2.17d are possible. Because of the complexity of this group of bids, they are not crowded onto the bid spread sheet, but are simply identified there by the numbers 1, 2, 3, 4, and 5 (see Fig. 2.18b).

	1	2	3	4	5
Sewer	U.G. Spec.	U.G. Spec.	Low temp	Low temp	Allco
Water	Budget	Budget	incl.	incl.	incl.
Plumbing	Plumco	Plumco	Plumco	Plumco	incl.
Air Cond.	Low temp	Comfort	Low temp	Comfort	incl.
Heating	Budget	incl.	Budget	incl.	incl.

Figure 2.17d

2.18 Putting the Bid Together

The bid day is the "birthday" of a construction project, in that its idea becomes reality through the transitional activity of bidding and contract. The bidder's previously diversified activities of making and inviting a great number of estimates and quotations now concentrates into one strenuous effort of receiving, sorting, comparing, choosing, and assembling the data—in short, putting the bid together. Figure 2.12a illustrates the convergence of the many independent sub-bids to a point just before the bid deadline. Tensions rise because of the mental concentration required, the chance of error, and the mutual commitments and apprehensions regarding success or failure.

An experienced bidder realizes that a thoroughly planned bidding procedure, managed with perfect control, can suddenly be thrown into chaos by the sheer quantity of incoming bids, hasty analyses, and

unverified computations. Such collapses in the bidding process occur when the complexity of the incoming data exceeds the capability of the bidding team within the given time frame. These collapses can happen in spite of superior preparation and teamwork; the bidder is always looking for means to improve the bid day routine.

In the previous section, we developed the spread sheet as far as the available data permitted. Now, the sub-bids rapidly accumulate on forms such as Fig. 2.18a (also see the Means "Telephone Quotation" sheet, Appendix E).

Telephone Quotation

Project _Science Lab_   Bid Date ____9/18/84____

Subcontractor _Histackers_   Date Received _9/18/84_

Person Quoting ___Davis___   Time Received ___1:05 p.m.___

Item/Trade ___04200 Masonry___

Per P&S ✔ Addenda _1,2 & 3_ Installed___ For Job___ Taxes Included ✔

Inclusions	Prices
Rebar	482,482
Hoisting	

Exclusions
  Shoring of openings
  Miscellaneous inserts

Figure 2.18a

The bid takers should be experienced in receiving phoned-in bids, asking relevant questions, and accurately recording the information. Figure 2.18a exhibits an example of a typical phoned-in sub-bid with relevant qualifications and stipulations. This form may also be used as a flyer for recording early conversations with subs prior to receipt of their firm bid prices (see Sec. 2.17, Preparing To Bid).

The spread sheet started in Fig. 2.12b and developed to an intermediate level in Fig. 2.17b is now shown completed in Fig. 2.18b. Combinations of sub-bids selected as "best" (not necessarily the lowest) are circled, summed up, and entered in their boxes. All base bid figures are added together and the total amount is entered opposite Base Bid Cost in the upper of the three summary blocks in the lower right-hand corner of the spread sheet.

1100	GENERAL CONDITIONS	250,792	1,533,092
2050	DEMO. FOR REMODELING	68,400	
3100	C.I.P. CONCRETE	972,560	
5100	INSTALL MISC. METAL	33,000	
6100	CARPENTRY - ROUGH	109,950	
	CARPENTRY - FINISH	81,790	
7900	CAULKING & SEALANTS	36,600	
		1,533,092	

PROJECT: SCIENCE LAB. LOCATION
BID DATE: SEPT. 18, 1984 COMPLE

01050 DEMOLITION — 442,500

02200 EARTHWORK — 112,500

	DEMO	EARTH WORK	ALT. 1
HEADACHE	175,000	No	42,000
DOZERS	No	267,500	70,500
DO-ALL	500,000	YES	130,300

02400 ASPHALT CONC. PAVING — 81,034 / 6,800

	A.C. PAVING	HEADERS	STRIPING	ALT. 1
BUDGET	79,284	YES	1,750	6,800
BLAZERS	82,360	YES	No	7,000

02450 CHAIN LINK FENCE — 22,100 / 1,100

	FENCE	ALT. 1
PARTITIONERS	22,100	1,100
OBSTACLES, INC.	26,000	1,800
STOP-ALL	24,400	1,300

02480 IRRIGATION & LANDSCAPING — 90,000

	IRRIG.	LAND-SCAPE
GREEN I.	33,000	No
BEAN S.	No	65,700
PLANTON	90,000	YES

03200 REINFORCING STEEL — 86,300 / 7,500

	HOISTING	WELDING	ALT. 1
BUDGET	1,800	3,000	
FAST B.	83,300	YES	No	7,500
BETTER R.	85,000	NO	No	8,000

04200 MASONRY — 364,800 / 25,000

	RE-BAR	SHORING	ALT. 1
		2,800	
BUDGET		2,800	
HIGH ST.	393,000	YES	No	22,000
BROCKSON	362,000	YES	No	25,000

05100 STRUCTURAL & MISC. METAL — 736,000 / 62,000

	BUDGET	STRUC.	MISC.	ALT. 1
RINGER	(INCL.)	736,000	YES	62,000
PIZZA	4,800	731,260	YES	67,000
RUSTY	6,000	729,000	YES	70,000

06100 MILLWORK — 63,600

	DOOR LOUVERS	LAM. PLASTIC
BUDGET	1,200	12,000
JOINTSPL	50,400	No	No
MITER SQ.	66,600	No	No

07100 ROOFING & ROOF INSULATION — 69,750

	ROOFING	INSUL.
TOPPERS	52,250	No
NO-LEAK	64,000	YES
CRACKFILL	No	17,500

07200 WALL & CEILING INSULATION — 62,550

	WALLS	CEILINGS
BATCO	45,000	21,400
COZY	41,150	No
COMFY	65,000	YES

07600 SHEET METAL — 35,100 / 3,000

	WALL LOUVERS	ALT. 1
BUDGET	3,700	
LEADERS	39,000	YES	2,700
FLASHER	35,100	YES	3,000
GUTTER	33,300	YES	3,250

08100 FINISH HARDWARE — 18,990

	HARDWARE
BUDGET	22,000
HARDY	25,255
LAUREL	18,990
HOLDER	22,200

08200 METAL DOORS & FRAMES — 37,480

	DOORS	FRAMES
SLAMMER	37,480	YES
ACCESS	39,977	YES

08500 METAL WINDOWS & GLAZING — 72,000

	WINDOWS	GLAZING	SLIDE. DOORS
SLIDERS	No	No	18,500
SEE-THRU	No	29,000	No
WIDEOPE	33,500	No	No

08700 STEEL OVERHEAD DOORS

	DOORS	INSTALL
BUDGET	No	20,000
OVER DR.	64,444	YES
SLIDE UP	40,000	No

09100 PAINTING & WALL COVERI

	PAINTING	WALL COVER	ALT. 1
SMEARS	101,500	YES	9,7??
HIDEALL	108,000	YES	10,000
COVERCO.	98,800	YES	8,20?

09200 CERAMIC TILE

	LATH & SCRATCH	ALT. 2
BUDGET	1,800	
CERTILE	No	22,40?
FACIA	No	22,20?

09300 LATHING & PLASTERING

SANTEX	49,720	
TROWEL	52,800	
FASTER	54,000	

09400 METAL FRAMING & GYP. BO

	METAL FRAMING	GYP. BOARD
WALLERS	No	102,102
GYPERS	YES	180,000
GOGUYS	YES	125,500

09500 RESILIENT FLOORING
09600 CARPETING

	RESIL. FLOOR	CARPET
BUDGET		19,000
UNDER FT.	78,800	No	DEDUC
RECARP	No	21,200	ADD -
FLOORER	84,000	No

09700 ACOUSTIC TILE

	ACOUSTIC TILE	SUSP. CLG.
TILESPEC	73,150	YES
SQUARE	67,500	YES
DROPPER	70,000	YES

09800 GLAZED WALL COATING

			ALT. 2 DEDUC
2-TONE	30,000		9,20?
GOLD	34,700		9,000
SILVER	35,240		9,50?

Figure 2.18b

LOCATION Long Beach, Calif.

COMPLETION TIME 600 Cal. Days

COLOR CODE { Base Bid ——— / Alt. 1 – – – – / Alt. 2 oooooooo

…erhead Doors — 60,000

…rs	Install
…	20,000
…44	Yes
…00	No

… & Wall Covering — 98,800 (Alt. 1: 8,200)

…ting	Wall Cover	Alt. 1
…500	Yes	9,790
…000	Yes	10,000
…300	Yes	8,200

… Tile — (Alt. 2: 24,000)

…n & …tch	Alt. 2
…00	
…o	22,400
…	22,200

… & Plastering — 49,720

…720
…300
…000

…ming & Gyp. Board — 125,500

…al …ing	Gyp. Board
…o	102,102
…s	180,000
…s	125,500

… Flooring — 78,800 (Alt. 2: 12,200)

…s …il. …r	Carpet		Alt. 2
	19,000		
…300	No	Deduct	9,000
…	21,200	Add	21,200
…00	No		

… Tile — 67,500

…stic …e	Susp. Clg.
…50	Yes
…500	Yes
…500	Yes

… Wall Coating — 30,000 (Alt. 2: 9,200 Deduct)

	Alt. 2 Deduct
…000	9,200
…100	9,000
…240	9,500

10100 Toilet Partitions — 11,175

Partitions Inc.	13,150
Specco	11,175
Screens	12,000

10201 Building Specialties — 37,000

	Bath Access.	Flag Pole	Ven. Blinds
Budget	No	2,800	No
Specco	11,000	No	No
Screens	No	No	23,200
Alspec	40,000	Yes	Yes

10300 Portable Partitions — 20,000

		Doors & Hardware
No Fold	20,000	Yes
Sturdy	23,300	Yes

11100 Adjustable Loading Ramp — 28,880

Lifters	28,880
Dropper	33,330

11600 Dental Casework & Equip. — 199,400

		Install
Budget		75,000
Science	210,000	Yes
Daquip	124,400	No

12100 Fixed Theater Seats — 35,000

Rokers	35,000
Lofers	39,900

13100 Radiation Protection — 93,300

Protech	99,999
Ratech	93,300

13200 Walk-In Refrigerator — 39,500

		Floor Insulate
Budget		2,500
Walkins	37,000	No
Colbox	45,000	Yes
Costore	43,430	Yes

13300 Integrated Ceiling — 40,150

2-Kinds	44,440
Clg-Fix	40,150

14200 Hydraulic Elevator — 250,000

		Drill Shaft
Upson	262,200	Yes
Downs	250,000	Yes
2-Ways	267,700	Yes

15000 Mechanical — 1,242,979 (Alt. 2: 105,000)

(See separate sheet) Alt. 2

Combination #5 Allco

16000 Electrical — 800,000 (Alt. 2: 45,200)

		Alt. 2
Total Elec.	880,000	49,000
Static	800,000	45,200
Magnet	845,450	42,500

Base Bid

	Cost	6,953,000
8%	Mark-up	556,240
	Subtotal	7,509,240
.47%	Bond Cost	35,293
Less	Adjustment	(17,700)
	Total	7,526,833

Alt. 1

	Cost	316,100
8%	Mark-up	25,288
	Subtotal	341,388
.47%	Bond Cost	1,605
	Adjustment	————
	Total	342,993

Alt. 2

	Cost	86,800
8%	Mark-up	6,944
	Subtotal	93,744
.47%	Bond Cost	441
	Adjustment	————
	Total	94,185

Figure 2.18b (cont.)

All alternative No. 1 figures are also added together and the total amount is carried down. Alternative No. 2 presents a special case in that glazed wall coating and electrical are deductive items, while resilient flooring and carpeting combined produce a net addition. Boxes for these deductive items should be shaded in with color as a reminder and warning. The total cost of alternative No. 2 is a net addition to the base bid. The base bid and each alternative bid now receive the following markups. For this example, using the markup finder scale in Fig. 2.6k, and assuming a d-rating of 88, we come up with 8%, and will use this markup for the alternative bids as well. The bond cost factor for a project in the bid amount of 7 to 9 million dollars is found from Fig. 2.7a to be .0047.

The work of addition and double or triple checking takes time. The bidder must start this summation before all of the sub-bids are received. Final adjustments are usually necessary and are accomplished most quickly and with the least risk of error by subtracting or adding *one net lump sum*, as in Fig. 2.18c. This work sheet may then be stapled or otherwise attached permanently to the spread sheet. The bidding work is now finished, except for filling in the bid form and delivering it to the sponsor.

Figure 2.18c

| | Adjustment to the Bid | |
	Cut	Add
Earthwork	3,200	—
Struc. Steel	—	5,000
Masonry	7,500	—
Electrical	12,000	—
Total	22,700	5,000
Net cut	17,700	

2.19 Submitting the Bid

Since the last few minutes before the deadline can be critical to the success or failure of the bid, it is common practice for bidders to send a team member ahead to a telephone station near the point of delivery, positioned to receive a "forward pass." The runner carries the bid papers, which are completely filled in except for the final dollar amounts of the bid items (see Appendix A for an example of a bid form).

The time provided the runner to write in the amounts and deliver the sealed bid may be a matter of two or three minutes. The formal opening of bids usually begins on the exact minute of the opening deadline, and the customary rule is that a bid arriving after the opening ritual begins will not be accepted. Figure 2.19a is a visual example of a typical bid form custom-made by the sponsor, filled in by the bidder, with prices written in by the runner. Other sheets, including bid bond, that are part of the submittal are not shown here, since the focus of attention by both bidder and runner is on the dollar amounts.

Bid Form
(Construction Contract)

Name and Location of Project   <u>Sept. 18, 1984</u>
                                                                                     (Date)

Science Lab
Long Beach, CA.

To: Storky & Hitch, Architects
      100 Pulitzer St.
      Los Angeles, CA.

In compliance with the invitation for bids, all requirements of the contract documents and addenda _____ , the undersigned proposes to furnish all labor, material and equipment as required for the said <u>Science Lab, Long Beach</u> for the following amounts:

Base Bid   <u>Seven Million Five Hundred Twenty-Six</u>
<u>Thousand Eight Hundred Thirty-Three</u> ($ 7,526,833)

Alternate Bid 1   Add   ($ 342,993)
Alternate Bid 2   Add   ($ 94,185)
Enclosed is a bid guarantee consisting of: _____

Bidder: Your Company   By: *Alphonso Builder*
            13 Sandfill Road
            San Diego, CA.   Alphonso Builder, Pres.

Figure 2.19a

We have previously noted that a bidder has the doubly difficult task of producing both a low and a potentially profitable bid. At the deadline, the bidder needs to receive the latest, often lowest sub-bids, and then submit the bid before the deadline. To play it safe on the time element is to risk a noncompetitive bid. However, the experienced bidder practices the principle: *any bid delivered on time is better than a late, disqualified, low bid.*

Although the success or failure of a bid is often determined in the last few minutes before the deadline, the probability of that happening can be decreased by energetic preparations. Thorough researching of prospective sub-bidders (and the resulting knowledge) can provide reasonable assurance in the final moments of the assembly that the critical sub-bids have, in fact, all been received, and that it is safe to submit the bid *before* the final moment.

2.20 Postmortems

The expression "postmortem," borrowed from the medical profession, is often used figuratively for the analysis of bidding results. Bidders, sub-bidders, and others exchange information and attempt to explain what went wrong—or what went right. Postmortems greatly influence the d-ratings of future projects.

One prime bidder and *one* subcontractor in each trade will be successful, and all others will need to be assured that competition was fair. Justly or unjustly, many decisions are made affecting future relationships with subs, suppliers, and sponsors. All that remains for the unsuccessful bidders is knowledge gained from the experience that might be helpful in future bidding. He gains inside information about the current market, competition, profit margins, and so forth—information that cannot be learned from books. Figure 2.20a is an example of a bid result.

Figure 2.20a

Bid Result, Example 1:

		Bids Received		
Bidder	**Base Bid**	**Alt. 1**	**Alt. 2**	**Alt. 3**
A	2,999,000	43,000	210,000	66,000
B	2,992,500	39,250	218,180	69,900
C	2,987,350	41,720	209,000	62,250
D	2,986,000	38,880	212,500	65,400
E	2,980,150	39,000	200,000	60,000
F	2,976,000	42,500	200,000	69,330
X	2,960,000	43,400	220,000	72,000

Bidder X's position stresses the importance of carefulness in the figuring of alternative bids. Depending on the sponsor's choice, if any, of alternative bids, Bidders X, F, and E are all eligible for the award of the contract, as the following grouping of bids show:

	X	**F**	**E**
Base bid	2,960,000	2,976,000	2,980,150
Alt. 1	43,400	42,500	39,000
Sub total (a)	3,003,400	3,018,500	3,019,150
Alt. 2	220,000	200,000	200,000
Sub total (b)	3,223,400	3,218,500	3,219,150
Alt. 3	72,000	69,300	60,000
Sub total (c)	3,295,400	3,287,800	3,279,150

If the alternative bids are taken progressively, Bidder X could lose the contract to Bidder F on alternative No. 2, or to Bidder E on alternative No. 3. If the alternative bids are taken separately, other choices of low bidders are possible.

The example in Fig. 2.20a is one of tight bidding; there is a spread in base bids between the lowest bid (X) and the highest bid (A) of only $39,000, or 1.3%. Since this difference is well within all the bidder's markups, any one of them might have produced the low bid by lowering markup, or some other tightening up of their estimates. In this instance, if Bidder X could have foreseen losing on alternatives 2 and 3, those areas might have been tightened up.

Bid Result, Example 2:

Bidder	Base Bid	Bids Received Alt. 1	Base & Alt.
A	5,505,000	175,000	5,680,000
B	5,498,300	169,900	5,668,200
C	5,450,000	168,000	5,618,000
X	5,422,750	168,500	5,591,250
D	5,400,000	168,000	5,568,000
E	4,690,880	152,000	4,842,880
F	4,655,000	170,000	4,825,000

Figure 2.20b

Figure 2.20b is an example of bid results in which Bidder X would have had no chance of being low bidder.

The bids of Bidders A, B, C, X, and D are comparable; Bidders E and F form a separate comparable group, appearing much too low compared to the majority. Bidder F has the possible false security of E's close confirmation, but should Bidders E and F both withdraw their bids on evidence of a gross error, Bidder X would still lose to Bidder D.

Bid Result, Example 3:

Bidder	Bids Received Base Bid
X	4,025,000
A	3,980,445
B	3,977,277
C	3,970,000
D	3,966,666
E	3,964,000
F	3,959,500

Figure 2.20c

Figure 2.20c is an example in which Bidder X is the highest bidder in spite of a strong competitive effort. Bidder X is acquainted with Bidder D who, not being low bidder, candidly discusses the project. No adequate explanation appears that would account for the lower bids. Bidder X's fault, if any, may have been in the original analysis of the project for desirability (Sec. 1.4, Analyzing a Project for Desirability). Hindsight, which may have some value for future bidding, indicates that he would have to bid $65,000 (1.6%) lower to equal the low bid. He must now determine whether he should have raised the d-value of the job or not have bid at all.

Postmortems sharpen the skills used in desirability analysis and are comparable to checking the targets after competitive shooting. From the results, better techniques for future attempts can be deduced. It is interesting to note that bidding "targets" can be seen only *after* the shooting.

2.21 Follow-up Work

After the postmortems, follow-up on unsuccessful bids is minor, consisting of (1) filing away the bid package for future reference, and (2) answering the questions of sub-bidders. Follow-up work is more extensive in cases of successful bids. The bidder cannot, without penalty

to the project, turn it over to the superintendent without further comment. At this point no one knows the project as well as the bidder.

Part IV of this book is devoted exclusively to follow-up work. Therefore, this section provides only a brief outline. The main steps, roughly in the order of occurrence, are:

1. Decide upon subcontractors and suppliers in conference with company management staff.
   a. Inform the unsuccessful sub-bidders of their status, as a courtesy. It is good policy for the bidder to perform this public relations function personally, rather than delegating it to assistants.
   b. Notify the successful sub-bidders of your intention of awarding them contracts. This should be done in writing, but it is sometimes advisable to precede the written notice with a telephone call clarifying terms and details.
   c. Obtain firm prices and commitments on any items previously only estimated or budgeted. Neglect of this operation could cause delays later in the progress of the construction.
   d. Write all subcontracts and purchase orders.
2. Provide the project superintendent with all the data needed to construct the project, such as:
   a. Drawings, specs, and addenda
   b. Copies of subcontracts and purchase orders
   c. Copies of estimates, budgets, and cost-control paperwork
   d. Concepts of construction methods upon which the bid was based
   e. Progress charts designed to bind all subs and other participants to a time schedule
   f. Format and data for monthly progress payments
3. Prepare for continuing follow-up:
   a. Schedules for expediting shop drawings and material samples requiring A&E approval
   b. Quality control, material testing, and inspection
   c. Change orders
   d. Value Engineering
   e. Regular cost records
   f. Progress schedule updating

A thorough "briefing" of the project superintendent will minimize the time required in follow-up by the bidder. In addition to all of the data outlined above, two other aids are:

1. A written information/instruction sheet (see Fig. 2.21a).
2. A set of specifications containing marginal notations naming subs and other sources of materials and work and/or services.

These documents ideally leave no important questions unanswered. Figure 2.21a is a suggested format for the superintendent's information/instruction sheet. Only content headings are shown in this example, but a filled in form will be demonstrated in Part IV. Let us now review and briefly explain each of the follow-up duties as outlined above.

Selecting subs and suppliers. Some subs and suppliers are readily recognized as the best on the basis of complete coverage, low prices, and performance on other contracts. These bids should be promptly accepted.

Some of the sub-bids may require clarifications before commitments are made. In Sec. 2.18, Putting the Bid Together, examples were given

Superintendent's Information/Instruction Sheet

For Project _____

General Information:

    Starting Date _____ Completion Date _____

    A&E _____

       Representative _____ Phone _____

    Owner (Sponsor) _____

    Subcontractors

       Trade   Sub Contractor   Representative Phone

    Material Suppliers & Other Services

       Mat'l Service   Supplier   Representative Phone

    Superintendent Will Do:

    Office Will Do:

    Special Information:

Figure 2.21a

of sub-bids that were qualified so that a single choice based on price alone was not possible. The hasty choices made in the bidding process may not be accurate enough for actual contract commitments.

Figure 2.21b is an example of three steel sub-bids which illustrates the problem in selecting subcontractors from the face value of their bids. Ringer Steel Company is the only complete bidder. The other two bids can be completed by either (1) asking the bidders to provide firm bids for the excluded items, or (2) obtaining independent quotations from others. The first method raises a question of ethics, since after the bidding it would be easy for L.T. Pizza and Rusty Fabricators to learn the amount of Ringer Steel's bid, and then adjust their own new quotations accordingly.

Steel Sub-bids

	Bid	Exclusions	Budget	Total
Ringer Steel Co.	736,000	none	—	736,000
L.T. Pizza Iron	731,260	Alum. railings	4,800	736,060
Rusty Fabricators	729,600	Alum. railings & M.H. covers	6,000	735,600

Figure 2.21b

If independent quotations confirm the budgeted values of the excluded items, Ringer Steel is the favored sub for the following reasons: (1) Although a small savings can be made by subletting to Rusty Fabricators, it is better for management and field supervision to have *one* subcontractor responsible for full coverage (see Sec. 2.10, General Bidding Strategies), and (2) the practice of awarding contracts to subs who conscientiously bid full coverage tends to raise the general standard of subcontractor bidding.

There are no fixed rules. Every set of sub-bids poses unique conditions. The following is a list of typical guidelines for making selections under various conditions:

1. When the low bid is clearly evident, consider any gross differences in the subs' abilities and performances.
2. Favor the most complete in coverage, as Ringer Steel in Fig. 2.21b.
3. When price difference is trivial, favor the sub whose financial and/or performance record is superior, but consider the possible penalty in loss of goodwill on the part of the disappointed sub.
4. Favor subs with superior technical ability. Often a low bid proves to be more costly in the long run.
5. Favor subs with proven ability to meet tight time schedules.
6. When only one sub-bid is received for a trade, consider, with due regard to ethical and public relations, obtaining one or two additional bids. If the single bid appears to be competitive, it might be advisable to sublet without inviting additional bids.
7. If prices are equivalent, favor a sub whose proposed method of construction appears advantageous.

An unfortunate consequence of the competitive bidding system is that the bidder is often forced to do business with inferior subcontractors. Bidders must honor low sub-bids for both economic and ethical reasons. To keep a competitive edge, the bidder must not discourage too many low-bidding subs by contracting with more desirable subs at slightly higher prices. While it may be true that low bidders who perform poorly prove to be the most costly choice in the end, there is no guarantee that a higher-priced sub will deliver a superior performance. Either way, the bidder takes a risk.

Writing subcontracts. Since contractors customarily use printed subcontract forms of either standard or custom design, the writing is a matter of filling in the blanks with specific details of the desired agreement. (See Appendix Q for an example of a subcontract form.) The main terms of subcontracts already exist in the bid day communications, so that writing of contracts is mostly a matter of faithfully transferring those facts and conditions to the subcontract form. Writing of subcontracts is only a matter of formalizing the oral contracts—or to say it another way, formally accepting the sub's offer.

A written contract must be more precise than the typical telephone sub-bid, since it might have to be interpreted months in the future by persons other than the original signers. Thus, a contract contains three main categories, explained with examples as follows.

1. The specifics and terms as quoted by the sub-bidder. Typical examples are:
   a. Identification of the trade (sheet metal, painting, etc.)
   b. Definition of the scope of work (section of the specs, drawing sheet numbers, etc.)
   c. Included items noted for clarification (to avoid future disputes)
   d. Excluded items identified by name, drawing detail designation,

and/or spec page numbers
  e. The price as quoted, including alternative bids, unit prices, etc.
2. The statements binding the subcontractor to responsibilities and participation in the project, beyond the narrow scope of a specific trade, but which are essential to the teamwork between the prime contractor and all subcontractors. Examples are:
  a. Complying with time (progress) schedules
  b. Delivery and protection of materials
  c. Hoisting and scaffolding
  d. Safety provisions
  e. Evidence of required insurance
  f. Cleaning up
  g. Special terms of payment
  h. Requirements, if any, for bonding
  i. Material testing and inspection
3. The standard clauses as printed on the contract form. These clauses are so general in effect that they pertain to most contractual relations with no need for change. It is usually the duty of the sub to challenge any of the standard clauses which may seem unsuitable. Typically, these clauses would include:
  a. General and special conditions of the specs
  b. Monthly payment retentions
  c. Equal opportunity laws
  d. Environmental protection laws
  e. Warranties and indemnifications
  f. Damages caused by delays
  g. Licensing
  h. Labor relations
  i. Arbitration
  j. Safety laws

An effort is made to write contracts for *all* materials and work in the project, except for the labor which the prime bidder's company will furnish. It is desirable to leave no loose ends for others to do, to forget to do, or to refuse to do.

Briefing the superintendent. Sometimes the prospective project superintendent participates in the bidding activity and is familiar to a degree with the details. Usually, however, the superintendent is introduced to the project *after* the bidding and requires a complete briefing.

Since the bidder's main duty in the company is the continuous bidding of projects, it is inappropriate to be overly involved in the follow-up work. The briefing of the superintendent amounts to a nearly complete transfer of the project. The more calculated the risks that were taken in the bidding activity, the more urgent it is: (1) to have the most competent superintendent available, and (2) to perform a thorough job of briefing.

All of the data given to the superintendent is for guidance of costs, methods, and time periods. It is understood that the superintendent will strive to hold all activities and expenditures within the bid limitations, and will accomplish, if possible, further savings without sacrificing acceptable quality of materials and workmanship.

Cost records and cost control systems pertain only to that work that is not sublet. The work that is sublet is firm and requires no accounting, except for purposes of progressive payments is described as follows.

Figure 4.8a provides an example of a form used for recording field costs and comparing them to the estimated costs. This activity serves two main purposes: (1) a budget control marking limits of expenditures permissible on each element of the contract, and (2) a permanent record of unit costs, which is valuable for estimating and bidding.

Without such a guide the superintendent would be working blindly, the project costs would tend to exceed the estimates, and future bidding would be less accurate. A cost record system is demonstrated in Part IV.

Progress charts serve to budget and control time in the same way that cost control systems control costs, that is, by assigning appropriate time to each construction activity. The format used depends on the requirements of the job.

1. The spec requirements.
   a. A single, fully described scheduling system such as CPM, manually prepared or computerized.
   b. Two or more systems briefly described and left to the bidder's choice.
   c. No specific description other than "an approved system."
2. The project requirements. The size and complexity of the project is the main deciding factor, but it is not always easy to recognize the line between small/simple and large/complex. In Parts III and IV, examples of the two typical systems, the bar chart and the CPM system, are shown in simplified form. For a complete presentation of the CPM system of progress charting, the reader is referred to *Means Scheduling Manual,* by F. William Horsley, and published by R.S. Means, Co., Inc. For a brief discussion of this subject, see Sec. 2.9, Construction Progress Schedules.

Progress payment schedules are sometimes integrated with the CPM system, but the traditional method still applies to the majority of projects and will be our focus. Figure 4.7a is a typical progress payment schedule form. Part IV demonstrates its use.

In this section, we have discussed each element of the bidding process and the interaction of sponsor, A&E, general contractor, sub-bidder, and material supplier. We have discussed what to do when we are an "also ran," learning where our bid went astray and how to avoid the same errors in future bidding. We have also examined the next steps to take when we are the successful low bidder. In Part III, we will use this valuable information to prepare an actual bid.

Part III: Bidding a Project

Step 1: Choosing a Project and Analyzing it for Desirability

Let us imagine that six construction jobs are available for bidding. From their advertised descriptions three of them appear suitable to our company's present need. We obtain the sponsor's bid packages (Sec. 1.2) for all three projects and, using a very brief version of our system for rating projects for desirability (Sec. 1.4), we find that two of the projects, if taken separately, are too small to be desirable. If taken together, they would equal the third project in desirability, but due to the bid dates it is impractical to bid all three projects. We select the third project for two reasons: (1) the probability of a low bid on a single try is higher than that of two consecutive low bids, and (2) contract administration is simpler in one large contract than in two smaller ones.

At this point the selection is only tentative. We now apply the d-rating system more methodically. Significant information is as follows:

Name of project:	Administration Building and Fire Station
Location:	Picacho, California
Purpose:	Office for Public Works, Law Enforcement, and Fire Chief
Completion time:	365 calendar days
Liquidated damages:	$500 per calendar day
Cost range:	$1,000,000 to $2,500,000
Time to estimate:	21 calendar days

This project is created for the purpose of demonstrating the step-by-step bidding procedure as outlined in Parts I and II. Figures 3.1a - 3.1e are plans and elevations of the project.

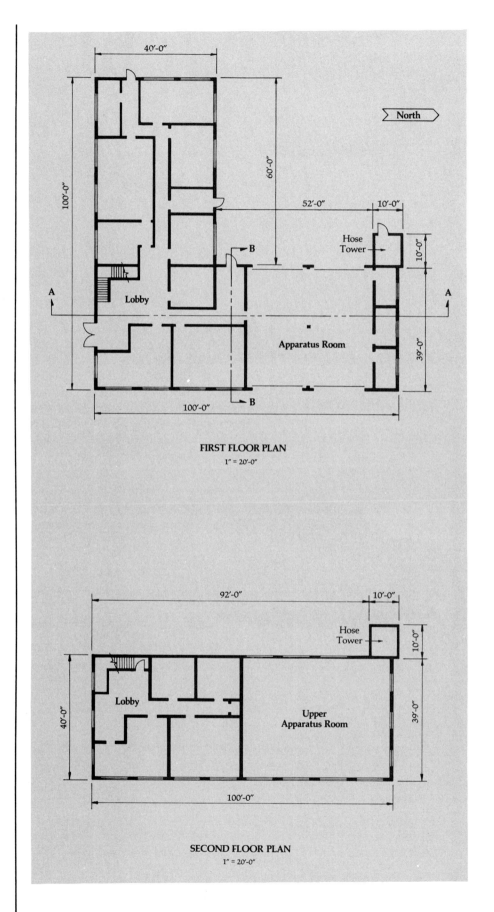

FIRST FLOOR PLAN
1" = 20'-0"

SECOND FLOOR PLAN
1" = 20'-0"

Figure 3.1a

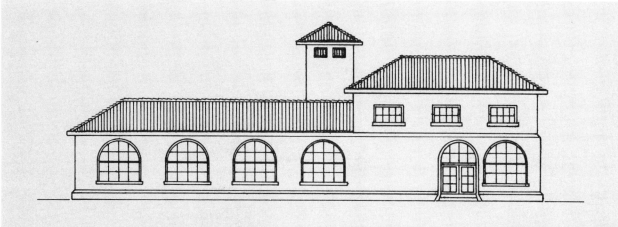

SOUTH ELEVATION
1″ = 20′-0″

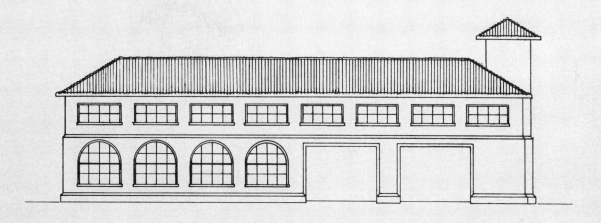

EAST ELEVATION
1″ = 20′-0″

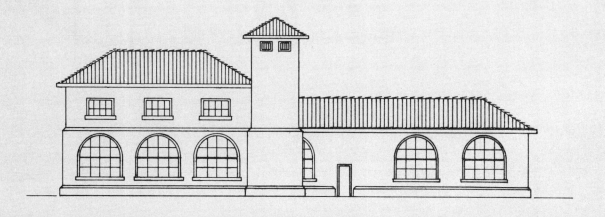

NORTH ELEVATION
1″ = 20′-0″

Figure 3.1b

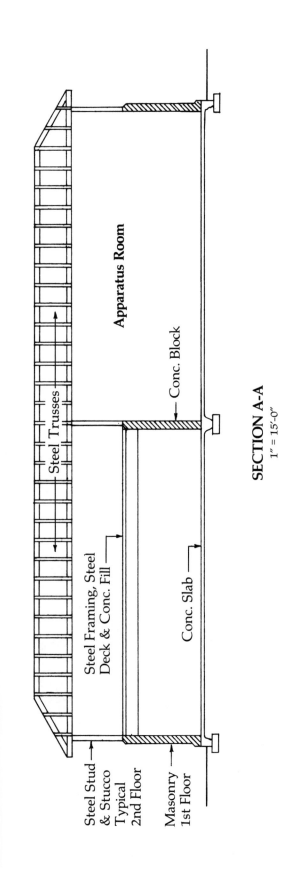

Steel Trusses

Apparatus Room

Conc. Block

Steel Framing, Steel
Deck & Conc. Fill

Conc. Slab

Steel Stud
& Stucco
Typical
2nd Floor

Masonry
1st Floor

SECTION A-A
1" = 15'-0"

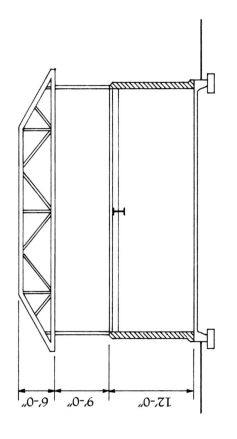

6'-0"

9'-0"

12'-0"

SECTION B-B
1" = 15'-0"

Figure 3.1c

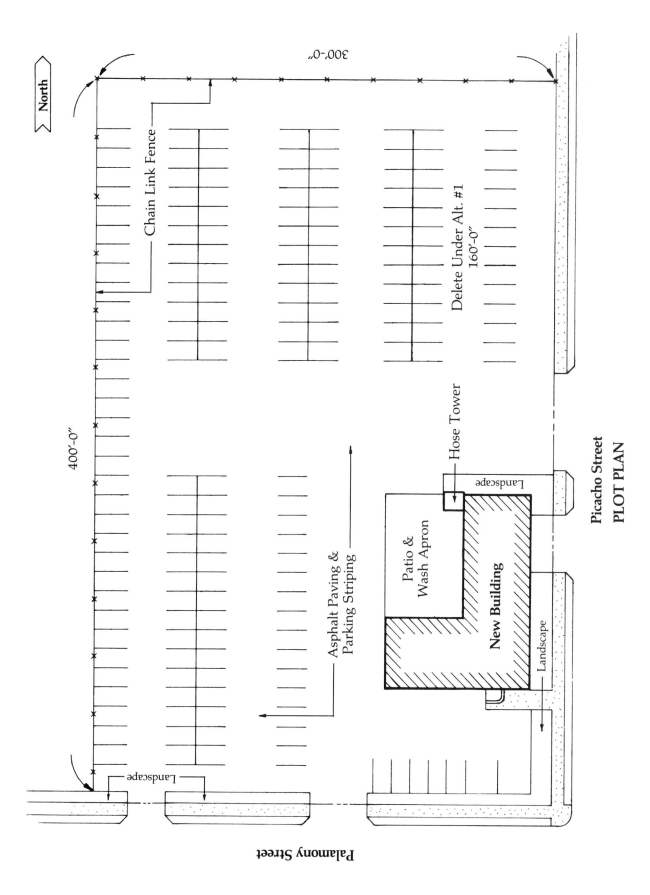

North

300'-0"

Chain Link Fence

Delete Under Alt. #1
160'-0"

400'-0"

Asphalt Paving &
Parking Striping

Hose Tower

Landscape

Patio &
Wash Apron

New Building

Landscape

Landscape

Palamony Street

Picacho Street
PLOT PLAN

Figure 3.1d

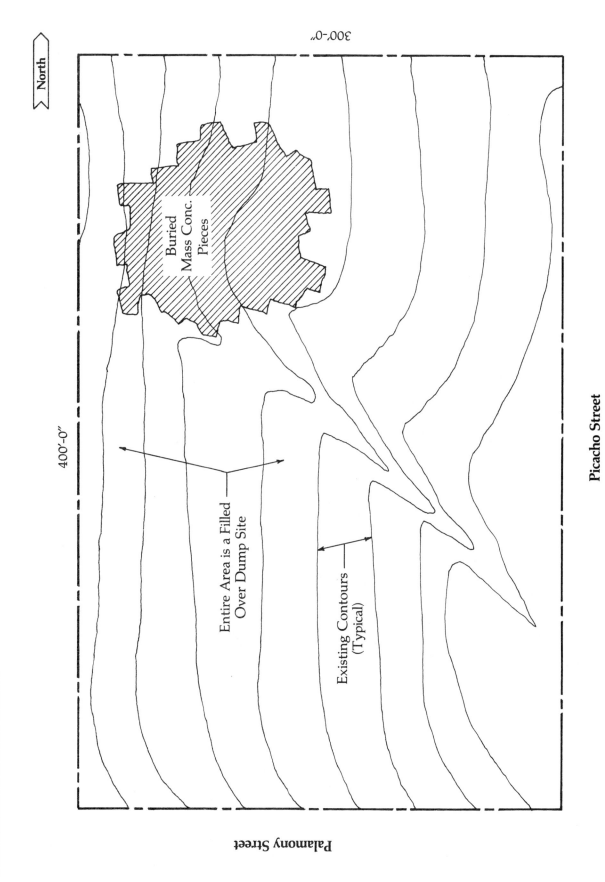

North

300'-0"

400'-0"

Buried Mass Conc. Pieces

Entire Area is a Filled Over Dump Site

Existing Contours (Typical)

Palamony Street

Picacho Street

GRADING PLAN

Figure 3.1e

The advertised cost range seems too wide. We can narrow the target by using square-foot cost records from similar completed projects. An experienced bidder can expect to guess the cost of a project within 30%, which is close enough for the first d-rating analysis. From Fig. 3.1a and 3.1d the approximate square-foot cost of the project can be determined as follows:

1st floor	100 x 40 = 4,000 sf
	60 x 40 = 2,400
	10 x 10 = 100
2nd floor	50 x 40 = 2,000
	10 x 10 = 100
Upper tower	10 x 10 = 100
Total	8,700 sf
Building	8,700 sf @ 95/sf = $ 826,500
Site work	120,000 sf @ 5/sf = $ 600,000
Total Cost Approximation	$1,426,500

Within 30% of accuracy, the cost range in rounded-off figures is $1,250,000 to $1,650,000. For d-rating analysis, let us use $1,215,000.

The above approximation method is sometimes called "parameter pricing." Its main application lies outside the field of competitive bidding. The reader who wishes to research this comparative cost system is referred to the current editions of *Building Construction Cost Data* and *Means Square Foot Estimating*, both published by R.S. Means Co., Inc.

Using the fourteen points discussed in Sec. 1.4 for analyzing desirability, our project can be analyzed as follows:

1. *The size of the project* is less than ideal. Our company's bonding capacity is $12,000,000, and we have $9,000,000 in uncompleted work on hand. Thus, the ideal size of any single project would be $3,000,000. Our contemplated project earns a weight of: 82.
2. *The location of the project* is only one mile distant from home office and receives the highest possible rating: 90.
3. *Sponsor relations* are unknown to us, suggesting that we exercise caution. The rating is thus: 70.
4. *The type of construction* is one in which our company has considerable experience, thus: 90.
5. *The competition* is known to us from the following sources: (a) the advertised list of prospective bidders, (b) our own experience bidding against them for other jobs, and (c) rumor and hearsay. The competition may be rated as follows, from expected least competitive to most competitive:

    (1) *Clawhammer Company* has many contracts on hand and no great need for work: +6.
    (2) *Taciturn Builders* is a mechanical contractor not experienced in prime bidding: +5.
    (3) *I.N. Valid Construction Company* is an out-of-town company and may not receive the best local prices: +4.
    (4) *Your Own Company* is not in great need of work, having $9,000,000 in work on hand: 0.
    (5) *Likable Construction* has recently shown a consistently competitive performance: -1.
    (6) *Will Bid & Sons* has no work on hand and is bidding many projects: -2.

(7) *Strategic Structures* is primarily a structural steel company that recently invested heavily in site engineering equipment. Steel and site work are both major portions of this project: -3.

Our company, if our assessment is correct, is exactly median, which suggests a median grade of: 75.

6. *Labor market conditions* in the small town of Picacho are below the standard of large cities, both in quantity of workmen and quality of skills: 80.
7. *Subcontract market conditions* are the same as the labor market; several subcontractors may have to commute 100 or more miles. Administrative and supervisory problems are probable: 80.
8. *The quality of drawings and specs* are rated as good: 90.
9. *The quality of supervision* is unknown; it will be necessary to hire a superintendent: 80.
10. *Special risks* are not anticipated: 90.
11. *Completion time and penalty* seem realistic. Liquidated damages of $500 per day may be high, but that risk is offset by a generous completion time of 365 calendar days: 85.
12. *Estimating and bidding time* is computed by the method in Sec. 2.9 (see Fig. 2.9a) as follows:

> Assume the complexity at midway between B and C;
> Net hours = 72;
> Net working days (4 effective hrs/day): 72/4   = 18
> Saturdays and Sundays   + 4
> **Total calendar days**   22

> Since this exceeds by only one calendar day the time available, we will allow a conservative estimate: 83.

13. *Need for work* is low, since our company has $9,000,000 in uncompleted work on hand. Our position may be regarded as one of "normal need," suggesting: 85.
14. *Other special advantages or disadvantages* exist, such as nearness to the jobsite, but only an above-average rating is justified: 90.

Summing up the individual ratings and dividing by 14, we have a d-rating for the project of 84, which is near the high point of the average range (80 to 85).

The above analysis is the process that bidders perform mentally, often subjectively and intuitively. All bidders, whatever their methods, establish an attitude toward a project from the beginning and maintain it throughout the bidding process, including the markup. Without itemizing, as we have just done, an experienced bidder would quickly rate this project at about 85 or, in classroom scoring, B+.

Conditions and knowledge may change regarding one or more of the 14 criteria, calling for an adjustment in the d-rating. For instance, the list of prospective bidders might change, affecting competition; one or more of the competitors might be successful bidder on some other project, decreasing competitiveness on this project. In unusual cases, conditions on bid day may be drastically different from when the documents were first viewed.

Step 2: Preliminary Steps

1. *Request a bid bond.* Use your company's regular bonding company. Submitted with the bid, the bid bond is the sponsor's assurance against default or the bidder's failure to perform. The bonding company "bets" on the bidder, cosigns for the obligation, and consequently imposes a financial ceiling, which bidders call "bonding capacity." We have established that our unused bonding capacity is $12,000,000 − $9,000,000 = $3,000,000. Since our project estimate is $1,500,000, we are confident of receiving a bond.

2. *Note significant miscellaneous conditions.*

    a. The bid schedule requests:
       A base bid for the complete project.
       An alternative bid No. 1 for the deletion of all site work, except fencing and modified excavation in the North 160 feet of the jobsite.

    b. The bid date and time: October 22, 1984, at 1:00 p.m. Bids to be delivered to: Old Public Works Building, Room 200.

    c. The present pay scales for trades.

	Base Pay per Hour ($)
Carpenters	19.94
Cement masons	19.00
Laborers	16.60
Foreman, Carpenter	21.19
Foreman, Cement mason	21.00
Foreman, Labor	17.35

      Fringe benefits, payroll taxes, and insurance, lumped together and termed Labor Overhead, average 47% for all trades.

    d. All costs of testing and inspecting will be paid by the sponsor, except for concrete compression tests and mix designs.

    e. The prime contractor may not sublet more than 75% of the total project.

    f. Since this is a city sponsored project, no charges for building permits and utility connections will be assessed. However, a pedestrian barricade will be required along both Picacho and Palamony streets, the full length of the project property lines.

3. *Advertise as a prospective bidder.* Use the local periodicals that specialize in the reporting of construction bidding activities. This is a general and nonspecific invitation to all subs and suppliers to offer their quotations. Even though it is impersonal, this blanket invitation will bring a majority of sub-bids, particularly those of a routine, noncritical kind.

It is a good policy to request listing as early as possible in order to be high on the list of bidders. An early listing gives your company an advantage at bid deadline.

Prospective Bidders Admin. Bldg. and Fire Station for City of Picacho, CA.

Your Own Company	Favorable position
Strategic Structures	
Likable Construction	
I.N. Valid Const. Co.	
Will Bid & Sons	
Clawhammer Company	Unfavorable position
Taciturn Builders	

Figure 3.2a

4. Search for sources and prices of critical, scarce, or hard to get items. A complete listing of all trades and items in the project will be made soon, but at this point we scan the drawings and specs and single out the following items for immediate investigation:

a. Earthwork—unusually extensive, as the project is an old dump site requiring extensive removal of waste material and the importing of select fill.

b. Asphaltic concrete paving—an unusually large area.

c. Structural steel and steel decking—this is a critical trade; we have noted that one of our competitors (Strategic Structures) has a bidding advantage in both steel and earthwork. We must try to obtain competitive sub-bids.

d. Masonry—a superior quality is required, calling for the need of prequalified subs.

e. Clay tile roofing—no known qualified subs are available locally.

f. Mechanical and electrical trades—these are critical because of their high cost and because they need special attention.

5. Inspect the jobsite. Having studied the drawings and specs pertaining to site preparation work (see Sec. 2.11) and underground utilities, we visit the site and make the following observations, as recorded in Fig. 3.2b.

a. *Distance from home office*, 1.2 miles (as found by odometer).

b. *Subsistence* is necessary for three-quarters of the total labor force, which must be imported [see item (f) below].

c. *Railroad spur* is not applicable to job needs.

d. *Working room* is ample due to large parking area.

e. *Equipment rental sources* are available locally, except motorized cranes, which must be imported a distance of 100 miles.

f. *Labor availability* is limited to about one-fourth of that needed for the total project.

g. *Subcontractor availability* is limited in Picacho to minor trades such as sheet metal, landscaping, insulation, plastering, drywall, and painting. Major trades, such as structural steel, a.c. paving, and mechanical and electrical will have to be imported from 50 miles or more.

h. *Source of water*, a fire hydrant, one block distant, is available for temporary supply until permanent water service is installed.

i. *Source of power*, a pole, exists at the corner of Picacho and Palamony streets, but a transformer will be required.

j. *Barricade* is required per specs. A flagman will be needed full time for four weeks during earthwork operations and periodically thereafter. Lights and portable barricades will be needed for curb cuts and utility connections.

k. *Soil conditions.* We confirm that the site is an old abandoned dump. All material, which is to be removed down to the original grade, is relatively soft and dry from natural drainage.

l. *Extent of clearing* requires all grass and weeds be stripped and disposed of integrally with the earth and debris.

m. *Location of disposal area.* All excavated material must be hauled 5 miles to the county dump; the fee is $15 per truck load.

n. *Source of borrow material* is not known. It is important that a source be found.

o. *Security requirements.* The site is centrally located, and the perimeter is constantly patrolled by city police.

p. *Source of materials.* Picacho Transit Mix Concrete is available; miscellaneous materials are available from local suppliers; unusual materials, most of which subs will provide, must be obtained from distant sources.

q. *Remarks.* Protruding blocks of concrete indicate that breaking and loading could be expensive. An educated guess of the quantity is unavoidable.

6. *Make the first routine inquiries.* Use prospective sub-bidders. The key word here is *routine*; these are the items, other than critical, scarce, or hard to get, which are dealt with separately above. Most of the routine sub-trades may be delegated to various office personnel. But first, let us make the *Estimate Summary Sheet*, Fig. 3.2c, which is a listing of the trades and cost categories as they are separated in the specifications.

Site Investigation Check Sheet

Project ___Admin. Bldg & Fire Sta.___   **Bid Date** ___Oct. 22, 1984___

Location ___Picacho, CA___   **A&E** ___Bell & Bell___

1. Distance from home office ___1.2 miles___

2. Subsistence for workmen required? yes ___X___ no ___(See G)___

3. Railroad spur available? ___NA___ how near? _____

4. Working room? none _____ little _____ ample ___X___

5. Equipment rental available? ___No crane___ how near? ___100 miles___

6. Labor available? ___Part___ quantity? ___1/4 of need___ skill? ___Part___

7. Subcontractors available? ___Few___

8. Source of water ___Hydrant one block distant___

9. Source of power ___Need transformer___ telephone ___Available___

10. Need fences, barricades, lights, flagmen? ___Barricade & flagman___

11. Soil conditions ___Old dump___ hardness ___Soft___ wetness ___Dry___

12. Extent of clearing, grubbing, trees, etc. ___Grass & weeds___

13. Location of disposal area ___5 miles___ fees ___$15/load___

14. Source of import fill material ___Not known___

15. Security requirements ___Local police patrols___

16. Source of concrete, lumber, etc. ___Local supply___

17. Remarks ___Indications of mass concrete pieces buried in the old fill.___
___About 1500 sf of shoring is required along Picacho Street___
___to prevent cave-in during excavation.___
_____
_____

Investigation made by ___S.T. & J.J.___ Date ___10/7/84___

Figure 3.2b

ESTIMATE SUMMARY SHEET

Project **Admin. Bldg. & Fire Sta.** Bid Date **10/22/84**

Location **Picacho, CA** Calendar Days to Complete **365**

Spec.	Section and Heading	Base Bid	Alt. No. 1	Distr.
01100	General Conditions	X		E
02200	Clearing & Earthwork	X	X	B, C, S
02444	Chain Link Fence	X		S
02640	A.C. Paving	X	X	B, C, S
02800	Landscaping	X	X	S
03300	C.I.P. Concrete	X	X	E
03320	Reinforcing Steel	X		S
04000	Masonry	X		B, C, S
05120	Structural Steel	X		C, S
05300	Miscellaneous Metal	X		E S
05320	Steel Decking	X		C, S
06000	Carpentry & Millwork	X		E, B
07230	Wall & Ceiling Insulation	X		S
07240	Roof Insulation	X		S
07430	Clay Tile Roofing	X		C, S
07600	Sheet Metal	X		S
07950	Caulking & Sealants	X		E
08100	Hol. Metal Doors & Frames	X		S
08330	Rolling Steel Doors	X		S
08400	Aluminum Windows	X		S
08720	Glass & Glazing	X		S
08800	Finish Hardware	X		S
09110	Lathing & Plastering	X		S
09250	Metal Framing & Gypsum Board	X		B, S
09310	Ceramic Tile	X		S
09500	Acoustical Tile	X		S
09650	Resilient Flooring	X		S
09110	Painting	X		S
10100	Building Specialties	X		S
15000	Mechanical	X		C, S
16000	Electrical	X	X	C, S

X = prices under the base bid and Alternative 1.

E = items and trades to be figured by our Estimating Department.

B = items and trades to be budgeted.

C = critical trades; the bidder will research for dependable and competitive sub-bids.

S = depend entirely upon sub-bids for these trades.

Figure 3.2c

The estimating department will figure the cost of general conditions, concrete, installation of miscellaneous metal, carpentry, and caulking. The estimating department will also make up budget costs for clearing and earthwork, a.c. paving, masonry, millwork and metal framing, and gypsum board. These budget figures are intended for incorporation into the bid only if dependable sub-bids are not obtained.

The bidder will investigate sources of the following critical cost items as decided in preliminary Step 4: earthwork, a.c. paving, masonry, structural steel, steel decking, tile roofing, mechanical, and electrical. All other trades and items on the summary sheet will be researched for coverage by office personnel on the bidding team.

Step 3: Reviewing the Estimates

Our estimating department has produced the estimate sheets, Figs. 3.3a, 3.3b, and 3.3c. Compared to the estimates made for a real project, these are simplified and condensed, but they are suitable to demonstrate our project. One important sheet, general conditions, is reserved for a later step because it requires special attention.

Using our formula in Fig. 2.15a, we can expect the general conditions to cost about $120,000 ($1,500,000 x 0.08). Mentally adding all the estimates and general conditions, we can predict that our own work will total less than the required 25% of the total project costs. Thus, we might not be able to sublet as much of the work as customary. This decision will have to be made before bid deadline. We reason that the unusually high proportion of site work was not considered when the sponsor specified a 75% limitation of sub work. Therefore, we might request an addendum from the sponsor to raise the percentage of work that may be sublet.

As we review these estimates of our company's own work (not to be sublet), let us keep in mind all that contributes to our d-rating of 84. We consider the figures generally neither tight nor loose. We adjust line items 1b, 2f, 4a, and 12a under C.I.P. Concrete & Struc. Excav. We make no changes in either Miscellaneous Metal or Caulking. We adjust only line items 4a and 4b in Carpentry. Note that Caulking is listed under the subcontract column for easy comparison to possible sub-bids. Note also that Millwork is estimated in the Carpentry sheet under the subcontract column in readiness for the option of subletting.

At this point, a value judgment has to be made. Since the portion of the project to be accomplished by our own company (not sublet) is relatively small, a significant amount of competitiveness cannot be accomplished by cutting our own work. Unless we have the lowest (sub items) for the major cost items, such as earthwork and structural steel, the probability of our being low bidder is slight. However, assuming that an addendum will be issued to raise the allowable percentage of subcontract work, we may reduce our final markup in a valid competitive effort.

PROJECT	ADMINISTRATION BLDG. & FIRE STATION	CLASSIFICATION	
LOCATION	PICACHO, CALIFORNIA	ARCHITECT	DATE 10-22-1984
TAKE OFF BY PJC	QUANTITY BY PJC	PRICES BY PJC EXTENSIONS BY MD	CHECKED BY JM

DESCRIPTION	NO.	QUANTITY	UNIT	MATERIAL UNIT	MATERIAL TOTAL	LABOR UNIT	LABOR TOTAL	SUBS UNIT	SUBS TOTAL	TOTAL UNIT	COST TOTAL
C.I.P. CONCRETE & STRUC. EXCAV.											
FOOTINGS - LAYOUT, BATTER BDS, ETC.	1.A	1200	LF	0.10	120	0.88	1056			0.98	1176
MACHINE EXC.	B	320	CY	8.00 (9.23 struck)	2560 (2954 struck)		0			8.00 (9.23 struck)	2560 (2954 struck)
HAND TRIM TRENCHES	C	2800	SF		0	0.40	1120			0.40	1120
FORMING	D	1200	LF	0.90	1080	2.95	3540			3.85	4620
CONCRETE & PLACING	E	220	CY	65.00	14300	8.26	1817			73.26	16117
CONCRETE CURING FOOTING TOPS	F	1200	LF	.035	42	0.35	420			0.39	462
DISPOSAL EXCESS DIRT TO 5 MILES	G	220	CY	8.25	1815		0			8.25	1815
BACKFILL & TAMP	H	100	CY	5.50	550	13.45	1345			18.95	1895
FLOOR SLAB ON GRD. - LAYOUT & LEVEL	2.A	6400	SF	0.03	192	0.12	768			0.15	960
FINE GRADE FOR GRAVEL BASE	B	6400	SF	0.05	320	0.13	832			0.18	1152
4" GRAVEL BASE COURSE	C	95	CY	12.00	1140	9.37	890			21.37	2030
6 MIL VAPOR BARRIER	D	7000	SF	0.07	490	0.07	490			0.14	980
2" SAND & FINE GRADE	E	48	CY	12.00	576	12.37	594			24.37	1170
FORM SLAB EDGES	F	800	LF	0.56	448	1.40 (3.40 struck)	1120 (2720 struck)			1.96 (3.96 struck)	1568 (3168 struck)
FORM DEPRESSIONS	G	164	LF	0.60	98	2.90	476			3.50	574
ANCHOR BOLTS FOR WALL SILLS	H	200	EA	1.50	300	5.70	1140			7.20	1440
SET SCREEDS	I	6400	SF	0.04	256	0.10	640			0.14	896
CONCRETE & PLACING	J	90	CY	65.00	5850	8.26	743			73.26	6593
ADD PUMPING (1/2 OF SLAB)	K	45	CY	12.00	540		0			12.00	540
FINISH & CURE	L	6400	SF	0.03	192	0.30	1920			0.33	2112
SEALER PER FINISH SCHEDULE	M	4000	SF	0.07	280	0.07	280			0.14	560
STEPS ON GRD. (TREAD LENGTH)	3.A	22	LF	2.50	55	7.60	167			10.10	222
STAIRS TO 2ND FLOOR FORMING	4.A	640	SF	2.80	1792	5.90 (6.20 struck)	3776 (3968 struck)			8.70 (9.00 struck)	5568 (5760 struck)
CONCRETE & PUMPING	B	6	CY	80.00	480	22.00	132			102.00	612
FINISH & CURE	C	240	SF	0.20	48	1.20	288			1.40	336
FILL ON STEEL DECK - SET SCREEDS	5.A	2200	SF	0.06	132	0.12	264			0.18	396
CONCRETE & PUMPING	B	22	CY	85.00	1870	18.00	396			103.00	2266
FINISH & CURE	C	2200	SF	0.03	66	0.30	660			0.33	726
CARRY FORWARD					35986 (struck) / 35592		26666 (struck) / 24874				62652 (struck) / 60466

Figure 3.3a

PROJECT	ADMINISTRATION BLDG. & FIRE STATION		CLASSIFICATION				SHEET NO. 2 OF 7
LOCATION	PICACHO, CALIFORNIA		ARCHITECT				ESTIMATE NO.
TAKE OFF BY PJC	QUANTITY BY PJC		PRICES BY PJC	EXTENSIONS BY MD			DATE 10-22-1984
							CHECKED BY JM

DESCRIPTION	NO.	QUANTITY	UNIT	MATERIAL UNIT	MATERIAL TOTAL	LABOR UNIT	LABOR TOTAL	SUBS UNIT	SUBS TOTAL	TOTAL UNIT	COST TOTAL
C.I.P CONCRETE FORWARDED					~~35986~~ 35592		~~26666~~ 24874				~~62652~~ 60466
CURBS ON SLABS	6.A	68	LF	3.50	238	2.75	187			6.25	425
LOCKER BASES	7.A	50	SF	7.50	375	4.00	200			11.50	575
EQUIPMENT SLABS	8.A	60	SF	15.50	930	5.50	330			21.00	1260
SPLASH BLOCKS	9.A	6	EA	32.00	192	32.00	192			64.00	384
SIDEWALKS & APRON	10.A	6150	SF	1.90					11685	1.90	11685
CURBS-GUTTER TYPE	11.A	600	LF	9.25					5550	9.25	5550
DRIVEWAYS	12.A	1000	SF	2.75 ~~2.25~~					2750 ~~2250~~	2.75 ~~2.25~~	2750 ~~2250~~
CATCH BASINS	13.A	4	EA	255.00	1020	480.00	1920			735.00	2940
SUB TOTAL					~~38741~~ 38347		~~29495~~ 27703		~~19485~~ 19985		~~86035~~ ~~87721~~
FB 47% OF LABOR											13020 ~~13863~~
TOTAL											~~101584~~ 99055
INSTALL MISC. METAL											
FIREMAN'S POLE	1.A	1	EA			80.00	80				
LADDERS	2.A	2	EA			28.50	57				
CHANNEL DOOR FRAMES	3.A	4	EA			40.00	160				
DOOR CORNER GUARDS @ JAMBS	4.A	8	EA			19.00	152				
LINTELS OVER DOORS	5.A	4	EA			60.00	240				
GUARD POSTS, PIPE W/CONC. FILL	6.A	12	EA			9.50	114				
DETENTION BAR ASSEMBLIES	7.A	2	EA			160.00	320				
STAIR RAILINGS	8.A	80	LF			3.00	240				
SUB TOTAL							1363				
FB 47% OF LABOR							641				
TOTAL							2004				
CAULKING & SEALANTS											
DOOR & WINDOW FRAMES	1.A	1600	LF	1.25					2000	1.25	2000
BLOCK TO STUCCO TO FACIA	2.A	680	LF	2.00					1360	2.00	1360
TOTAL									3360		3360

Figure 3.3b

PROJECT   ADMINISTRATION BLDG. & FIRE STATION   CLASSIFICATION   SHEET NO. 3 OF 7
LOCATION   PICACHO, CALIFORNIA   ARCHITECT   ESTIMATE NO.
TAKE OFF BY PJC   QUANTITY BY PJC   PRICES BY   PJC   EXTENSIONS BY   MD   DATE   10-22-1984
                                                                                                   CHECKED BY   JM

DESCRIPTION	NO.	QUANTITY	UNIT	MATERIAL UNIT	MATERIAL TOTAL	LABOR UNIT	LABOR TOTAL	SUBS UNIT	SUBS TOTAL	TOTAL UNIT	COST TOTAL
CARPENTRY											
DOORS - HOLLOW METAL	1.A	6	EA			39.88	239			39.88	239
WOOD, S. C.	B	18	EA			39.88	718			39.88	718
DOOR FRAMES - HOLLOW METAL	2.A	24	EA			29.91	718			29.91	718
DOOR HARDWARE - CLOSERS	3.A	12	EA			19.94	239			19.94	239
EXIT DEVICES	B	3	EA			39.88	120			39.88	120
THRESHOLDS	C	6	EA			29.91	179			29.91	179
SEALS	D	6	EA			39.88	239			39.88	239
WINDOW FRAMES (ARCHED) W/CASINGS	4.A	9	EA	880.00		199.70 / ~~79.76~~	1797 / ~~718~~		7920	1079.70 / ~~959.76~~	9717 / ~~8638~~
RECTANGULAR W/CASINGS	B	25	EA	225.00		159.00 / ~~59.82~~	3975 / ~~1496~~		5625	384.00 / ~~284.82~~	9600 / ~~7121~~
SINGLE STORAGE SHELVING	5.A	38	LF	3.00		3.50	133		114	6.50	247
RECEPTIONIST COUNTER	6.A	24	LF	60.00		7.00	168		1440	67.00	1608
LAM. PLASTIC TOP & FRONT	B	144	SF	6.00					864	6.00	864
BASE CABINETS W/LAM. PLASTIC TOPS	7.A	30	LF	65.00		7.00	210		1950	72.00	2160
JANITOR SHELF	8.A	12	LF	3.00		3.50	42		36	6.50	78
FIREMEN'S BUNKS	9.A	2	EA	480.00		80.00	160		960	560.00	1120
KITCHEN BASE CAB. W/LAM.PL. TOP	10.A	10	LF	70.00		8.00	80		700	78.00	780
OVERHEAD CABINET	B	30	SF	12.00		4.50	135		360	16.50	495
WORKBENCH	11.A	12	LF	40.00		6.00	72		480	46.00	552
WALL SHELVING UNITS	12.A	160	SF	4.00		2.00	320		640	6.00	960
CLOSET SHELVES	13.A	36	LF	3.00		2.50	90		108	5.50	198
POLES	B	36	LF	2.50		1.50	54		90	4.00	144
SHOWER BENCH	14.A	8	LF	30.00		8.00	64		240	38.00	304
NAILERS ON ROOF 2 X 4 & 2 X 6	15.A	400	LF	0.70	280	0.70	280			1.40	560
ROOF FASCIA 2 X 12	16.A	480	LF	1.60	768	1.20	576			2.80	1344
MISC. ROUGH HARDWARE	17.A	LS			150						150
INSTALL TOILET ACCESSORIES (FURN. BY OTHERS)	18.A	24	HRS			19.94	479			19.94	479
SUB TOTAL					1198		~~7529~~ / 11087		21527		~~33812~~ / 30254
FB 47% OF LABOR											5211 / ~~3539~~
TOTAL											~~39023~~ / 33793

Figure 3.3c

Step 4: Making Up the Bid Spread Sheet

At this early stage we can enter in the upper-left block the estimated costs of our company's own work, less the general conditions costs. Next, enter the subcontract trade headings with names of a few expected sub-bidders and separate boxes for the base bid and alternative bid No. 1. We can also start a more detailed breakdown under each block. Under masonry, for example, there are three questionable items: reinforcing steel, precast concrete window sills, and shoring for openings. Questions answered in the bidding stage minimize disputes later.

The spread sheet in Fig. 3.4a is a model of one used in bidding, except the number of lines under each heading are fewer. A real spread sheet provides enough lines to list eight or ten sub-bidders. The standard sheet may be reduced for a simple job by cutting, or it may be widened for a complex job by splicing.

		ALT. 1	BASE BID		PROJECT	ADMINISTRATION BUILDING & FIRE STATION		LOCAT
01100	GENERAL CONDITIONS				BID DATE	OCTOBER 22, 1984		COMP
03300	C.I.P. CONCRETE	320	99,055					
06000	CARPENTRY		17,497					
	MILLWORK		21,527					
07950	CAULKING & SEALANTS		3,360					
06300	INSTALL MISC. METAL		2,004					

05120	STRUCTURAL STEEL

07950	CAULKING & SEALANTS

06300	MISCELLANEOUS METAL

08100	HOLLOW METAL DOORS & F
	H.M. DOORS & FRAMES	WOOD DOORS

02200	CLEARING & EARTHWORK

05320	STEEL DECKING
	HOISTING

08330	OVERHEAD STEEL DOOR
	ELEC. OPER.

02444	CHAIN LINK FENCE

06000	MILLWORK
	LAM. PLASTIC

08400	ALUMINUM WINDOWS
	CAULKING

02640	A.C. PAVING

07320	WALL & CEILING INSULATION
	FURRING

08720	GLASS & GLAZING

02800	LANDSCAPING
	SPRINK-LERS

07240	ROOF INSULATION

08800	FINISH HARDWARE

03320	REINFORCING STEEL
	HOISTING	MASONRY REINF.

07320	CLAY TILE ROOFING

09110	LATHING & PLASTERING
	LATH & SCRATCH TILE

04000	MASONRY
	REINF. STEEL	P.C. WDW SILLS

07600	SHEET METAL
	WALL LOUVERS

09250	METAL FRAMING & GYP.
	CAULKING

Figure 3.4a

& SEALANTS			09310	CERAMIC TILE						16000	ELECTRICAL				
				LATH & SCRATCH											

AL DOORS & FRAMES			09500	ACOUSTIC TILE											
S WOOD S DOORS				SUSP. CL'G											

STEEL DOORS			09650	RESILIENT FLOORING											

WINDOWS			09110	PAINTING											

GLAZING			10100	BUILDING SPECIALTIES											
				TOILET ACCESS.	TOILET PARTN'S	VEN. BLINDS	F.E. CAB'S								

RDWARE					KIT. UNIT	FLAG POLE	ROOM NUMBERS								

PLASTERING			15000	MECHANICAL					
					SAN. SEWER	STORM DRAINS	EXTERIOR WATER	EXTERIOR GAS	

BASE BID

	COST	
	MARK-UP	
	SUBTOTAL	
	BOND COST	
	ADJUSTMENT	
	TOTAL	

ING & GYP. BOARD									
S					PLUMBING	HEATING	VENT. & A.C.	HOSE REELS	

ALT. 1

	COST	
	MARK UP	
	SUBTOTAL	
	BOND COST	
	ADJUSTMENT	
	TOTAL	

Figure 3.4a (cont.)

In alternative bid No. 1, finish grade is to be left two feet lower than the base bid elevation. Therefore, excavation will be a deductive item. The paving contractor will have a large deductive price for less paving and a small additive price for an additional temporary berm which is quoted as a net deduction. It is a good idea to print the deductive price for excavation and paving in red pencil.

Over the few days that the bidding process takes place, a trickle of information will be entered on the spread sheet, leaving that much less work to do on bid day.

Step 5: Researching for Sub-Bids

Subtrades were delegated, in preliminary Steps 4 and 6, to the bidder's team members for contacting subs and eliciting their "yes" or "no" responses (see Sec. 1.8). A passive approach could fail to bring in some of the best and lowest sub-bids. It is possible, however, to overdo this effort. We not only want the contract, but we want to make money. To be the low bidder is not to "win the race," but only to qualify for the real contest that lies ahead—the construction. It is good planning to contact the subs that we consider best qualified to do the work. Our call sheet contains only those subs we consider acceptable, based on our first-hand experience with them and on their reputations. We do not have to contact weak, low-bidding subs.

Our basic purpose is to find out *who* will bid *what*, so that we can get the best possible coverage on all the items of work. Subs have their own systems of d-rating projects. Therefore, we prime bidders have only limited influence on whether they bid to *us*, and at what level of competitiveness. In a sub's d-rating of a project, the prime bidder is one of several variables, just as the sponsor is one of several variables to the prime bidder.

Step 6: Reviewing the General Conditions

In Step 3 we reviewed all of the estimated costs of our own company's portion of the project (not to be sublet), except the general conditions. Approaching the bid day, we now have enough information to price the general conditions needs of the project. The specs allow us 365 calendar days to complete the project. Let us confirm or adjust the completion time by use of a bar graph, as in Fig. 3.6a.

We will use the estimate sheet, Fig. 3.2c, to construct our graph. From experience we know that a project of this type and size should not take 365 days to complete, but we note that site earthwork is unusually massive and will require about five weeks. No other work can start until earthwork is completed. Most of the other site work (a.c. paving, concrete walks, curbs, landscaping, and fencing) occur in the final weeks.

Masonry work cannot start until concrete footings are completed. The majority of the structural steel can proceed only after the second floor decking is in place. Most of the architectural trades occur in the eighth, ninth, and tenth months.

Under ideal conditions we can complete the project in eleven months. Allowing for unpredictable delays, time to make the final corrections, cleaning up, and negotiating the sponsor's acceptance of the project, the specified twelve months is realistic. We have thus far taken a well-balanced view on d-rating, reviewing the estimates, and researching for qualified subs. Let us therefore agree for consistency to base our general conditions cost on the realistic twelve months completion time.

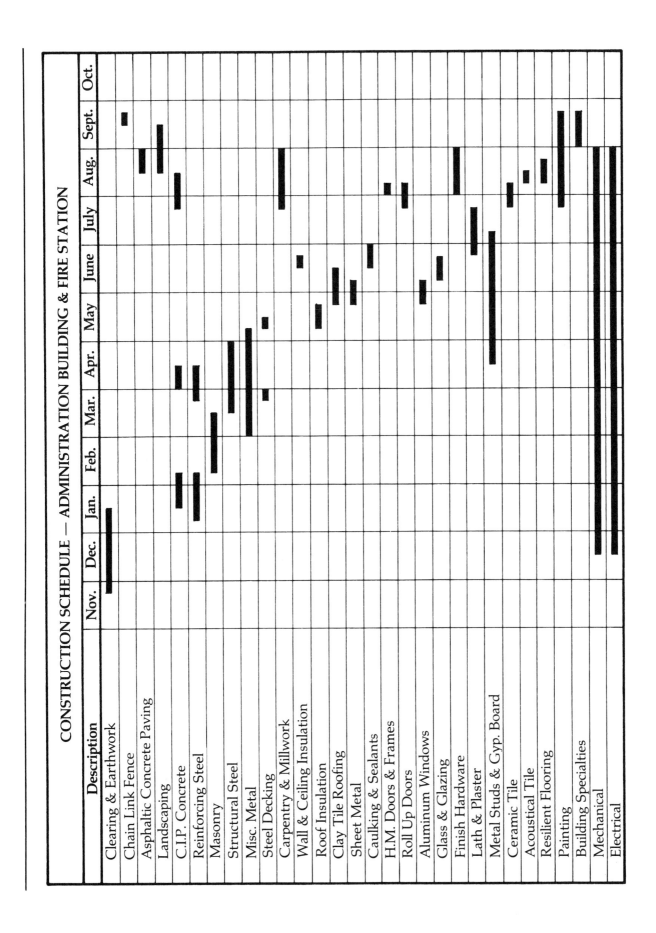

Figure 3.6a

Our review of the general conditions estimate, Fig. 3.6b, begins with the check list in Sec. 2.15. Because earthwork is unusually extensive, surveying is an important and expensive item that should be kept separate for comparison with possible sub-bids. We therefore provide a budget figure for it in the upper-left corner block of the spread sheet. Two other items are also carried over to the upper-left block: (1) window and fixture cleaning, and (2) progress schedule. These items will probably not be sub-let, but our budget costs may easily be compared with sub-bids.

CONSOLIDATED COST ANALYSIS

SHEET NO. 4 OF 7
ESTIMATE NO.

PROJECT ADMINISTRATION BLDG. & FIRE STATION   CLASSIFICATION
LOCATION PICACHO, CALIFORNIA   ARCHITECT   DATE 10-22-1984
TAKE OFF BY PJC   QUANTITY BY PJC   PRICES BY PJC   EXTENSIONS BY MD   CHECKED BY JM

DESCRIPTION	NO.	QUANTITY	UNIT	MATERIAL UNIT	MATERIAL TOTAL	LABOR UNIT	LABOR TOTAL	SUBS UNIT	SUBS TOTAL	TOTAL UNIT	COST TOTAL
GENERAL CONDITIONS											
SURVEYING (SEE SPREAD SHEET)	1										
LAYOUT FOR STRUCTURES	2	48	HRS	3.00	144	52.61	2525			55.61	2669
FIELD OFFICE	3	12	MO	85.00	1020					85.00	1020
STORAGE SHED	4	12	MO	75.00	900					75.00	900
TOILETS 2 EA.	5	12	MO	95.00	1140					95.00	1140
TELEPHONE	6	12	MO	150.00 ~~100.00~~	1800 ~~1200~~					150.00 ~~100.00~~	1800 ~~1200~~
WATER HOOKUP & METER	7.A		LS		300		300	1500			2100
WATER MONTHLY CHARGES	B	12	MO	60.00	720					60.00	720
ELECTRICAL SERVICE & TRANSFORMER	8.A		LS		400		500	1800			2700
ELECTRICAL MONTHLY CHARGES	B	12	MO	70.00	840					70.00	840
SECURITY YARD FENCE	9	200	LF	10.00				2000		10.00	2000
PROJECT SIGN	10		LS		100		100	250			450
TEMP WEATHER CLOSURES @ DRS & WDWS	11		LS		250		800				1050
OFFICE SUPPLIES	12	12	MO	35.00	420					35.00	420
SMALL TOOLS	13	12	MO	200.00	2400					200.00	2400
MISC. RENTAL EQUIPMENT	14	12	MO	400.00 ~~200.00~~	4800 ~~2400~~					400.00 ~~200.00~~	4800 ~~2400~~
OIL, FUEL, REPAIRS, SERVICING	15	12	MO	150.00	1800					150.00	1800
CLEANUP, PROGRESSIVE	16.A	12	MO	100.00	1200	1200.00	14400			1300.00	15600
CLEANUP, FINAL	B	120	HRS	2.00	240	25.00	3000			27.00	3240
WDWS & FIXT. CLNG (SEE SPRD SHT)	17										
SUPERINTENDENT	18	12	MO			3236.40	38837			3236.40	38837
SUBSISTENCE FOR IMPORTED LABOR	19	209	DAYS	20.00	4180					20.00	4180
BARRICADES - 8' HIGH PLYWOOD	20	700	LF	6.00	4200	6.00	4200			12.00	8400
NIGHT LIGHTS ON BARRICADES	21	12	MO	60.00	720					60.00	720
PROGRESS SCHD (SEE SPRD SHT)	22										
SAFETY RAILINGS AT ROOF	23	280	LF	1.00	280	1.50	420			2.50	700
SUBTOTAL					~~24854~~ 27854		65082		5550		~~95486~~ 98486
FB 47% OF LABOR											30588
TOTAL											~~126074~~ 129074

Figure 3.6b

108

Most of the general conditions are expressed in cost per month, although some of them are not clearly meaningful in that form. The usefulness of this practice is its uniformity when bidding various projects. It provides an efficient system for keeping actual cost records, and it simplifies the adjustment of costs in the event the number of months for completion is revised.

Four items (water meter, transformer, security yard fencing, and project sign painting) are entered under the subcontract column for future negotiation with subs. These are allowances rather than budgets.

We adjust only two items: (1) telephone is increased due to many out-of-town subs and sources of supply, and (2) rental equipment is increased due to mobilization from distant cities.

We compare the total estimated cost to the rough formula in Fig. 2.15a. Note that as the project size decreases, the percentage of general conditions cost rises. For 1.5 million dollar project taking twelve months to complete, we may interpolate and approximate about 8%; thus, $1,500,000 x 0.08 = $120,000, which is less than the estimated $129,074. Have we overestimated the cost of general conditions? A careful checking of all items convinces us that we have not; therefore, we enter the estimated amount in the line reserved for it in the upper-left block of the spread sheet.

Step 7: Budgets, Plug-in Figures, and Allowances

Budgets, plug-in figures, and allowances should be made for all items which may not be adequately covered by sub-bids, as well as for items on which we know we will not get a figure until the last minute. This allows us to make lump sum adjustments to our bid without holding up its preparation.

For this project, in preparatory Step 6 above, we decided to prepare budgets for earthwork, a.c. paving, masonry, millwork, metal framing, and gypsum board. We did this not only because of the predictable scarcity of sub-bids, but because of the limitation by the specs of sub-letting 75% of the project. These trades (Figs. 3.7a, 3.7b, and 3.7c) were budgeted by our estimating department.

Earthwork. From the drawings, specs, and site investigation we learned that the site is a filled-over dump containing large pieces of concrete. We made an educated guess of the quantity of buried concrete by exploratory drilling and by questioning former dump employees. According to the specs, all material must be removed, down to the original, undisturbed grade. New select fill will then be imported, brought up to the finish grade in the base bid, or left two feet below finish grade, as in alternative bid No.1. We have located a source of borrow fill material from a supplier at $2.95 per cubic yard, delivered to the site. We have also determined sources and rental rates for earthmoving equipment, since we must spread and compact this fill.

Based on the above considerations, we have applied a 20% markup to the estimated bare cost in order to equate to possible sub-bids, or to allow for risk should our own company undertake the earthwork.

A.C. paving. The budget indicates that competitive bids will be about $200,000 for the base bid.

Masonry. This is a quality masonry job. For an out-of-town subcontractor, our budget is probably minimal.

CONSOLIDATED COST ANALYSIS

PROJECT ADMINISTRATION BLDG. & FIRE STATION CLASSIFICATION ESTIMATE NO.
LOCATION PICACHO,CALIFORNIA ARCHITECT DATE 10-20-1984
TAKE OFF BY PJC QUANTITY BY PJC PRICES BY PJC EXTENSIONS BY MD CHECKED BY JM

DESCRIPTION	NO.	QUANTITY	UNIT	MATERIAL UNIT	MATERIAL TOTAL	LABOR UNIT	LABOR TOTAL	SUBS UNIT	SUBS TOTAL	TOTAL UNIT	COST TOTAL
EARTHWORK BUDGET BASE BID											
EXC DOWN TO OLD DUMP SURFACE	1.A	17000	CY	0.80					13600		
LOAD, HAUL 5 MILES & RETURN	B	17000	CY	2.05					34850		
EXC. TYPICAL DEBRIS	2.A	20000	CY	1.13					22600		
LOAD, HAUL 5 MILES & RETURN	B	20000	CY	2.25					45000		
BREAK UP MASS CONCRETE	3.A	5000	CY	7.68					38400		
LOAD, HAUL 5 MILES & RETURN	B	5000	CY	3.92					19600		
PURCHASE IMPORT FILL MATERIAL	4.A	45000	CY	2.95					132750		
SPREAD & COMPACT THE FILL	B	45000	CY	0.90					40500		
FINE GRADE OVERALL	5	120000	SF	0.03					3600		
EROSION PROTECTION OF SLOPES	6	9000	SF	0.15					1350		
DUMP FEES	7	2200	LDS	15.00					33000		
EQUIPMENT MOVE ON & OFF	8	80	HRS	50.00					4000		
SUPERVISION	9	5	WK	1176.00					5880		
COST OF EXPLORATORY DRILLING	10	60	LF	20.00					1200		
SUB TOTAL									396330		
MARKUP 20 %									79266		
TOTAL									475596		
ALTERNATE #1 DEDUCTIVE											
IMPORT FILL MATERIAL	4.A	10500	CY	2.95					30975		
SPREAD & COMPACT THE FILL	B	10500	CY	0.90					9450		
SUBTOTAL									40425		
MARKUP 20%									8085		
TOTAL									48510		

Figure 3.7a

CONSOLIDATED COST ANALYSIS

PROJECT	ADMINISTRATION BLDG. & FIRE STATION	CLASSIFICATION			ESTIMATE NO.	
LOCATION	PICACHO, CALIFORNIA	ARCHITECT			DATE 10-20-1984	
TAKE OFF BY PJC	QUANTITY BY PJC	PRICES BY PJC	EXTENSIONS BY MD		CHECKED BY JM	

DESCRIPTION	NO.	QUANTITY	UNIT	MATERIAL UNIT	MATERIAL TOTAL	LABOR UNIT	LABOR TOTAL	SUBS UNIT	SUBS TOTAL	TOTAL UNIT	COST TOTAL
A.C. PAVING BUDGET BASE BID											
FINE GRADE & ROLL THE SUBGRADE	1	108000	SF	0.05					5400		
6" AGGREGATE BASE COURSE	2	2400	CY	12.00					28800		
3" A.C. PAVING	3	108000	SF	1.35					145800		
SAND & SEAL COAT	4	108000	SF	0.07					7560		
SUBTOTAL									187560		
MARKUP 15%									28134		
TOTAL									215694		
ALTERNATE BID #1											
DEDUCT PAVING	1	45000	SF	1.73					77850		
ADD BERM	2	300	LF	2.45					735		
NET SUBTOTAL									77115		
MARKUP 15%									11567		
TOTAL									88682		
MASONRY BUDGET											
CONC BLK 8" X 12" X 16" INT CLR SG	1	3500	SF	7.95					27825		
REINFORCING STEEL	2	3500	SF	0.80					2800		
SHORE OPENINGS	3	36	EA	21.94					790		
PC WINDOW SILLS	4	36	EA	30.70					1105		
SUBTOTAL									32520		
MARKUP 20%									6504		
TOTAL									39024		

Figure 3.7b

DESCRIPTION	NO.	QUANTITY	UNIT	MATERIAL UNIT	MATERIAL TOTAL	LABOR UNIT	LABOR TOTAL	SUBS UNIT	SUBS TOTAL	TOTAL UNIT	COST TOTAL
METAL FRAMING & GYPSUM BOARD											
METAL FRAMING											
6" 25 GA GALV STUDS, 16" O.C.	1	600	SF	1.50					900		
3 5/8" 25 GA GALV STUDS, 16" O.C.	2	6000	SF	1.05					6300		
3 5/8" 18 GA GALV STUDS, 16" O.C.	3	3200	SF	1.20					3840		
7/8" FURRING ON BLOCK WALLS	4	3500	SF	0.76					2660		
CHANNEL FRAMED CEILING	5	1200	SF	1.40					1680		
CEILING ACCESS PANELS	6	8	EA	60.00					480		
GYPSUM BOARD											
RIGID INSULATION (NOT INCLUDED)											
5/8" G.B SCREWED TO STUDS	1	13200	SF	0.70					9240		
5/8" G.B GLUED TO INSULATION	2	3500	SF	0.60					2100		
5/8" G.B SCREWED TO CEILING FRMG	3	1200	SF	0.90					1080		
MISC. METAL TRIM	4	3600	LF	0.65					2340		
EXPANSION JOINT	5	16700	SF	0.15					2505		
SUBTOTAL									33125		
MARKUP 15%									4969		
TOTAL									38094		

PROJECT ADMINISTRATION BLDG. & FIRE STATION
LOCATION PICACHO, CALIFORNIA
TAKE OFF BY PJC   QUANTITY BY PJC
CLASSIFICATION
ARCHITECT
PRICES BY   PJC   EXTENSIONS BY   MD
SHEET NO. 7 OF 7
ESTIMATE NO.
DATE   10-20-1984
CHECKED BY   JM

Figure 3.7c

Metal framing and gypsum board. Our own company is experienced in this trade and will not sublet this portion of this project for more than $40,000.

All of these budgets are entered in their respective blocks on the spread sheet where they may, or may not, eventually be selected and made part of the total bid in lieu of sub-bids.

Step 8: Preparing to Bid

Everything we do in this step is intended to save time and to avoid errors in the last few hours of putting the bid together. The submittal package (bid forms, bond forms, etc.) is filled in completely, except for the amounts of the base bid and the alternative bid. We now analyze, tabulate, and enter on the bid spread sheet the information contained on flyers (Fig. 2.17a) mailed in by subs. Then we review the addenda and assure ourselves that we have not overlooked any changes having monetary value. Next, we complete the researching for sub-coverage. Finally, we organize and brief the members of the bidding team and arrange the bid room to deal efficiently with the action that is about to start. A minimum team for this particular project is:

Bidder	1
Assistant bidders	2
Sub-bid receivers	6
Total	**9**

The main purpose of our earlier d-rating, Step 1, was to decide: (1) whether to bid the job or not, and (2) the level of competitiveness. Now

we need to review that d-rating to determine the markup. A change has occurred in point 5, the competition. Will Bid & Sons is reported to have received a large new contract, and presumably will be less competitive in this project. This positive effect is offset by the possibility that our company might perform a major subtrade, such as site excavation, because of the 75% subwork limitation. This lowers the grade for point 10, special risk.

If we agree to retain our original d-rating of 84 and to use it to find the markup, then we may apply a positive or negative contingency allowance (add or cut) as a part of the final adjustment to the total bid. If our project cost is $1.5 million and the d-rating is 84, the markup finder scale (Fig. 2.6k) will suggest a 12% markup, which includes 4% for overhead. The breakdown would be as follows:

Overhead	$1,500,000 x .04 =	$ 60,000
Profit	$1,500,000 x .08 =	120,000
Total	$1,500,000 x .12 =	$180,000

This tentative evaluation of the markup may prevent a hasty decision and mistake of judgment at the bid deadline.

Step 9: Putting the Bid Together

Since this project is for demonstration purposes, a variety of typical problems calling for decisions are created and explained in this step. Figure 3.9a is the completed bid spread sheet.

PROJECT ADMINISTRATION BUILDING & FIRE STATION   LOCATIO...

BID DATE OCTOBER 22, 1984   COMPLE...

GEN. CONT. WORK

		ALT. 1	BASE BID	297,627
01100	GENERAL CONDITIONS		129,074	
03300	C.I.P. CONCRETE	320	99,055	320
06000	CARPENTRY		17,497	
	MILLWORK		21,527	
07950	CAULKING & SEALANTS		3,360	
06300	INSTALL MISC. METAL		2,004	
	SURVEYING		8,000	
	WINDOW CLEANING		2,200	
	PROGRESS SCHEDULE		6,750	
	SHORE PICACHO ST.		8,160	
		(320)	(297,627)	

02200 CLEARING & EARTHWORK — 475,596 / 48,510

	EROSION CONTROL	DUMP FEES	ALT. 1	BASE BID
BUDGET	441,256	1,350	33,000	48,510 / 475,596
LEVELERS	595,000	YES	YES	60,510 / 595,000

02444 CHAIN LINK FENCE — 10,500

		BASE BID
OBSTACLES, INC.		10,500
STOP-ALL		11,260
PROP-DIVIDER		10,900

02640 A.C. PAVING — 209,200 / 82,000

	PARKING STRIPING	ALT. 1	BASE BID
BUDGET	1200	88,682	215,694
BLAZERS	208,000	No	82,000 / 209,200
HARDPAK	218,900	YES	90,000 / 218,900
HILINE	223,000	YES	91,500 / 223,000

02800 LANDSCAPING — 12,222 / 2,000

	SPRINKLERS	ALT. 1	BASE BID
BEANSTIK	15,500	YES	2,990	15,500
PLANTON	14,000	YES	2,850	14,000
GREENER	12,222	YES	(2,000)	(12,222)

03320 REINFORCING STEEL — 14,850

	HOISTING	MASONRY REINF.	BASE BID
BUDGET	(600)	2,800	
BETBAR	(14,250)	No	No	14,850
STRAPTIE	18,000	YES	YES	18,000
BENDER	21,300	YES	YES	21,300

04000 MASONRY — 42,000

	REINF. STEEL	P.C. WDW SILLS	SHORE OPENINGS	BASE BID
BUDGET	37,864	2,800	1,080	2,880	39,024
HISTACK	36,320	No	(YES)	No	42,000
WALLMEN	48,500	YES	YES	YES	48,500
BLOKSON	47,000	YES	YES	YES	47,000

05120 STRUCTURAL STEEL — 156,600

	STRUC. STEEL	MISC. METAL	BASE BID
L.T. PIZZA	142,200	No	142,200
RINGER	(156,000)	(YES)	(156,600)
W.F. BEAM	149,000	No	149,000

06300 MISCELLANEOUS METAL

		MISC. METAL	BASE BID
ALUM.		18,188	18,188
CARBON		17,000	17,000
ZINC		18,990	18,990

05320 STEEL DECKING — 21,240

	HOISTING	ROOF DECK	FLOOR DECK	BASE BID
HORIZON	24,400	YES	YES	YES	24,400
DEKKO	21,240	YES	YES	YES	(21,240)

06000 MILLWORK   SEE GEN. CONTR. WORK

	LAM. PLASTIC	BASE BID
SPLICERS	27,777	YES	27,777
TERMITES	23,000	YES	23,000

07320 WALL & CEILING INSULATION — 6,100

	FURRING	BASE BID
COMFY	6,100	YES	(6,100)
COZY	12,000	YES	12,000

07240 ROOF INSULATION — 12,352

		BASE BID
ENERGY		14,140
2-COURSE		14,000
AMPLE		(12,352)

07320 CLAY TILE ROOFING — 30,000

		BASE BID
TILETOP		(30,000)

07600 SHEET METAL — 3,800

	WALL LOUVERS	BASE BID
BUDGET	(960)	
FLASHER	4,400	YES	
LEADER	2,840	No	(3,800)
DRYER	3,220	No	4,180

07950 CAULKING & SEALANTS

LINERS		

08100 HOLLOW METAL DOORS & FR...

	H.M. DOORS & FRAMES	WOOD DOORS
BUDGET		1,260
SLAMMER	2,100	/No
ACCESS	2,800	/No
OPEN	3,000	No

08330 OVERHEAD STEEL DOORS

	ELEC. OPER.	
SLAMMER	7,900	No	INCO...
SLIDEUP	8,800	YES	

08400 ALUMINUM WINDOWS

	CAULKING	INSTALL
SLIDEIN	10,500	No	No	INCO...
SEETHRU	10,750	YES	YES	
SHINY	12,880	YES	YES	

08720 GLASS & GLAZING

	GLASS IN DOORS	MIRRORS
BRITTLE	4,200	YES	YES
GLOSSY	4,890	YES	YES
SPARKLE	5,500	YES	YES

08800 FINISH HARDWARE

HOLDER		
TIGHTEN		
CONNECT		

09110 LATHING & PLASTERING

	LATH & SCRATCH TILE	
SCRATCH	29,150	800
TROWEL	33,000	No
FASTER	29,000	YES

09250 METAL FRAMING & GYP. B...

	CAULKING	
BUDGET	38,094	600
GYPERS	47,000	1,000
UPRITE	40,000	YES

Figure 3.9a

LOCATION __PICACHO, CALIFORNIA__

COMPLETION TIME __365 DAYS__

COLOR CODE { BASE BID ——— / ALT. 1 – – – – –

& SEALANTS	SEE GEN. CONTR. WORK	⊠
	BASE BID	
	3,550	

09310 CERAMIC TILE — 3,850

		LATH & SCRATCH		BASE BID
KAINSCO	4,240	No		4,250
TILERS	5,000	-800		4,200
MOSAIC	3,850	No		(3,850)

16000 ELECTRICAL — 68,000 / 3,000

		DOOR OPER.	ALT. 1	BASE BID
SHOCKER		No	3,440	75,500
STATIC		No	3,700	71,440
SPARKS		No	(3,000)	(68,000)

TAL DOORS & FRAMES — 3,360

	WOOD DOORS		BASE BID
	(1,260)		
	/No		(3,360)
	/No		4,060
	No		4,260

09500 ACOUSTIC TILE — 3,600

		SUSP. CL'G	METAL TRIM	BASE BID
T. SQUARE	4,141	YES	YES	4,141
CHECKER	3,600	YES	YES	(3,600)
SANTEX	5,000	YES	YES	5,000

STEEL DOORS — 8,800

		BASE BID
		INCOMPLETE
		(8,800)

09650 RESILIENT FLOORING — 7,500

	RISIL. FLOOR	CARPET	BASE BID
TREADS	5,900	1,600	(7,500)
HISTEP	8,300	YES	8,300
TRIPPER	6,000	No	7,600

WINDOWS — 10,750

	INSTALL	BASE BID
	No	INCOMPLETE
	YES	(10,750)
	YES	12,880

09110 PAINTING — 28,000

		BASE BID
SMEARS	28,000	(28,000)
DAUBERS	28,000	(28,000)
STREAKS	31,400	31,400

GLAZING — 4,200

	MIRRORS	BASE BID
	YES	(4,200)
	YES	4,850
	YES	5,500

10100 BUILDING SPECIALTIES — 6,930

	TOILET ACCESS.	TOILET PARTNS	VEN. BLINDS	F.E. CABS
SPECCO	1,220	1,400	No	(200)
FURNALL	1,510	(1,330)	No	220
ANYTHING	1,700	1,660	(2,000)	300

ARDWARE — 3,870

	BASE BID
	(3,870)
	4,420
	4,400

	KIT. UNIT	FLAG POLE	ROOM NUMBERS
SPECCO	(780)	1,100	450
FURNALL	No	(980)	500
ANYTHING	900	1,000	(420)

PLASTERING — 29,000

	BASE BID
	29,950
	33,800
	(29,000)

15000 MECHANICAL — 98,500

	SAN. SEWER	STORM DRAINS	EXTERIOR WATER	EXTERIOR GAS
UTILITY	33,000	YES	YES	YES
PIPER	(13,500)	(YES)	(14,500)	(YES)
FIXTURES	31,000	YES	YES	YES

BASE BID

	COST	1,607,141
12% MARK-UP		192,856
	SUBTOTAL	1,799,997
0.6% BOND COST		10,800
DEDUCT - ADJUSTMENT		(14,594)
	TOTAL	1,796,203

AMING & GYP. BOARD — 38,694

	BASE BID
	(38,694)
	48,000
	40,000

	PLUMBING	HEATING	VENT. & A.C.	HOSE REELS
UTILITY	(25,900)	46,000	YES	(2,100)
PIPER	78,000	YES	YES	YES
FIXTURES	30,000	(42,500)	(YES)	No

ALT. 1

	COST	135,830
12% MARK UP		16,300
	SUBTOTAL	152,130
0.6% BOND COST		913
	ADJUSTMENT	– – – –
DEDUCTIVE TOTAL		153,043

Figure 3.9a (cont.)

115

General conditions. We immediately sum up the items in the upper-left block that are the estimated costs of the work our company will perform. We can tell at a glance that the total amount falls roughly $100,000 below the 25% required by the contract documents. A section of concrete sidewalk is to be deducted under alternative bid No. 1:

> Base bid: $475,596
> Alt. 1, deduct: $320

Clearing and earthwork has been our main focus of concern from the start, because of its massiveness, its cost, and the assumption we made in Step 1, d-rating, that our competitor, Strategic Structures, had a strong motive to estimate this item very low. We have one sub-bid from Levelers, approximately $100,000 above our own budget, and have been unable to obtain other sub-bids. We reason that Levelers is aware that theirs is the only sub-bid. This knowledge, coupled with the buried concrete risk factor, influences them to bid high. We decide to use our own budget, which also solves the problem of the 75% subcontract limitation:

> Base bid: $475,596
> Alt. 1, deduct: $48,510

Chain link fence will clearly be sublet to Obstacles, Inc.:

> Base bid: $10,500

A.C. paving presents an ethical problem. Is Blazer's bid too low? Should they be notified? Our own budget is helpful in this decision. Since Blazer's bid is above our anticipated median of $200,000 and is above our budgeted bare cost of $187,560, we may be justified in regarding Blazer's bid as not grossly out-of-line:

> Base bid: $209,200
> Alt. 1, deduct: $82,000

Landscaping, including irrigation sprinklers, will be sublet to the obvious low bidder, Greener:

> Base bid: $12,222
> Alt. 1, deduct: $2,000

Reinforcing steel and masonry presents a joint problem. Betbar is low bidder on rebar and Histack is low bidder on masonry, but neither of them includes steel for the masonry. Our only valuation for masonry steel is our own budget of $2,800. By combining it with Histack's bid, we temporarily solve the problem. The actual amount can be negotiated with either of the subcontractors later. We add hoisting cost to Betbar's bid of $14,250.

> $14,250 + $600 = $14,850
> Base bid: $14,850

We then add rebar from our budget ($2,800) and shoring of openings from our budget ($2,880) to Histack's bid of $36,320.

> $36,320 + 2,800 + 2,880 = $42,000
> Base bid: $42,000

Structural steel and miscellaneous metal also present a combination problem. Ringer Steel's combination bid of Structural Steel and Miscellaneous Metals is lower than any combination. None if the three separate miscellaneous metal bids will be used, so we cross out the box for that trade. It is usually preferable to sublet work in one contract, rather than in separate contracts for each trade. Structural steel and miscellaneous metal:

Base bid: $156,600

Steel decking will be sublet to Dekko on the legitimate low bid of:

Base bid: $21,240

Millwork is presently included in our own work (upper-left block) in the amount of $21,527, which is slightly lower than Termite's bid. Let us postpone the decision of subletting this work.

Wall and ceiling insulation presents the problem of a great spread between two sub-bids. We phone Comfy and question them regarding the materials and quantities in their bid, at the same time avoiding reference to their extremely low status. They assure us of their willingness to stand firm on the price. Although a potential risk is involved, we tentatively enter their bid in the box:

Base bid: $6,100

Roof insulation. Ample has a poor performance record, but this bid is notably lower than the others and demands our acceptance if we hope to remain competitive.

Base bid: $12,352

Clay tile roofing. In spite of the special research effort given this trade, we were quoted by only one sub:

Base bid: $30,000

Sheet metal. By combining our budget for wall louvers with Leader's sub-bid, we get:

Base bid: $3,800

Caulking and sealants is quoted by one sub, Liners, at very nearly the same amount we have allowed for it in our own work (upper-left block). We cross out the price box and postpone the decision on subletting.

Hollow metal doors and frames. We combine a budget for the previously overlooked item, wood doors, with Slammer's sub-bid:

Base bid: $3,360

Roll-up steel doors. Slammer's bid for this item was not complete. Lacking a budget for electric door operators, we are forced to use Slideup's bid:

Base bid: $8,800

Aluminum windows. Slidin's bid is only $250 below Seethru's—not enough to cover installation and caulking. Therefore, we accept the complete bid of Seethru:

Base bid: $10,750

Glass and glazing will be sublet to Brittle at their all-inclusive bid:

Base bid: $4,200

Finish hardware. Holder is the apparent low bidder:

Base bid: $3,870

Lathing and plastering and ceramic tile present joint problems. We have no valuation for lathing and plaster scratch coat for ceramic tile other than Scratch's $800. We use this to equate all of the plastering bids (to include lath and scratch) and all of the ceramic tile bids (to exclude lath and scratch):

Lath and plaster — Base bid: $29,000
Ceramic tile — Base bid: $3,850

Metal framing and gypsum board. Our previous decision, in Step 7, was not to sublet this trade for more than $40,000. Uprite's quotation of $40,000 is acceptable, but we postpone the decision to sublet and enter our own budget in the box:

Base bid: $38,694

Acoustical tile will be sublet to Checker:

Base bid: $3,600

Resilient flooring. We use Tread's valuation of $1,600 for carpeting to equate Tripper's bid to the other bids. Tread is low bidder:

Base bid: $7,500

Painting. A tie is involved here that cannot be resolved at this time. In the bid form we can list our proposed subcontractor as Smears/Daubers:

Base bid: $28,000

Building specialties will be divided between each of the bidders, subletting individual items to the low bidders. Total combination is:

Base bid: $6,930

Mechanical Work will be sublet to different bidders for the low bids, as quoted separately:

Base bid: $98,500

Electrical will be sublet to Sparks:

Base Bid: $68,000
Alt. 1, deduct: $3,000

We can now sum up all of the base-bid boxes and all of the alternative-bid No. 1 boxes to find the total of the project:

	Base Bid	Deductive Alt. 1
	$1,607,141	$135,830
12% markup:	$ 192,856	$ 16,300
Subtotal:	1,799,997	152,130
Bond cost (0.6%):	10,800	913
First Total bid amount:	$1,810,797	$153,043

We may now consider changes and adjustments, using an add/cut sheet. But first, let us decide which trades our company will *not* sublet.

The 75% subcontract limitation is: $1,810,797 x 0.75% = $1,358,098. Our company's work cannot be less than: $1,810,797 x 0.25% = 452,699.25. Earthwork alone ($475,596) exceeds this limit. Therefore, by not subletting earthwork, we can sublet the entire balance of the project, assuming that we have acceptable sub-bids. Within economic limitations, it is desirable to sublet the maximum possible.

Earthwork appears to be the key to success in the bidding of this project. A decision not to sublet increases risk, but the risk is tempered by the 20% markup included in our earthwork budget. We therefore decide to make no additional adjustments.

On the other hand, general conditions costs appear high relative to our company's other work, such as concrete and carpentry. Let us reconsider the completion time, as charted in Step 6, and reduce it from 12 to 11 months, which reduces certain monthly based costs by $7,977. The following trades, for which the decision to sublet has been previously made, are as follows:

	Add	Cut
(Reduced monthly costs)	—	$7,977
Millwork	$1,473	—
Caulking	190	—
Surveying	—	800
CPM progress schedule	—	750
Metal framing and gyp. bd.	1,306	—
	$2,969	$9,527
		- 2,969
		$6,558

The adjustment ($6,558) is a net cut to the base bid.

Can we, or should we, make any further changes? At this point of submitting the bid, a bidder's mind is almost inevitably open to psychological and intuitive influences. How do we *feel* about our competitors? Our subs? How do we *feel* about the tightness, looseness, or risks in our own bid package?

If our company were in greater need of work, of if we had an earthwork sub-bid equal to or lower than our budget, we would surely reduce the markup so that our base bid would be below $1,800,000. Those conditions do not exist, but two lesser influences do exist: (1) our total bid amount greatly exceeds the educated guess of $1.5 million, which we made in Step 1, leading us to the likely conclusion that the sponsor's budget is lower than our base bid, and that the alternative, deductive bid will probably be accepted, and (2) Strategic Structures cannot be ignored as a keen competitor.

Let us agree to reduce our original base bid markup to 11-1/2% on the base bid only, but to retain the full 12% on the alternative bid (which in effect amounts to a cut). Our final adjustment, then, is as follows:

	Cut
Base bid, as itemized:	$ 6,558
Markup, 0.5%:	8,036
Total cut:	$14,594

	Base Bid	**Alt. No. 1, Deductive**
First total bid amount:	$1,810,797	$153,043
Adjustment cut:	14,594	—
Final bid amount:	$1,796,203	$153,043

Step 10: Submitting the Bid

At the bid reception point, our runner has all bid submittal papers, presigned and complete, except for the two bid amounts. We transmit that information to the runner by phone. Fig. 3.10a and 3.10b show the two most significant pages of the bid submittal forms on which the runner enters the data by hand. The list of subcontract trades was typed previously to reduce the writing-in time. Because the writing in of subs takes the greatest portion of the few remaining minutes, their names are transmitted first. The bid amounts are given last. We now await the runner's phone call reporting the bid results.

Bid Form
(Construction Contract)

Page 1 of 2

Name and Location of Project
Administration Bldg. & Fire Station
Picacho, California

Oct. 22, 1984
(Date)

To: Public Works Dept.
Picacho, California

In compliance with the invitation for bids, all requirements of the contract documents and addenda 1 & 2 the undersigned proposes to furnish all labor, material and equipment as required for the said Administration Bldg. and Fire Station for the following amounts:

Base Bid One Million Seven Hundred Ninety-Six Thousand Two Hundred Three Dollars ($1,796,203)

Alternate Bid #1 Deduct ($ 153,043)

Enclosed is a bid guarantee consisting of: Bid bond in the amount of 10% of the total bid

Bidder: Your Own Company
Palamony St.
Picacho, CA.

By: M.B. Lucky
M. B. Lucky, Pres.

Figure 3.10a

Project Admin. Bldg. and Fire Sta., Picacho, CA

Our proposed subcontractors are:

Portion of Project	Name	% of Total Bid
Millwork	Termites	.013
Caulking	Liners	.002
Surveying	Sight Bros.	.005
CPM schedule	Charters	.003
Chain link fence	Obstacles, Inc.	.006
A.C. paving	Blazers	.116
Landscaping	Greener	.007
Reinforcing steel	Betbar	.008
Masonry	Histack	.023
Structural steel/misc. metal	Ringer	.087
Steel decking	Dekko	.012
Wall & ceiling insulation	Comfy	.003
Roof insulation	Ample	.007
Clay tile roofing	Tiletop	.017
Sheet metal	Leaders	.002
H.M. doors & frames	Slammer	.002
Coiling steel doors	Slideup	.005
Aluminum windows	Seethru	.006
Glass & glazing	Brittle	.002
Lathing & plastering	Faster	.017
Met. framing & gyp. board	Upright	.022
Ceramic tile	Mosaic	.002
Acoustical tile	Checker	.002
Resilient flooring	Treads	.004
Painting	Smears/Daubers	.016
Building specialties	Specco/Furnall ⎫ Anything ⎭	.004
Mechanical	Utility/Piper ⎫ Fixture ⎭	.055
Electrical	Sparks	.038
		.486

Figure 3.10b

Step 11: Postmortem

The bidding of this project has been relatively simple because of the single alternative bid, which involved only a few sub-bids. From the start we exercised realistic rather than tight choices and decisions. Therefore, a degree of slack may exist. Compensating for that probability, we cut the general conditions and the markup at the end in a mathematical, rather than an arbitrary, manner. A number of imperfections still exist:

1. The project was more expensive than our first guess in Step 1. Will it exceed the sponsor's budget or the company's ability or willingness to proceed with a contract?
2. Having no acceptable earthwork sub-bid, we face a do-it-yourself risk. Earthwork must begin immediately, allowing no time for organizing and economizing.
3. A smaller percentage of the project cost than is desirable will be subbed out.

4. Not all of our budgets were replaced by firm sub-bids (for example, reinforcing steel for masonry, parking striping, wall louvers, and wood doors).
5. Only one sub-bid was received for clay tile roofing.
6. A great disparity exists between the two insulation bids.
7. Two painting sub-bids are tied for low position.
8. Mechanical work is divided between three subs. One all-inclusive bid would have been preferred.

In spite of these imperfections, we consider ours to be a *good* bid, and the bid results confirm this belief, as follows:

Bids for Administration Building and Fire Station, Picacho, CA.

Name of Bidder	Base Bid ($)	Deductive Alt. No. 1 ($)
Taciturn Builders	1,863,700	178,200
Clawhammer Co.	1,859,999	180,000
Likeable Construction	1,839,700	166,700
I.N. Valid Const. Co.	1,842,220	170,000
Strategic Structures	1,831,320	180,660
Will Bid & Sons	1,830,900	161,200
Your Own Company	1,796,203	153,043
Picacho City budget	$1,650,000	$100,000

The bid results also confirm roughly our educated guess about the order of the bidders. Our guess that Will Bid & Sons would not be competitive due to their receiving a large new contract was incorrect. However, Strategic Structures' alternative bid No. 1, subtracted, places them below Will Bid & Sons. Since the sponsor will probably accept a base bid, less deductive alternative bid, let us list all of the bids as they would be after subtracting the alternatives:

Name of Bidder	Base Bid Less Alt. No. 1
Taciturn Builders	$1,685,500
Clawhammer Co.	1,679,999
Likeable Construction	1,673,000
I.N. Valid Const. Co.	1,672,220
Will Bid & Sons	1,669,700
Strataegic Structures	1,650,660
Your Own Company	1,643,160

Our final adjustment proved fortuitous. If we had not cut the markup by 0.5%, our net bid would have been $1,651,196 ($1,643,160 + $8,036), and we would have lost the contract to Strategic Structures by $536! We are pleased to note that our net bid of $1,643,160 is within the sponsor's base bid budget of $1,650,000. Reasoning that this money is already in the town's budget and that the town managers would rather forego the parking space deleted in alternative No. 1 than abandon the project, we feel confident of a contract award.

One further conclusion we are tempted to draw because all of the bids are grouped so closely is that the bidders all budgeted the earthwork, as did we, or that they succeeded in obtaining a competitive sub-bid, which was close to the amount we budgeted.

Our bid *looks* good. But unless we (with the cooperation of many other people) conduct a tight follow-up procedure, the final accounting could prove otherwise. The next section demonstrates the follow-up to the bidding of this same project.

Part IV: Project Management (Bidding Follow-up)

As low bidder and recipient of the prime contract, we have obtained only the opportunity to invest capital and a lot of energy, for either gain or loss. (Breaking even is a *loss*, due to the sacrifice of capital and energy that could have produced a profit in some other venture.)

Some understaffed bidders turn over the bid package to a superintendent and never participate further in the project. Some bidders are interested only in procuring contracts, not fulfilling them. However, the superintendent, the project, and the company all benefit from bidder participation in the field work.

Most bid packages, and our Administration/Fire Station is no exception, contain loose ends and potential technical and human relations (subcontractor) problems. The packages have been in the design stage for many months; sponsors are eager to "break ground." The clock has started for our project, with its twelve-month commitment to the sponsor (eleven months to ourselves). Hereafter, let us use the term "super" for superintendent.

Very large projects may support a full-time project manager in addition to the super. Management of smaller projects, such as ours, is customarily shared by the super and the bidder, or company general manager. The prime contractor's management priorities, roughly in order of importance, are as follows:

1. Inform subcontractors of their competitive positions in their respective trades.
2. Notify successful subs of your intention to award them subcontracts.
3. Resolve loose ends.
4. Write subcontracts and purchase orders.
5. Brief the super.
6. Prepare a construction progress schedule.
7. Prepare a progress payment schedule.

8. Set up a cost record-keeping system.
9. Expedite the project; make periodic job inspections; consult with super; participate in the change-order negotiations and in the final "selling" of the job.

4.1 Inform the Unsuccessful Sub-Bidders

This is the first priority because it is involuntary and thrust upon the bidder immediately after the prime bidding results are known. Projects that do not require the naming of subcontractors as a part of the bidding submittal can pose public-relations problems, since the prime bidder is not forced to make hasty selections and sometimes goes "bid shopping" after the award. Our Administration/Fire Station project required selection of subs *before* the bid deadline. The sponsor's reasons were twofold: (1) promotion of fair play between prime bidders and subs, and (2) establishment of a degree of control at the very beginning of the project through early commitments between parties. The sponsor could, in extreme cases, reject certain proposed subs, or even reject the entire package of the low prime bidder.

Since our chosen subs are known to the public, we need only report the facts to unsuccessful subs, thank them, and wish them "better luck next time." Disappointments, particularly when sub-bids are very close, are to be expected. Slammer, for instance, is happy to receive the hollow metal work, but unhappy to lose the roll-up steel doors, due to omission of power operators, which they insist "we could have negotiated." Ours was both an ethical and a long-view decision, even though it contradicted the general rule favoring one instead of two or more subcontracts.

4.2 Notify the Successful Sub-Bidders

It is good practice, although not essential, to send selected subs notices of your intention to award subcontracts pending written confirmation of their telephone quotations. The reasons for this are: (1) legal proof that an offer had indeed been made, (2) statement of terms, conditions, inclusions, and exclusions to be made part of the contract, in order to minimize future disputes, and (3) clarification of certain details not previously discussed (clarification does not mean a *change in the bid*).

Our project contains twenty-eight subcontract items. A form letter such as Fig. 4.2a is therefore suggested. Naming our proposed subs with the submitted bid package is a form of contractual commitment. Notice of intention to award contracts is more binding. It signals subs to prepare paperwork, shop drawings, shop arrangements, and human resources, and to acquire materials and equipment.

Letter of Intent

To: Blazers
    770 Interloper Place
    Toolow, CA.

Att: Mr. Trail Blazer, Manager
Re: Administration Bldg. & Fire Station, Picacho, CA.

Dear Sirs:

  Pending receipt of a written confirmation of your telephone bid quoted to us on 10/22/84, it is our intention to award you the subcontract for <u>Section 02640</u>

<u>   Asphalt Concrete Pavement   </u>

for the sum of <u>$127,200.00 (Base bid less Alt. No. 1)</u>

Very truly yours,
Your Own Company

By *E.T. Being*
        Vice Pres.

Figure 4.2a

Notices of intention to award subcontracts, sent out promptly, provide us with a few additional days to prepare formal subcontracts with care.

4.3
Resolve Loose Ends

Not all of the loose ends can be resolved before the project starts, but we wish to resolve as many as possible. Not all are even known. Let us list those loose ends we do know and our proposed method of resolving them.

Loose Ends	Method of Resolution
1. Design a method of earth shoring at Picacho Street.	Discuss with super and agree. Budget is $8,160.
2. Final cleaning of windows and fixtures.	Delegate entirely to the super. The budget is $2,200.
3. No sub for parking striping.	Hire men, equipment, and material on a time and material (T&M) basis. The budget is $1,200.
4. Masonry reinforcing steel.	Ask Betbar for a firm quotation. The budget is $2,800. Also, ask Histack for a quotation.
5. Wall louvers.	Ask Leaders for a firm quotation. The budget is $960.
6. Wood doors.	Obtain two or more quotations. The budget is $1,260.
7. Site work concrete.	Obtain two or more quotations. The budget is $19,985.

This list of loose ends, and any others that may be discovered, can be pinned to a tackboard as a visual reminder to expedite them. They should be checked off as they are resolved.

4.4
Write Subcontracts and Purchase Orders

Many generalities regarding subcontract writing are discussed in Sec. 2.21, Follow-up Work. The reader is advised to review that section with reference to the following demonstrations.

Figures 4.4a and 4.4b are the face sheets of Associated General Contractors' popular *Standard Form Subcontract*, which is one of several forms available to contractors. The opposite sides of these sheets, shown in Appendix Q, contain detailed provisions of the subcontract, such as liens, insurance, labor relations, indemnification, and arbitration. These standards may *not* cover certain provisions important to our project and the unique subcontractor relationships we have established previously. We need to specify, even to the point of redundancy, every aspect of each sub-trade that is a potential matter of dispute. To do this, we draw upon both experience and imagination.

It is good practice to write and issue the subcontracts as soon as possible so that subs can order material and equipment requiring long lead times, prepare shop drawings, and coordinate manning requirements. The bar chart (Fig. 3.6a) guides us as follows:

1. Mechanical; electrical
2. Reinforcing steel; masonry*; hollow metal work; aluminum windows

3. Structural steel and miscellaneous metal
4. Steel decking
5. Painting
6. Millwork*
7. Roof insulation; clay tile roofing; sheet metal; metal framing and gypsum board
8. Wall and ceiling insulation
9. Lathing and plastering
10. Caulking and sealants
11. Finish hardware*
12. Glass and glazing
13. Ceramic tile; building specialties
14. Roll up steel doors; acoustical tile; resilient flooring

*Certain items above are not, strictly speaking, subcontract work; they are only materials supplied to the jobsite. For these, a purchase order such as Fig. 4.4c is used.

Standard Form Subcontract

Subcontract No. __1__

THIS AGREEMENT, made and entered into at _____Picacho, CA_____ this __1st__ day of
_____November_____ , 19 _84_ , by and between _____Your Own Company_____
hereinafter called CONTRACTOR, with principal office at _____Picacho, CA_____ , and
_____Piper Piping Company_____ hereinafter called SUBCONTRACTOR,
with principal office at _____ .

RECITALS

On or about the __30th__ day of _____October_____ , 19 _84_ , CONTRACTOR entered into a prime contract
with _____City of Picacho, CA_____
hereinafter called OWNER, whose address is _____Old Public Works Bldg., Picacho, CA_____
to perform the following construction work:

Administration Building and Fire Station

Said work is to be performed in accordance with the prime contract and the plans and specifications. Said plans and specifications have
been prepared by or on behalf of_____Bell & Bell_____ , ARCHITECT.

SECTION 1 — ENTIRE CONTRACT

SUBCONTRACTOR certifies and agrees that he is fully familiar with all of the terms, conditions and obligations of the Contract Documents, as hereinafter defined, the location of the job site, and the conditions under which the work is to be performed, and that he enters into this Agreement based upon his investigation of all of such matters and is in no way relying upon any opinions or representations of CONTRACTOR. It is agreed that this Agreement represents the entire agreement. It is further agreed that the Contract Documents are incorporated in this Agreement by this reference, with the same force and effect as if the same were set forth at length herein, and that SUBCONTRACTOR and his subcontractors will be and are bound by any and all of said Contract Documents insofar as they relate in any part or in any way, directly or indirectly to the work covered by this Agreement. SUBCONTRACTOR agrees to be bound to CONTRACTOR in the same manner and to the same extent as CONTRACTOR is bound to OWNER under the Contract Documents, to the extent of the work provided for in this Agreement, and that where, in the Contract Documents reference is made to CONTRACTOR and the work or specification therein pertains to SUBCONTRACTOR'S trade, craft, or type of work then such work or specification shall be interpreted to apply to SUBCONTRACTOR instead of CONTRACTOR. The phrase "Contract Documents" is defined to mean and include:

The drawings, Pages 1 through 48 and the specifications,
Sections 01100 through 16440, all dated September 3, 1984
titled Administration Building and Fire Station for the
City of Picacho, CA, prepared by architects Bell & Bell.
Addenda 1 and 2 are included.

SECTION 2 — SCOPE

SUBCONTRACTOR agrees to furnish all labor, services, materials, installation, cartage, hoisting, supplies, insurance, equipment, scaffolding, tools, utilities, storage and other facilities of every kind and description required for the prompt and efficient execution of the work described herein and to perform the work necessary or incidental to complete _Sanitary sewers, storm drains,_
exterior water and exterior gas.

for the project in strict accordance with the Contract Documents and as more particularly, though not exclusively, specified in:

Sections 15100, 15150, 15200, and 15250

SECTION 3 — CONTRACT PRICE

CONTRACTOR agrees to pay SUBCONTRACTOR for the strict performance of his work, the sum of:
_____Twenty eight thousand dollars_____ ($ ___$28,000.00___),
subject to additions and deductions for changes in the work as may be agreed upon, and to make payment in accordance with the
Payment Schedule, Section 4.

Figure 4.4a

128

SECTION 4 — PAYMENT SCHEDULE

CONTRACTOR agrees to pay SUBCONTRACTOR in monthly payments of __90__ % of labor and materials which have been placed in position and for which payment has been made by OWNER to CONTRACTOR. The remaining __10__ % shall be retained by CONTRACTOR until he receives final payment from OWNER, but not less than thirty-five days after the entire work required by the prime contract has been fully completed in conformity with the Contract Documents and has been delivered and accepted by OWNER, ARCHITECT, and CONTRACTOR. Subject to the provisions of the next sentence, the retained percentage shall be paid SUBCON-TRACTOR promptly after CONTRACTOR receives his final payment from OWNER. SUBCONTRACTOR agrees to furnish, if and when required by CONTRACTOR, payroll affidavits, receipts, vouchers, releases of claims for labor, material and subcontractors per-forming work or furnishing materials under this Agreement, all in form satisfactory to CONTRACTOR, and it is agreed that no payment hereunder shall be made, except at CONTRACTOR'S option, until and unless such payroll affidavits, receipts, vouchers or releases, or any or all of them, have been furnished. Any payment made hereunder prior to completion and acceptance of the work, as referred to above, shall not be construed as evidence of acceptance of any part of SUBCONTRACTOR'S work.

SECTION 5 — GENERAL SUBCONTRACT PROVISIONS

General Subcontract Provisions on back of Pages 1 and 2 are an integral part of this Agreement.

SECTION 6 — SPECIAL PROVISIONS

1. Included by subcontractor:

   a. Shoring of trenches when required

   b. All catchbasins, manholes, and covers

   c. Lights, barricades, and flagmen for Picacho street work

   d. Cost of leakage and sterilization tests

2. Not included by subcontractor:

   a. Costs of tests and inspections other than 1d above

3. Additional agreements:

   a. Subcontractor will make connection to city water main as soon as possible.

Contractors are required by law to be licensed and regulated by the Contractors' State License Board. Any questions concerning a contractor may be referred to the registrar of the board whose address is:

Contractors' State License Board, Sacramento, California

IN WITNESS WHEREOF: The parties hereto have executed this Agreement for themselves, their heirs, executors, successors, adminis-trators, and assignees on the day and year first above written.

SUBCONTRACTOR	CONTRACTOR
Piper Piping Company	_Your Own Company_
By _Pied Piper, Pres._	By _E. T. Being_ _Vice Pres._
Name Title	Name Title
[X] Corporation [ ] Partnership [ ] Proprietorship	
(Seal)	
Contractor's State License No. _SYX420_	Contractor's State License No. _1CYW561_

Revised 11/81

Published by AGC of California

Page 2 of 2

Figure 4.4b

Purchase Order

To: Slammer Door Co.
1220 Locktite Lane
Entercity, Arizona

Date 11/3/84

Project: Administration Bldg. & Fire Station
Picacho, California

Please Supply the Following:

All hollow metal doors and frames required for the project in accordance with the drawings and specifications and addenda #1 and #2 for the lump sum of- - - - - - - $2,100.00

Terms: FOB Jobsite ____Yes____
FOB Supplier Warehouse ________
Sales Tax ____Included____
Payment ____Full by 10th of mo. following del.____
Time of Delivery ____January 15, 1985____

Your Own Company

By *E. T. Being*
E. T. Being, Mgr.

Figure 4.4c

We start with the mechanical and electrical trades, since these subs will begin the underground portions of their work immediately and need long lead times for their equipment. The general definitions and descriptions of the project, as shown in Figs. 4.4a and 4.4b, will be repeated in all subcontracts. Only the names of the subs, the trades, the dollar amounts, and any clarifying information will differ, as follows:

Sub: Piper (see Figs. 4.4a and 4.4b)

Sub: Utility
Trade: Plumbing; hose reels
Price: $28,000
Inclusions: pipe insulation; access panels
Exclusions: formed concrete work; painting

Sub: Fixture
Trade: Heating, ventilating, and air conditioning
Price: $42,500
Inclusions: access panels
Exclusions: gas piping (see plumbing)

Sub: Sparks
Trade: Electrical
Price: $65,000 (base bid less alt. No. 1)
Inclusion: wiring to door operators
Exclusion: furnishing of door operators

Sub: Betbar
Trade: Reinforcing Steel
Price: $14,250
Inclusion: mesh in second-floor slab
Exclusions: hoisting; masonry reinforcing steel

Sub: Histack
Trade: Masonry
Price: $36,320
Inclusions: window sills; install (only) reinf. steel
Exclusions: furnishing of reinf. steel; shoring openings

Supplier: Slammer (see Fig. 4.4c, Purchase Order)

Sub: Seethru
Trade: Aluminum Windows
Price: $10,750
Inclusions: installation; caulking
Exclusion: wood frames

Sub: Ringer
Trade: Structural Steel and miscellaneous iron
Price: $156,600
Inclusion: furnishing misc. metal
Exclusions: installing misc. metal; steel decking

Sub: Dekko
Trade: Steel Decking
Price: $21,240
Inclusions: roof & floor decking; hoisting
Exclusion: cutting openings for other trades

Sub: Daubers
Trade: Painting
Price: $28,000
Inclusions: scaffolding; paint exposed pipes
Exclusion: prime painting of metal items

Supplier: Termites (purchase order)
Trade: Millwork
Price $23,000
Inclusion: laminated plastic
Exclusion: wood doors

Sub: Ample
Trade: Roof Insulation
Price: $12,352
Inclusion: wood nailers
Exclusion: cant strips

Sub: Tiletop
Trade: Clay Tile Roofing
Price: $30,000
Inclusion: closures
Exclusion: roof jacks

Sub: Leader
Trade: Sheet Metal
Price: $2,840
Inclusion: roof jacks
Exclusion: wall louvers

Sub: Uprite
Trade: Metal Framing & Gypsum Board
Price: $40,000
Inclusions: scaffolding; caulking of gypsum board
Exclusion: rigid wall insulation

Sub: Comfy
Trade: Wall and Ceiling Insulation
Price: $6,100
Inclusions: furring; rigid wall insulation
Exclusion: gypsum board

Sub: Faster Plaster Co.
Trade: Lathing and Plastering
Price: $29,000
Inclusions: lath & scratch for tile; scaffolding
Exclusion: metal framing

Sub: Liners
Trade: Caulking and Sealants
Price: $3,550
Inclusion: caulking of block to stucco at fascia
Exclusion: caulking of gypsum board

Supplier: Holder (purchase order)
Material: Finish Hardware
Price: $3,870

Sub: Brittle
Trade: Glass and Glazing
Price: $4,200
Inclusions: mirrors; glass in doors
Exclusions: cleaning; replacing of breakage by others

Sub: Mosaic
Trade: Ceramic Tile
Price: $3,850
Inclusion: waterproofing behind wainscot
Exclusion: lath and scratch coat

Sub: Specco
Trade: Toilet Accessories; Fire-Extinguisher Cabinet; Kitchen Unit
Price: $2,200
Inclusion: installation (except toilet accessories)
Exclusions: plumbing hookup; installation of toilet accessories

Sub: Furnall
Trade: Toilet Partitions; Flagpole
Price: $2,310
Inclusion: installation
Exclusion: concrete base for flagpole

Sub: Anything Supply Co.
Trade: Venetian Blinds; Room Numbers
Price: $2,420
Inclusion: installation
Exclusion: layout for room numbers

Sub: Slideup
Trade: Roll-up Steel Doors
Price: $8,800
Inclusion: electric operators
Exclusion: steel channel frames

Sub: Checker
Trade: Acoustical Tile
Price: $3,600
Inclusions: suspended ceiling; metal trim
Exclusion: access panels

Sub: Treads
Trade: Resilient Flooring and Carpeting
Price: $7,500
Inclusions: cove base; door strips
Exclusion: preparation of underlayment

Before subcontracts and purchase orders are sent out, have someone other than the original writer proofread for names, spelling, punctuation, and numbers. Give particular attention to dollar amounts. Sending subcontracts is an order for subs to perform. We therefore include with the subcontract a letter of transmittal, such as Fig. 4.4d, giving information, requests, and instructions. When all subcontracts and purchase orders are completed, the super must coordinate them to make the project flow. This involves speeding up slow performers, slowing down the overly fast, lining up the dependent ones, and guiding the independent ones. For field supervision, the super should help prepare a progress schedule. But first, let us brief the super and transfer the entire package.

Your Own Company
1000 Palamony Street
Picacho, California

November 7, 1984

Mr. Pied Piper, President
Piper Piping Company
510 Electrolysis Ave.
Fallingrock, California

Re: Administration Building and Fire Station, Picacho, CA

Dear Mr. Piper:

Enclosed is your contract for exterior sewers, storm drains, water and gas. Please retain one copy and return the others to us.

1.) Submit to our office as soon as possible all samples, shop drawings, catalog data and certifications of materials for approval.
2.) Submit certificates of required insurance.
3.) Be prepared to begin site work as soon as rough grading is completed (approximately 60 days from this date).

Very truly yours,

E. T. Being

E. T. Being,
Vice-President

Enclosure

Figure 4.4d

4.5 Brief the Superintendent

Our super for this project is selected on the basis of experience in earthmoving work, as well as in general building construction. We provide a set of drawings and specs specially marked; the margins of each page of the specs contain the names of subs, suppliers, or others responsible for the various items. In addition to the vocal briefing, we supply the super with the *Superintendent's Information/Instructions Sheet*, Fig. 4.5a, which acts both as a check list for the briefing and a record for the super's reference.

Superintendent's Information/Instructions Sheet

For Project: __Admin. Bldg. & Fire Sta., Picacho, CA__

General Information:

Starting Date: __Nov. 5, 1984__ Completion Date:

Official: __Nov. 5, 1985__

Proposed: __Oct. 5, 1985__

A & E: __Bell & Bell Architects__

Representative: __Chris Bell__ Phone: __777-7777__

Sponsor: __City of Picacho, CA__ __737-7373__

Representatives:

Contract Administrator __H. Stern__

Building Inspector __N. Picky__

Project Inspector __Not known__

Subcontractors:

Trade	Sub	Rep	Phone
Millwork	Termites	Sawyer	737-7373
Caulking	Liners	Bill	544-5444
Surveying	Sight Bros.	O.O. Sight	555-5552
CPM schedule	Charters	Diane	737-4872
Chain link fence	Obstacles	?	297-7414
A.C. paving	Blazers	T. Blazer	554-2496
Landscaping	Greener	Joe	676-6766
Reinforcing steel	Betbar	?	474-8888
Masonry	Histack	Curtis	757-0930
Struc. steel/misc. met.	Ringer	Paul	545-2200
Steel decking	Dekko	Phil E.	676-1084
Wall & clg., insulation	Comfy	Jean	297-7077
Roof insulation	Ample	?	554-5554
Clay tile roofing	Tiletop	Swanson	676-1111
Sheet metal	Leaders	Al Barnes	345-5000
H.M. Doors & frames	Slammer	Johnson	666-6666
Roll up steel doors	Slideup	Barbara	336-5678
Aluminum windows	Seethru	Janine	767-7666
Glass & glazing	Brittle	?	336-6787
Lathing & plastering	Faster	Neil	676-4444
Met. framing/gyp. board	Upright	Wally	297-6283
Ceramic tile	Mosaic	Muriel	666-7575
Acoustical tile	Checker	Murray	545-8080
Resilient flooring	Treads	A. Vallin	474-2121
Painting	Daubers	P. Daubers	345-1383
Toilet accessories F.E. cabinets Kitchen units	Specco	G. Welch	741-9124
Toilet partitions Flagpoles	Furnall	Burroughs	737-3002

Figure 4.5a

Venetian blinds Room numbers	} Anything	F. Lee	757-2900
Sewer; storm drains; Exter. Water; gas	} Piper	P. Piper	336-0621
Plumbing; hose reels	Utility	Sullivan	776-7766
Heating & ventilating	Fixture	E. Stewart	346-2002
Electrical	Sparks	E.C. Static	767-1000

Material Suppliers & Services (suggested sources)

Import fill	Scoop's Soils Co. ($2.95/cy)
Concrete	Picacho Transit Mix Co.
Lumber/plywood	Tall Timbers
Rough hardware	Tall Timbers
Finish hardware	Holder Hardware Co.
Sand & gravel	Volcanic Distributors
Rental equipment	Picacho Rentals

Superintendent Will Do:
a. Consult with the engineer designing the progress schedule.
b. Design and build the pedestrian barricade.
c. Maximize local hiring of workmen to minimize subsistence costs (budget: $4,180).
d. Arrange for temporary water and power services.
e. Consult with engineer designing earth shoring.
f. Search for more economical sources of import fill.
g. Note the list of loose ends and help resolve them.
h. Arrange for field office, storage shed, toilets, security fence, telephone, project sign, and other temporary facilities.
i. Search for sources of heavy earthmoving rental equipment, and supervise the grading work.
j. Provide shoring for all openings in masonry walls.
k. Provide hoisting for rebar to second floor and above.
l. Provide formed concrete work for mechanical trades.
m. Provide cant strips for roofing sub.
n. Provide concrete base for flagpole.
o. Purchase directly small quantities of materials as needed.

Office Will Do:
a. Furnish a progress schedule (see subcontract list).
b. Furnish cost record keeping program.
c. Order large quantities of materials through purchase orders.
d. Perform general expediting of sub's submittals.

Special Information and Instructions
a. All costs of testing and inspection will be borne by the sponsor, except for concrete compression tests and mix designs.
b. If possible, excavate footings neatly (no side forms).
c. Eliminate disposal of excess footing excavation material by using as site fill. This will also save a small amount of borrow material.
d. Arrange for installation of toilet accessories by company employees. Subs will install all other building specialties.

Figure 4.5a (cont.)

When we have completed subcontracts and purchase orders, resolved loose ends, and briefed the super, we have thoroughly provided for every detail of the project. Its successful fulfillment now depends upon the super, our project management, the performance of the subs, and certain unpredictable "luck" factors (for instance, no natural disasters during construction).

4.6 Prepare a Construction Progress Schedule

In this project we have sublet the progress schedule to Charter, a specialist in this type of work (see Sec. 2.9 and Fig. 2.9d). It is to Charter's and our own company's mutual advantage that we provide them with as much information as possible. Figure 4.6a is the completed schedule for posting in the field office.

The figure is a time scale CPM chart, showing activities, events, and the critical path. It considers only working days and covers the estimated eleven-month construction time span. This master progress schedule may be updated periodically if actual progress varies significantly. Certain major subs may be given copies of this schedule, and all subs are asked to familiarize themselves with the copy posted in the field office.

We may, if we choose, read and update this schedule "manually," or we can program it for computer readout. It is worth repeating again that the reader who wishes to learn more about network scheduling is advised to study *Means Scheduling Manual*, by F. W. Horsley and published by R. S. Means Co., Inc.

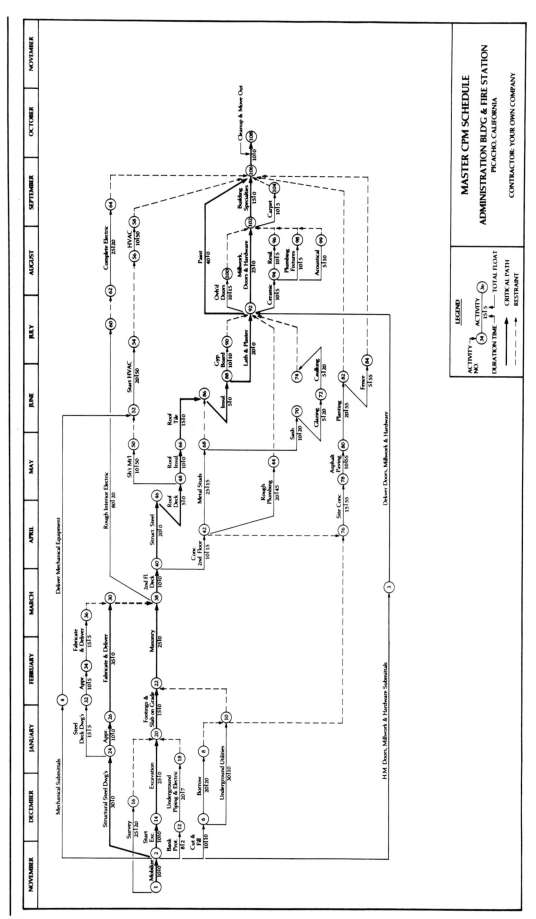

Figure 4.6a

4.7
Develop a Progress Payment Schedule

The first 30 days or so into construction are financed by our own company and our subcontractors. Since we have not sublet the expensive earthmoving work, we could face a capital outlay of a quarter of a million dollars or more before receiving compensation. Perhaps we should have included a cost item in our bid for interest on capital removed from other investments. Had we done so at the rate of $250,000 x 10% for one month, the addition to our bid would have been $2,083. Not to sublet earthwork was a bit unusual for our company and was a last-minute decision (although we had early warning of the possibility). This illustrates a common error case that could be classified as a slip (see Sec. 2.16). We can, however, partially compensate by "loading" the first billing, as explained a few paragraphs later, to receive payment from the sponsor *before* our accounts payable to subs and suppliers are due.

The progress payment schedule could have been incorporated in the CPM schedule. In very large and complex projects that would be a good procedure, but in this relatively small project we have chosen the traditional method.

Figure 4.7a is our master breakdown, which is constructed directly from the bid spread sheet, augmented by detailed information from (1) our own estimate sheets (see Fig. 3.3a,b,c), and (2) breakdowns provided by subs.

The master payment schedule requires that general conditions, markup, and bond costs be distributed in some manner between the other cost items. The sponsor tends to prefer an even prorating, whereas we (the contractor) feel that an irregular distribution is both more equitable and expedient. The final schedule is usually a compromise between the sponsor and contractor. Figure 4.7a accomplishes the following objectives:

1. Most of the sub-trades are listed in the exact amounts of the sub-bids (contract amounts), which simplifies the mathematics of their monthly paychecks.

2. Certain major sub-trades carry an identical percentage, in this case 25%, of the overhead and profit—again to simplify the mathematics of payments.

3. The remainder of the overhead and profit to be distributed is placed in one lump sum in the earliest on-site work—in this case, earthwork.

4. The front end is loaded as heavily as the sponsor will permit in order to minimize the use of our company's own capital.

The prices in the material/equipment column for earthwork and the column for earthwork and a.c. paving appear high because they include the wages of equipment operators.

Figure 4.7b shows the first request for payment on this contract. It is important to submit this request punctually and to demand prompt payment from the sponsor. With 10% withheld, this barely covers costs for our subs, suppliers, and ourselves. We have expended our money and we must get it back quickly. At the beginning of any project, the sponsor is always ahead, and we must get our expenses back as soon as possible.

Figure 4.7c shows a later billing, April 5, 1985 which is typical of all other payment requests. We may estimate our own company's portion, without regard to pickups or losses as indicated:

Administration Building and Fire Station
Picacho, California

Master Progress Payment Schedule

Pay Item	Cost Code	Work Description	Quantity	Labor		Mat'l./Equip.		Total	Notes
				U/C	Total	U/C	Total		
100	A100	Move on	L.S.	L.S.	5,000	L.S.	4,890	9,890	(1)
120	B100	Surveying	sub	L.S.	8,000	L.S.	1,000	9,000	(1)
121	B110	Progress schedule	sub	L.S.	7,000	L.S.	500	7,500	(1)
122	A130	Earth shoring	L.S.	L.S.	5,108	L.S.	5,092	10,200	(1)
123	A131	Earthwork	45,000 cy	.48	21,600	10.00	450,000	471,600	(2)
130	B111	Ch. link fence	540 lf	8.44	4,558	11.00	5,940	10,498	
131	B112	A.C. paving, base course	2,400 cy	1.75	4,200	12.00	28,800	33,000	(1)
131	B113	A.C. paving, finish course	108,000 sf	.12	12,960	2.00	216,000	228,960	(1)
132	A150	Parking striping	3,000 lf	.30	900	.10	300	1,200	
133	B114	Landscaping	sub	L.S.	3,000	L.S.	3,000	6,000	
133	B115	Irrigation sprinklers	sub	L.S.	2,222	L.S.	2,000	4,222	
134	B116	Reinforcing steel	28,500 lb	.25	7,125	.25	7,125	14,250	
135	B117	Masonry	3,500 sf	5.00	17,500	6.18	21,630	39,130	
136	B118	Structural steel	2,326 ton	25.00	58,150	50.00	116,300	174,450	(1)
136	B119	Miscellaneous metal	11,333 lb	.75	8,500	.75	8,500	17,000	
137	B120	Steel Decking–2nd floor	2,000 sf	.70	1,400	1.23	2,460	3,860	
137	B121	Steel Decking–roof	9,000 sf	1.00	9,000	.93	8,370	17,370	
138	A151	Concrete (except site work)	352 cy	117.24	41,268	107.39	37,801	79,069	
139	A180	Carpentry, rough & finish	L.S.	L.S.	10,731	L.S.	6,766	17,497	
139	A181	Install miscellaneous metal	L.S.	L.S.	2,004	—	—	2,004	
140	B122	Millwork	sub	—	—	L.S.	23,000	23,000	
141	A182	Wood doors	18 ea	—	—	70.00	1,260	1,260	
142	B123	Wall & ceiling insulation	12,200 sf	.25	3,050	.25	3,050	6,100	
143	B124	Roof insulation	9,000 sf	.60	5,400	.77	6,930	12,330	
144	B125	Clay tile roofing	9,000 sf	1.16	10,440	3.00	27,000	37,440	(1)
145	B126	Sheet metal	1,420 lb	1.00	1,420	1.00	1,420	2,840	
146	A183	Wall louvers	8 ea	40.00	320	80.00	640	960	
147	B127	Caulking & sealants	2,280 lf	1.00	2,280	.55	1,254	3,534	
148	B128	Hollow metal doors & frames	24 ea	—	—	87.50	2,100	2,100	
149	B129	Roll up steel doors	4 ea	500.00	2,000	1700.00	6,800	8,800	
150	B130	Aluminum windows	34 ea	150.00	5,100	166.17	5,650	10,750	
151	B131	Glass & glazing	1,680 sf	1.00	1,680	1.50	2,520	4,200	
152	B132	Finish hardware	sub	—	—	L.S.	3,870	3,870	
153	B133	Lathing & plastering	2,416 sy	8.00	19,328	7.00	16,912	36,240	(1)

Figure 4.7a

Administration Building and Fire Station
Picacho, California

Master Progress Payment Schedule

Pay Item	Cost Code	Work Description	Quantity	Labor U/C	Labor Total	Mat'l./Equip. U/C	Mat'l./Equip. Total	Total	Notes
154	B134	Metal framing & gyp. board	2,777 sy	10.00	27,770	8.00	22,216	49,986	(1)
155	B135	Ceramic tile	550 sf	3.50	1,925	3.50	1,925	3,850	
156	B136	Acoustical tile	3,000 sf	.60	1,800	.60	1,800	3,600	
157	B137	Resilient flooring	8,000 sf	.30	2,400	.43	3,440	5,840	
158	B138	Carpeting	100 sy	6.00	600	10.00	1,000	1,600	
159	B139	Painting	100,000 sf	.17	17,000	.18	18,000	35,000	(1)
	B140	Toilet accessories	20 ea	—	—	61.00	1,220	1,220	
	B141	F.E. cabinets	4 ea	—	—	50.00	200	200	
	B142	Kitchen unit	1 ea	280.00	280	500.00	500	780	
160	B143	Toilet partitions	8 ea	66.25	530	100.00	800	1,330	
	B144	Flagpole	1 ea	180.00	180	800.00	800	980	
161	B145	Venetian blinds	25 ea	30.00	750	50.00	1,250	2,000	
	B146	Room numbers	42 ea	2.50	105	7.50	315	420	
162	B147	Sanitary sewer	sub	L.S.	4,000	L.S.	6,000	10,000	(1)
	B148	Storm drains	sub	L.S.	3,000	L.S	3,875	6,875	(1)
	B149	Exterior water	sub	L.S.	4,250	L.S.	7,000	11,250	(1)
	B150	Exterior gas	sub	L.S.	2,875	L.S.	4,000	6,875	(1)
163	B151	Plumbing	sub	L.S.	11,000	L.S.	21,375	32,375	(1)
	B152	Hose reels	sub	L.S.	625	L.S.	2,000	2,625	(1)
164	B153	Heating	sub	L.S.	10,938	L.S.	20,312	31,250	(1)
	B154	Air conditioning	sub	L.S.	9,875	L.S.	12,000	21,875	(1)
165	B155	Electrical, underground	sub	L.S.	8,000	L.S.	14,500	22,500	(1)
	B156	Electrical, bldg. rough	sub	L.S.	20,000	L.S.	20,000	40,000	(1)
	B157	Electrical, bldg. finish	sub	L.S.	3,000	L.S.	7,000	10,000	(1)
	B158	Electrical, parking lot	sub	L.S.	3,000	L.S.	5,750	8,750	(1)
166	A184	Window & fixture cleaning	L.S.	L.S.	2,200	—	—	2,200	(1)
167	A185	Site concrete work	L.S.	L.S.	12,655	L.S.	7,000	19,655	(1)
		Totals			430,002		1,213,158	1,643,160	

Notes:
(1) Increased 25% for distribution of general conditions, markup, and bond costs.
(2) Includes the remainder of the distribution not covered in (1).

Legend: Cost Code A: Items to be accomplished by our own company (see cost record sheets).
Cost Code B: Items to be accomplished by subcontractors.

Figure 4.7a (cont.)

Administration Building and Fire Station Picacho, California

Request for Payment, Dec. 5, 1984

Pay Item	Cost Code	Work Description	Quantity	Labor		Mat'l./Equip.		Total	Notes
				U/C	Total	U/C	Total		
100	A100	Move on	100%	L.S.	5,000	L.S.	4,890	9,890	
120	B100	Surveying	85%	L.S.	6,800	L.S.	850	7,650	(3)
121	B110	Progress schedule	80%	L.S.	5,600	L.S.	400	6,000	(4)
122	A130	Earth shoring	90%	L.S.	4,597	L.S.	4,582	9,179	(5)
123	A131	Earth moving	22,500 cy	.48	10,800	10.00	225,000	235,800	
		Total Amount Earned			32,797		235,722	268,519	
		Less 10% Retention by Sponsor						26,852	
		Amount Payable						241,667	

Notes: (3) Final grade stakes remain to be done.
(4) Periodic updating remains to be done.
(5) Removal of shoring remains to be done.

Figure 4.7b

Administration Building and Fire Station, Picacho, California — Request for Payment, April 5, 1985

Pay Item	Cost Code	Work Description	Quantity	Labor U/C	Labor Total	Mat'l./Equip. U/C	Mat'l./Equip. Total	Total	Notes
100	A100	Move on	100%	L.S.	5,000	L.S.	4,890	9,890	(1)
120	B100	Surveying	100%	L.S.	8,000	L.S.	1,000	9,000	(1)
121	B110	Progress schedule	90%	L.S.	6,300	L.S.	450	6,750	(1)
122	A130	Earth shoring	100%	L.S.	5,108	L.S.	5,092	10,200	(1)
123	A131	Earthwork	100%	L.S.	21,600	L.S.	450,000	471,600	(2)
134	B116	Reinforcing steel	100%	L.S.	7,125	L.S.	7,125	14,250	
135	B117	Masonry	100%	L.S.	17,500	L.S.	21,630	39,130	
136	B118	Structural steel	1,200 ton	25.00	30,000	50.00	60,000	90,000	(1)
137	B119	Miscellaneous metal	8,000 lbs	.75	6,000	.75	6,000	12,000	
	B120	Steel decking, 2nd floor	100%	L.S.	1,400	L.S.	2,460	3,860	
138	A151	Concrete	330 cy	117.24	38,689	107.39	35,438	74,127	
139	A180	Carpentry	10%	L.S.	1,073	L.S.	677	1,750	
	A180	Install misc. metal	20%	L.S.	401	—	—	401	
162	B147	Sanitary sewer	100%	L.S.	4,000	L.S.	6,000	10,000	(1)
	B148	Storm drains	100%	L.S.	3,000	L.S.	3,875	6,875	(1)
	B149	Exterior water	100%	L.S.	4,250	L.S.	7,000	11,250	(1)
	B150	Exterior gas	100%	L.S.	2,875	L.S.	4,000	6,875	(1)
163	B151	Plumbing	50%	L.S.	5,500	L.S.	10,688	16,188	(1)
164	B153	Heating (rough-in)	40%	L.S.	4,375	L.S.	8,125	12,500	(1)
	B154	Air conditioning (rough-in)	20%	L.S.	1,975	L.S.	2,400	4,375	(1)
165	B155	Electrical, underground	80%	L.S.	6,400	L.S.	11,600	18,000	(1)
	B156	Electrical, bldg. rough	20%	L.S.	4,000	L.S.	4,000	8,000	(1)
		Total Amount Earned			184,571		652,450	837,021	
		Less 10% Retention by Sponsor						83,702	
		Amount Payable						753,319	

Notes: (1) General conditions, markup, and bond cost distribution is 25%.
(2) Of this item, $44,514 is general conditions, markup, and bond cost distribution.

Figure 4.7c

25% of items with notation (1) on Figs. 4.7b and 4.7c	$52,503
Lump sum on earthwork	$44,514
Gross general conditions, markup, and bond	$97,017

Of the total project contract amount:

General conditions and bond	= 9.6%	= 45.5% of $97,017	= $44,143
Overhead	= 4.0%	= 19.0% of $97,017	= $18,433
Profit	= 7.5%	= 35.5% of $97,017	= $34,441

Total distribution = $97,017

Due to the sponsor's retention of 10%, however, we realize a current net surplus of $13,315 after five months of work! The "current net surplus" is defined as the total amount received for overhead and profit from the sponsor, less the sponsor's retention on payments ($97,017 - $83,702). The $83,702 retained by the sponsor is equivalent to money in the bank (although it yields no interest) and can be shown as an asset in our company's financial statement, thereby influencing an increase in our bonding capacity.

4.8 Set Up a Cost Record-Keeping System

Line items in the master progress payment schedule with cost codes starting with capital letter A (A100, etc.) will be prepared by employees of our own company and accounted for by our super and bookkeeping personnel. Reasons for keeping current cost records include the following:

1. The control of costs as they occur in the field, to prevent overruns and to achieve as many underruns as possible.
2. The accumulation of reference cost data useful in future estimating and bidding.
3. The establishment of proven standards for negotiating change orders.
4. The development of a more accurate concept of profit and loss.

Figure 4.8a shows the original breakdown of estimated quantities, unit prices, and extensions, adjusted to reflect the deductive alternative bid No. 1 and made into a *master cost record* from which all periodic records are derived. Through the use of pay item numbers and cost codes, we have tied these line items to the master payment schedule for cross-identification and ease of computer programming, should we wish to use that technology. (For further information on the appropriate technology, consult the estimating and scheduling programs produced by R.S. Means Co., Inc.)

In this breakdown, we intentionally omitted fringe benefits, as they are not relevant to our immediate cost record-keeping purposes. This omission accounts for the differences between certain prices for the same items, as shown on the master cost record and the master payment schedule (for example, earth shoring, parking striping, and wall louvers).

Let us now analyze the cost record form in general and Fig. 4.8a in particular:

1. Cost records usually focus on labor costs. Keep it simple by using time cards showing the hours expended by workmen on various cost-coded items.
2. Material costs are not easily separated into daily cost items, since materials such as lumber are usually bought in bulk. In our example, we have shown the materials separated. They can be prorated as the project progresses.
3. We extended underruns and overruns only for the completed items. By inspection of current unit costs, we are quickly alerted to items that are over or under the estimated costs.
4. We can expect some variations between estimated and actual costs. Identical costs would be coincidental. With careful and realistic estimates and good project management, most variations should be minor; the overruns and underruns should tend to cancel each other. Close bidding would ordinarily preclude significant cost savings in our own work. In this project, however, we have a few pickups in the earthwork due to two circumstances: (a) a disposal area is located near the jobsite for clean fill material, thus reducing the cost of hauling (A131-1b) and dumping (A131-7) fees, and (b) a source of less expensive borrow fill material (A131-4a) was located. Notice, however, that the cost of breaking up buried concrete (A131-3a) exceeded the estimated cost, due to quantity rather than unit cost. Also, recall that our earthwork budget included a markup of 20% or $79,266, which should not be regarded as a pickup, but as a risk-taking compensation.

Administration Building & Fire Station, Picacho, CA — Master Cost Record

Pay Item	Cost Code	Work Description	Quantity	Estimated Cost Labor U/C	Labor Total	Mat'l/Equip./Sub U/C	Mat'l/Equip./Sub Total	Total	Quantity	Actual Cost To Date Labor U/C	Labor Total	Mat'l/Equip./Sub U/C	Mat'l/Equip./Sub Total	Total	Under Run	Over Run
100	A100	**General Conditions**														
	A100—2	Layout of structures	48 hrs	52.61	2,525	3.00	144	2,669	41 hrs	52.61	2,157	3.90	160	2,317*	352	—
	A100—3	Field office	11 mo	—	—	85.00	935	935	6 mo	—	—	91.22	547	547	—	—
	A100—4	Storage shed	11 mo	—	—	75.00	825	825	6 mo	—	—	77.50	465	465	—	—
	A100—5	Toilets (2 ea)	11 mo	—	—	95.00	1,045	1,045	6 mo	—	—	93.00	558	558	—	—
	A100—6	Telephone	11 mo	—	—	150.00	1,650	1,650	6 mo	—	—	166.67	1,000	1,000	—	145
	A100—7a	Waterhookup & meter	L.S.	—	300	L.S.	1,800	2,100	L.S.	—	245	L.S.	2,000	2,245*	—	—
	A100—7b	Water monthly charges	11 mo	—	—	60.00	660	660	6 mo	—	—	55.20	331	331	—	—
	A100—8a	Elec. service & transf.	L.S.	—	500	L.S.	2,200	2,700	L.S.	—	600	L.S.	1,880	2,480*	220	—
	A100—8b	Elec. monthly charge	11 mo	—	—	70.00	770	770	6 mo	—	—	74.80	449	449	—	—
	A100—9	Security yard fence	200 lf	—	—	10.00	2,000	2,000	200 lf	—	—	2.25	450	450*	1,550	—
	A100—10	Project sign	L.S.	L.S.	100	L.S.	350	450	L.S.	L.S.	96	L.S.	300	396*	54	—
	A100—11	Temp. weather closures	L.S.	L.S.	800	L.S.	250	1,050	L.S.	L.S.	517	L.S.	156	673	—	—
	A100—12	Office supplies	11 mo	—	—	35.00	385	385	6 mo	—	—	29.16	175	175	—	—
	A100—13	Small tools	11 mo	—	—	200.00	2,200	2,200	6 mo	—	—	170.00	1,020	1,020	—	—
	A100—14	Misc. rental equipment	11 mo	—	—	400.00	4,400	4,400	6 mo	—	—	315.00	1,890	1,890	—	—
	A100—15	Oil, fuel, repair, service	11 mo	—	—	150.00	1,650	1,650	6 mo	—	—	146.67	880	880	—	—
	A100—16a	Cleanup—progressive	11 mo	1,200.00	13,200	100.00	1,100	14,300	6 mo	1,170.00	7,020	110.00	660	7,680	—	—
	A100—16b	Cleanup—final	120 hrs	25.00	3,000	2.00	240	3,240	—	—	—	—	—	—	—	—
	A100—17	Not Used	—													
	A100—18	Superintendent	11 mo	3,236.40	35,600	—	—	35,600	6 mo	3,280.00	19,680	—	—	19,680	—	—
	A100—19	Subsistence	209 day	—	—	20.00	4,180	4,180	80 day	—	—	20.00	1,600	1,600	—	—
	A100—20	Barricades (pedestrian)	700 lf	6.00	4,200	6.00	4,200	8,400	700 lf	5.15	3,605	6.20	4,340	7,945	—	—
	A100—21	Night lights	11 mo	—	—	60.00	660	660	6 mo	—	—	49.90	299	299	—	—
	A100—22	Not used	—													
	A100—23	Safety railings	280 lf	1.50	420	1.00	280	700	280 lf	1.18	330	1.10	308	638	—	—
122	A130	Earth Shoring	260 lf	10.67	2,774	15.69	4,079	6,853	260 lf	13.50	3,510	14.70	3,822	7,332*	—	479
123	A131	**Earthwork (Grading)**														
	A131—1a	Exc. down to buried mat'l	17,000 cy	—	—	.80	13,600	13,600	17,350 cy	—	—	.82	14,227	14,227*	—	627
	A131—1b	Haul away A131-1a mat'l	17,000 cy	—	—	2.05	34,850	34,850	17,350 cy	—	—	1.93	33,486	33,486*	1,364	—
	A131—2a	Exc. & load debris	20,000 cy	—	—	1.13	22,600	22,600	18,580 cy	—	—	1.20	22,296	22,296*	304	—
	A131—2b	Haul away A131-2a mat'l	20,000 cy	—	—	2.25	45,000	45,000	18,580 cy	—	—	2.38	44,220	44,220*	780	—
	A131—3a	Breakup concrete	5,000 cy	—	—	7.68	38,400	38,400	6,200 cy	—	—	7.40	45,880	45,880*	—	7,480
	A131—3b	Haul away A131-3a mat'l	5,000 cy	—	—	3.92	19,600	19,600	6,200 cy	—	—	3.30	20,460	20,460*	—	860
	A131—4a	Purchase import mat'l	34,500 cy	—	—	2.95	101,775	101,775	33,300 cy	—	—	2.80	93,240	93,240*	8,535	—
	A131—4b	Spread/compact	34,500 cy	—	—	.90	31,050	31,050	33,300 cy	—	—	.87	28,971	28,971*	2,079	—
	A131—5	Fine grade overall	120,000 sf	—	—	.03	3,600	3,600	120,000 sf	—	—	.035	4,200	4,200*	—	600
	A131—6	Erosion protection	9,000 sf	—	—	.15	1,350	1,350	10,000 sf	—	—	.21	2,100	2,100*	—	750
	A131—7	Dump fees	2,200 lds	—	—	15.00	33,000	33,000	1,652 lds	—	—	15.00	24,780	24,780*	8,220	—
	A131—8	Equip. move on/off	80 hrs	—	—	50.00	4,000	4,000	102 hrs	—	—	50.00	5,100	5,100*	—	1,100
	A131—9	Supervision	5 wks	—	—	1,176.00	5,880	5,880	5 wks	—	—	1,210.00	6,050	6,050*	—	170

* Line item completed

Figure 4.8a

Administration Building & Fire Station, Picacho, CA — Master Cost Record

Pay Item	Cost Code	Work Description	Quantity	Estimated Cost					Quantity	Actual Cost To Date					Under Run	Over Run
				Labor U/C	Labor Total	Mat'l/Equip./Sub U/C	Mat'l/Equip./Sub Total	Total		Labor U/C	Labor Total	Mat'l/Equip./Sub U/C	Mat'l/Equip./Sub Total	Total		
132	A150	Parking Striping	3,000 lf	.21	630	.10	300	930								
138	A151	Con. Work & Struc. Excav.*														
	A151-1a	*Footings, layout*	1,200 lf	.88	1,056	.10	120	1,176	1,200 lf	.78	936	.125	150	1,086*	90	—
	A151-1b	Machine excav.	320 cy	—	—	8.00	2,560	2,560	370 cy	—	—	7.17	2,653	2,653	—	93
	A151-1c	Hand trim trenches	2,800 sf	.40	1,120	—	—	1,120	2,990 sf	.44	1,316	—	—	1,316*	—	196
	A151-1d	Forming	1,200 lf	2.95	3,540	.90	1,080	4,620	1,200 lf	2.79	3,348	.84	1,008	4,356*	264	—
	A151-1e	Concrete & placing	220 cy	8.26	1,817	65.00	14,300	16,117	218 cy	7.55	1,646	65.70	14,323	15,969*	148	—
	A151-1f	Concrete cure ftg. tops	1,200 lf	.35	420	.035	42	462	1,200 lf	.275	330	.04	48	378*	84	—
	A151-1g	Disposal excess dirt	220 cy	—	—	8.25	1,815	1,815	230 cy	—	—	1.21	278	278*	1,537	—
	A151-1h	Backfill & tamp	100 cy	13.45	1,345	5.50	550	1,895	111 cy	9.90	1,099	2.88	320	1,419*	476	—
	A151-2a	*Flr. slab on grd. layout*	6,400 sf	.12	768	.03	192	960	6,400 sf	.14	896	.04	256	1,152	—	192
	A151-2b	Fine grade for gravel	6,400 sf	.13	832	.05	320	1,152	6,400 sf	.08	512	.055	352	864*	288	—
	A151-2c	4" gravel base course	95 cy	9.37	890	12.00	1,140	2,030	97 cy	11.22	1,088	20.28	1,967	3,055*	—	1,025
	A151-2d	6 mil. vapor barrier	7,000 sf	.07	490	.07	490	980	7,000 sf	.064	448	.045	315	763*	217	—
	A151-2e	2" sand & fine grade	48 cy	12.37	594	12.00	576	1,170	52 cy	13.30	692	23.25	1,209	1,901	—	731
	A151-2f	Form slab edges	800 lf	1.40	1,120	.56	448	1,568	800 lf	2.91	2,328	1.08	864	3,192	—	1,624
	A151-2g	Form depressions	164 lf	2.90	476	.60	98	574	170 lf	3.33	566	.55	94	660	—	86
	A151-2h	Anchor bolts for sills	200 ea	5.70	1,140	1.50	300	1,440	240 ea	3.15	756	.75	180	936*	504	—
	A151-2i	Set screeds	6,400 sf	.10	640	.04	256	896	6,400 sf	.085	544	.045	288	832*	64	—
	A151-2j	Concrete & placing	90 cy	8.26	743	65.00	5,850	6,593	89 cy	8.08	719	65.70	5,847	6,566*	27	—
	A151-2k	Con. pumping (½ of slab)	45 cy	—	—	12.00	540	540	44 cy	—	—	14.10	620	620*	—	80
	A151-2l	Finish & cure	6,400 sf	.30	1,920	.03	192	2,112	6,400 sf	.28	1,792	.03	192	1,984*	128	—
	A151-2m	Sealer per fin. sched.	4,000 sf	.07	280	.07	280	560	4,000 sf	.075	300	.065	260	560	—	—
	A151-3a	*Steps on grd. (tread lgth)*	22 lf	7.60	167	2.50	55	222	22 lf	22.22	489	2.90	64	553*	—	331
	A151-4a	*Steps to 2nd flr. forming*	640 sf	5.90	3,776	2.80	1,792	5,568	640 sf	6.60	4,224	2.36	1,510	5,734*	—	166
	A151-4b	Concrete and pumping	6 cy	22.00	132	80.00	480	612	6 cy	27.87	167	73.23	439	606*	6	—
	A151-4c	Finish & cure	240 sf	1.20	288	.20	48	336	240 sf	1.55	372	.28	67	439*	—	103
	A151-5a	*Fill on stl. deck screeds*	2,200 sf	.12	264	.06	132	396	2,200 sf	.17	374	.06	132	506*	—	110
	A151-5b	Concrete & pumping	22 cy	18.00	396	85.00	1,870	2,266	23 cy	12.2	281	78.83	1,813	2,094*	172	—
	A151-5c	Finish & cure	2,200 sf	.30	660	.03	66	726	2,200 sf	.33	726	.03	66	792*	—	66
	A151-6a	Curbs on slabs	68 lf	2.75	187	3.50	238	425	76 lf	3.03	230	.84	64	294*	131	—
	A151-7a	Locker bases	50 lf	4.00	200	7.50	375	575								
	A151-8a	Equipment slabs	60 sf	5.50	330	15.50	930	1,260								
	A151-9a	Splash blocks	6 ea	32.00	192	32.00	192	384								
	A151-13a	Catch basins	4 ea	480.00	1,920	255.00	1,020	2,940								
139	A180	**Carpentry**														
	A180-1a	Doors, Hollow metal	6 ea	39.88	239	—	—	239								
	A180-1b	Doors, wood	18 ea	39.88	718	—	—	718								
	A180-2a	Door frames, hol. met.	24 ea	29.91	718	—	—	718	12 ea	31.60	379	—	—	379		—
	A180-3a	Hardware, closers	12 ea	19.94	239	—	—	239								
	A180-3b	exit devices	3 ea	39.88	120	—	—	120								
	A180-3c	thresholds	6 ea	29.91	179	—	—	179								
	A180-3d	seals	6 ea	39.88	239	—	—	239								

* Line item completed

Figure 4.8a (cont.)

Administration Building & Fire Station, Picacho, CA — Master Cost Record

Pay Item	Cost Code	Work Description	Quantity	Est. Labor U/C	Est. Labor Total	Est. Mat'l/Equip./Sub U/C	Est. Mat'l/Equip./Sub Total	Est. Total	Act. Labor U/C	Act. Labor Total	Act. Mat'l/Equip./Sub U/C	Act. Mat'l/Equip./Sub Total	Act. Total	Under Run	Over Run
139	A180	**Carpentry (Cont'd)**													
	A180-4a	Window frames (arched)	9 ea	199.70	1,797	—	—	1,797							—
	A180-4b	Window frames (rect.)	25 ea	159.00	3,975	—	—	3,975							
	A180-5a	Single storage shelving	38 lf	3.50	133	—	—	133							
	A180-6a	Receptionist counter	24 lf	7.00	168	—	—	168							
	A180-7a	Base cabinets	30 lf	7.00	210	—	—	210							
	A180-8a	Janitor shelf	12 lf	3.50	42	—	—	42							
	A180-9a	Firemen's bunks	2 ea	80.00	160	—	—	160							
	A180-10a	Kitchen base cabinets	10 lf	8.00	80	—	—	80							
	A180-10b	Kitchen wall cabinets	30 sf	4.50	135	—	—	135							
	A180-11a	Work bench	12 lf	6.00	72	—	—	72							
	A180-12a	Wall shelving units	160 sf	2.00	320	—	—	320							
	A180-13a	Closet shelves	36 lf	2.50	90	—	—	90							
	A180-13b	Closet poles	36 lf	1.50	54	—	—	54							
	A180-14a	Shower bench	8 lf	8.00	64	—	—	64							
	A180-15a	Roof Nailers, 2x4; 2x6	400 lf	.70	280	.70	280	560							
	A180-16a	Roof fascia, 2x12	480 lf	1.20	576	1.60	768	1,344							
	A180-17a	Misc. rough hardware	L.S.	L.S.	—	L.S.	150	150							
	A180-18a	Install toilet accessories	24 hrs	19.94	479	—	—	479							
139	A181	**Install Misc. Metal**													
	A181-1a	Fireman's pole	1 ea	80.00	80	—	—	80							
	A181-2a	Ladders	2 ea	28.50	57	—	—	57							
	A181-3a	Channel door frames	4 ea	40.00	160	—	—	160	36.00	144	—	—	144*	16	—
	A181-4a	Door corner guards	8 ea	19.00	152	—	—	152							
	A181-5a	Lintels over doors	4 ea	60.00	240	—	—	240	52.00	208	—	—	208*	32	—
	A181-6a	Pipe guard posts	12 ea	9.50	114	—	—	114							
	A181-7a	Detention bars	2 ea	160.00	320	—	—	320							
	A181-8a	Stair railings	80 lf	3.00	240	—	—	240							
141	A182	**Purchase Wood Doors**	18 ea	—	—	70.00	1,260	1,260	—	—	63.30	1,139	1,139*	121	—
146	A183	**Wall Louvers**	8 ea	27.21	218	80.00	640	858							
166	A184	**Window & Fixture Clean.**	L.S.	L.S.	1,497	—	—	1,497							
167	A185	**Site Concrete Work**													
	A185-10a	Sidewalk & apron	6,150 sf	—	—	1.90	11,685	11,685							
	A185-11a	Curbs, gutter type	600 lf	—	—	9.25	5,550	5,550							
	A185-12a	Driveways	1,000 sf	—	—	2.75	2,750	2,750							

*Line item completed

Figure 4.8a (cont.)

4.9
Miscellaneous Management Duties

The bidder's personal participation in project expediting is irregular and is prompted only by unusual events, such as disputes with sponsors, subs, or suppliers regarding interpretations of drawings, specs, or contracts. Legal actions, public relations, and change orders might also require the bidder's attention.

Public relations are perhaps more relevant to the role of the bidder than to any other employee in the company. The super's primary concern is the current project. Superimposed on this immediate public relations responsibility is the need to procure new projects by maintaining goodwill with a majority of subs and suppliers in the industry. Therefore, if drastic steps appear to be necessary to obtain the proper performance from a sub or supplier, the bidder is usually the prime mover.

Public relations by both the bidder and the super also play a part in change orders. As a general principle, only large change orders are profitable. Small change orders disrupt the continuity of job progress, interrupt and change the progress schedule, complicate the bookkeeping, and produce insufficient compensation. It is often preferable to trade off small additive and small deductive changes in the field.

When change orders are large enough to warrant formal processing, depending on the sponsor's policies, the bidder usually submits the necessary detailed breakdown of labor, material, equipment, subcontract, and markup to prove the validity of the total price and to secure a prompt agreement. The importance of speed in the expediting of change orders cannot be overemphasized.

Figure 4.9a is a typical change-order cost breakdown to be submitted to the sponsor for approval and authorization to proceed. In this example, the city has requested a price for the addition of 1,000 square feet of concrete parking apron and credit for the displaced a.c. paving. Both wages and material costs have risen since the original bidding, justifying a unit price greater than our original of $1.90 (before fringe benefits). Our breakdown (Fig. 4.9a) comes to $2,347, or $2.35 per square foot, to which we add fringe benefits, overhead, and profit.

Involvement in the construction work provides the bidder with a practical basis for making sound value judgments. The on-site experience gained enables the bidder: (1) to verify production estimates for men and equipment, (2) to spot cost items easily overlooked by the estimator, (3) to clarify jurisdictional separations between subtrades, (4) to rate subs individually for dependability, and (5) to formulate policies for future relations with subs and suppliers. Experience also enables the bidder to rate the sponsor for desirability of future contracts; the super can be fairly rated for leadership and economic efficiency. All such knowledge contributes to the next bidding effort.

Request for Change Order

To: Public Works Department
Picacho, California

Project: Administration Building and Fire Station
Proposed Change: Additional 1,000 square feet of concrete parking apron and credit for 1,000 square feet of A.C. paving.

Pay item 131; cost code B112 & B113	Quantity	Labor		Mat'l/Equip./Sub		Total
		U/C	Total	U/C	Total	
Deductive (Subcontract)						
As quoted by Blazer	1,000 sf	—	—	1.92	1,920	$1,920
Your Own Company - overhead	—					—
Your Own Company - profit, 7½%		—	—	—	—	144
Total Credit:						$2,064
Pay Item 167; Cost Code A185						
Additive (Your Own Company)						
Fine grading	1,000 sf	.05	50	.05	50	100
Form headers	90 lf	2.80	252	1.00	90	342
Set screeds	1,000 sf	.10	100	.04	40	140
Concrete placing	20 cy	6.50	130	68.00	1,360	1,490
Finish and cure	1,000 sf	.25	250	.025	25	275
Sub Total:						$2,347
Payroll taxes/fringe benefits 47% of labor						368
Sub Total:						$2,715
Overhead 4% of total						109
Sub Total:						$2,824
Profit 7½% of total						212
Total Additive						$3,036
Net Additive Change Order ($3,036 – $2,064):						$ 972

Figure 4.9a

150

Part V: Appendixes

Printed forms are the main tools of the bidder. The possibilities for design variations of the forms to suit each individual are infinite. The samples in these appendixes are simplified versions and prototypes of the most commonly used forms, most of which were not directly involved in the central bidding procedure, and therefore were not shown in the text. They are, nevertheless, involved in the general activities associated with bidding.

Bidders, particularly if they are not also the estimator, need knowledge of current costs in order to make the best selections and adjustments in the estimates, budgets, quotations, and sub-bids that constitute their daily work. Appendixes I, J, K, L, M, N, and R contain examples of reference data of the kind available to bidders. These appendixes conclude with miscellaneous exhibits of forms commonly used in the construction industry.

Appendix A: Bid Forms

Figure 5.A1 is the type of form used for bidding U.S. Navy projects. Variations of this form are used by other federal agencies as well. The reverse side of the form is shown in Fig. 5.A2.

Some projects call for itemized bids. A form such as Fig. 5.A3 is given to all the bidders for the sake of uniformity, clarity, and for ease of comparing the different bids.

STANDARD FORM 21 DECEMBER 1965 EDITION GENERAL SERVICES ADMINISTRATION FED. PROC. REG. (41 CFR) 1-16.401 S/N-0109-200-1604	**BID FORM** (CONSTRUCTION CONTRACT)	REFERENCE
Read the Instructions to Bidders *This form to be submitted in* DUPLICATE		DATE OF INVITATION 1 July 1982
NAME AND LOCATION OF PROJECT	NAME OF BIDDER (*Type or print*)	

TO:
San Diego Branch
Western Division
Naval Facilities Engineering Command
1220 Pacific Highway
San Diego, California 92132

_____
(Date)

In compliance with the above-dated invitation for bids, the undersigned hereby proposes to perform all work for

in strict accordance with the General Provisions (Standard Form 23-A), Labor Standards Provisions Applicable to Contracts in Excess of $2,000 (Standard Form 19-A), specifications, schedules, drawings, and conditions, for the following amount(s)

ITEMS OF BID

Base Bid Item 1 .... $ _____

(Continue on other side)

Figure 5.A1

The undersigned agrees that, upon written acceptance of this bid, by Notice of Award mailed or otherwise furnished within sixty calendar days (60 calendar days) after the date of opening of bids, he will within 10 calendar days (unless a longer period is allowed) after receipt of the prescribed forms, execute Standard Form 23 Construction Contract and within 15 calendar days after date of notice of award give performance and payment bonds on Government standard forms with good and sufficient surety. The undersigned agrees, if awarded the contract, to commence the work and to complete the work within the time period set forth in Section 01100, Par. 4, of the Specification.

RECEIPT OF AMENDMENTS: *The undersigned acknowledges receipt of the following amendments of the invitation for bids, drawings, and/or specifications, etc. (give number and date of each):*

The representations and certifications on the accompanying STANDARD FORM 19-B are made a part of this bid.

ENCLOSED IS BID GUARANTEE, CONSISTING OF   IN THE AMOUNT OF

NAME OF BIDDER *(Type or print)*	FULL NAME OF ALL PARTNERS *(Type or print)*
BUSINESS ADDRESS *(Type or print) (Include "ZIP Code")* Telephone No.:	
BY *(Signature in ink. Type or print name under signature)*	
TITLE *(Type or print)*	

DIRECTIONS FOR SUBMITTING BIDS: *Envelopes containing bids, guarantee, etc., must be sealed, marked, and addressed as follows*

CAUTION—Bids should not be qualified by exceptions to the bidding conditions.

Figure 5.A2

I/WE AGREE TO FURNISH ALL MATERIAL AND PERFORM ALL WORK REQUIRED TO

Item No.	Estimated Quantity	Description and Price	Unit Price	Extensions
1	8 Ton	Bituminous Tack Coat at: _____ Dollars and _____ Cents per ton.	$ _____	$ _____
2	2,880 Ton	Bituminous Surface Course at: _____ Dollars and _____ Cents per ton.	$ _____	$ _____
3	190 Ton	Bituminous Cement - AR 8000 at: _____ Dollars and _____ Cents per ton.	$ _____	$ _____
4	700 LF	Grind Notch in Existing Bituminous Surface Course at: _____ Dollars and _____ Cents per linear foot.	$ _____	$ _____
5	7,050 LF	Saw & Seal Asphalt Concrete Joints at: _____ Dollars and _____ Cents per linear foot.	$ _____	$ _____
8	360 LF	Random Crack Repair at: _____ Dollars and _____ Cents per linear foot.	$ _____	$ _____
10	1,015 SF	Airfield Marking at: _____ Dollars and _____ Cents per square foot.	$ _____	$ _____
12	20 SY	Remove Paint from Pavement at: _____ Dollars and _____ Cents per square yard.	$ _____	$ _____
13	2,400 LF	Replace Defective Joint Seal At: _____ Dollars and _____ Cents per linear foot.	$ _____	$ _____
15	635 LF	Grout Void Below Joint - Prepare Joint and Place Grout at: _____ Dollars and _____ Cents per linear foot of joint.	$ _____	$ _____

Figure 5.A3

154

16   120 CF   Grout Void Below Joint - Furnish
Grout at:

_____ Dollars
and _____ Cents
per cubic foot of grout injected. $ _____ $ _____

Bid Schedule   **TOTAL** $ _____

* *

TOTAL BID: $ _____

NOTES: Award will be made on the basis of the total.

In the case of inconsistency between words and figures submitted by bidder, the words shall govern.

The Contractor shall pay all applicable sales and use taxes. Said sales and use taxes shall be included in the amount bid.

The District reserves the right to reject any or all bids and to waive any informality in any bids received.

The following Addenda have been noted: _____

Figure 5.A3 (cont.)

Appendix B: Bond Forms

Figure 5.B1 is a bid bond form for a federal (Navy) project. Figure 5.B2 shows the reverse side. Completion of this bond by an authorized surety guarantees that the bidder will accept the contract, or the surety will pay any additional costs to the sponsor caused by default of the bidder. A more general form of bid bond often used in private projects is shown in Fig. 5.B3.

A contract may specify a performance bond or a labor and material bond, or both. Figures 5.B4 and 5.B5 show AIA's performance bond form. Figures 5.B6 and 5.B7 show a labor and material bond form. Figures 5.B8 and 5.B9 are samples of federal (Navy) payment and performance and bond forms. Taken together, these bonds are often called "construction bonds."

STANDARD FORM **24** JUNE 1964 EDITION GENERAL SERVICES ADMINISTRATION FED. PROC. REG. (41 CFR) 1-16.801	**BID BOND** *(See Instructions on reverse)*	24–103	DATE BOND EXECUTED *(Must not be later than bid opening date)*

PRINCIPAL *(Legal name and business address)*	TYPE OF ORGANIZATION *("X" one)*
	☐ INDIVIDUAL ☐ PARTNERSHIP ☐ JOINT VENTURE ☐ CORPORATION
	STATE OF INCORPORATION

SURETY(IES) *(Name and business address)*

PENAL SUM OF BOND					BID IDENTIFICATION	
PERCENT OF BID PRICE	AMOUNT NOT TO EXCEED				BID DATE	INVITATION NO.
	MILLION(S)	THOUSAND(S)	HUNDRED(S)	CENTS		
					FOR *(Construction, Supplies or Services)*	

KNOW ALL MEN BY THESE PRESENTS, That we, the Principal and Surety(ies) hereto, are firmly bound to the United States of America (hereinafter called the Government) in the above penal sum for the payment of which we bind ourselves, our heirs, executors, administrators, and successors, jointly and severally: *Provided,* That, where the Sureties are corporations acting as co-sureties, we, the Sureties, bind ourselves in such sum "jointly and severally" as well as "severally" only for the purpose of allowing a joint action or actions against any or all of us, and for all other purposes each Surety binds itself, jointly and severally with the Principal, for the payment of such sum only as is set forth opposite the name of such Surety, but if no limit of liability is indicated, the limit of liability shall be the full amount of the penal sum.

THE CONDITION OF THIS OBLIGATION IS SUCH, that whereas the Principal has submitted the bid identified above.

NOW, THEREFORE, if the Principal, upon acceptance by the Government of his bid identified above, within the period specified therein for acceptance (sixty (60) days if no period is specified), shall execute such further contractual documents, if any, and give such bond(s) as may be required by the terms of the bid as accepted within the time specified (ten (10) days if no period is specified) after receipt of the forms by him, or in the event of failure so to execute such further contractual documents and give such bonds, if the Principal shall pay the Government for any cost of procuring the work which exceeds the amount of his bid, then the above obligation shall be void and of no effect.

Each Surety executing this instrument hereby agrees that its obligation shall not be impaired by any extension(s) of the time for acceptance of the bid that the Principal may grant to the Government, notice of which extension(s) to the Surety(ies) being hereby waived; provided that such waiver of notice shall apply only with respect to extensions aggregating not more than sixty (60) calendar days in addition to the period originally allowed for acceptance of the bid.

IN WITNESS WHEREOF, the Principal and Surety(ies) have executed this bid bond and have affixed their seals on the date set forth above.

PRINCIPAL			
Signature(s)	1. *(Seal)*	2. *(Seal)*	Corporate Seal
Name(s) & Title(s) *(Typed)*	1.	2.	

INDIVIDUAL SURETIES			
Signature(s)	1. *(Seal)*	2.	*(Seal)*
Name(s) *(Typed)*	1.	2.	

CORPORATE SURETY(IES)					
SURETY A	Name & Address		STATE OF INC.	LIABILITY LIMIT	Corporate Seal
	Signature(s)	1.	2.		
	Name(s) & Title(s) *(Typed)*	1.	2.		

Figure 5.B1

		CORPORATE SURETY(IES) (Continued)			

SURETY B	Name & Address		STATE OF INC.	LIABILITY LIMIT	Corporate Seal
	Signature(s)	1.	2.		
	Name(s) & Title(s) (Typed)	1.	2.		

SURETY C	Name & Address		STATE OF INC.	LIABILITY LIMIT	Corporate Seal
	Signature(s)	1.	2.		
	Name(s) & Title(s) (Typed)	1.	2.		

SURETY D	Name & Address		STATE OF INC.	LIABILITY LIMIT	Corporate Seal
	Signature(s)	1.	2.		
	Name(s) & Title(s) (Typed)	1.	2.		

SURETY E	Name & Address		STATE OF INC.	LIABILITY LIMIT	Corporate Seal
	Signature(s)	1.	2.		
	Name(s) & Title(s) (Typed)	1.	2.		

SURETY F	Name & Address		STATE OF INC.	LIABILITY LIMIT	Corporate Seal
	Signature(s)	1.	2.		
	Name(s) & Title(s) (Typed)	1	2.		

SURETY G	Name & Address		STATE OF INC.	LIABILITY LIMIT	Corporate Seal
	Signature(s)	1.	2.		
	Name(s) & Title(s) (Typed)	1.	2.		

INSTRUCTIONS

1. This form is authorized for use whenever a bid guaranty is required in connection with construction work or the furnishing of supplies or services. There shall be no deviation from this form without approval by the Administrator of General Services.

2. The full legal name and business address of the Principal shall be inserted in the space designated "Principal" on the face of this form. The bond shall be signed by an authorized person. Where such person is signing in a representative capacity (e.g., an attorney-in-fact), but is not a member of the firm, partnership, or joint venture, or an officer of the corporation involved, evidence of his authority must be furnished.

3. The penal sum of the bond may be expressed as a percentage of the bid price if desired. In such cases, a maximum dollar limitation may be stipulated (e.g., 20% of the bid price but the amount not to exceed _____ dollars).

4. (a) Corporations executing the bond as sureties must be among those appearing on the Treasury Department's list of approved sureties and must be acting within the limitations set forth therein. Where more than a single corporate surety is involved, their names and addresses (city and State) shall be inserted in the spaces (Surety A, Surety B, etc.) headed "CORPORATE SURETY(IES)", and in the space designated "SURETY(IES)" on the face of this form only the letter identification of the Sureties shall be inserted.

(b) Where individual sureties execute the bond, they shall be two or more responsible persons. A completed Affidavit of Individual Surety (Standard Form 28), for each individual surety, shall accompany the bond. Such sureties may be required to furnish additional substantiating information concerning their assets and financial capability as the Government may require.

5. Corporations executing the bond shall affix their corporate seals. Individuals shall execute the bond opposite the word "Seal"; and, if executed in Maine or New Hampshire, shall also affix an adhesive seal.

6. The name of each person signing this bid bond should be typed in the space provided.

★ U.S. GOVERNMENT PRINTING OFFICE : 1964 OF—703-284—91-D

Figure 5.B2

THE AMERICAN INSTITUTE OF ARCHITECTS

AIA Document A310

Bid Bond

KNOW ALL MEN BY THESE PRESENTS, that we

(Here insert full name and address or legal title of Contractor)

as Principal, hereinafter called the Principal, and

(Here insert full name and address or legal title of Surety)

a corporation duly organized under the laws of the State of
as Surety, hereinafter called the Surety, are held and firmly bound unto

(Here insert full name and address or legal title of Owner)

as Obligee, hereinafter called the Obligee, in the sum of

Dollars ($),

for the payment of which sum well and truly to be made, the said Principal and the said Surety, bind ourselves, our heirs, executors, administrators, successors and assigns, jointly and severally, firmly by these presents.

WHEREAS, the Principal has submitted a bid for

(Here insert full name, address and description of project)

NOW, THEREFORE, if the Obligee shall accept the bid of the Principal and the Principal shall enter into a Contract with the Obligee in accordance with the terms of such bid, and give such bond or bonds as may be specified in the bidding or Contract Documents with good and sufficient surety for the faithful performance of such Contract and for the prompt payment of labor and material furnished in the prosecution thereof, or in the event of the failure of the Principal to enter such Contract and give such bond or bonds, if the Principal shall pay to the Obligee the difference not to exceed the penalty hereof between the amount specified in said bid and such larger amount for which the Obligee may in good faith contract with another party to perform the Work covered by said bid, then this obligation shall be null and void, otherwise to remain in full force and effect.

Signed and sealed this   day of   19

_____

(Witness)

_____ (Principal)   (Seal)

_____ (Title)

_____

(Witness)

_____ (Surety)   (Seal)

_____ (Title)

AIA DOCUMENT A310 • BID BOND • AIA ® • FEBRUARY 1970 ED • THE AMERICAN
INSTITUTE OF ARCHITECTS, 1735 N.Y. AVE., N.W., WASHINGTON, D. C. 20006   **1**

Figure 5.B3

THE AMERICAN INSTITUTE OF ARCHITECTS

AIA Document A311

Performance Bond

KNOW ALL MEN BY THESE PRESENTS: that

(Here insert full name and address or legal title of Contractor)

as Principal, hereinafter called Contractor, and

(Here insert full name and address or legal title of Surety)

as Surety, hereinafter called Surety, are held and firmly bound unto

(Here insert full name and address or legal title of Owner)

as Obligee, hereinafter called Owner, in the amount of

Dollars ($),

for the payment whereof Contractor and Surety bind themselves, their heirs, executors, administrators, successors and assigns, jointly and severally, firmly by these presents.

WHEREAS,

Contractor has by written agreement dated   19   , entered into a contract with Owner for
(Here insert full name, address and description of project)

in accordance with Drawings and Specifications prepared by

(Here insert full name and address or legal title of Architect)

which contract is by reference made a part hereof, and is hereinafter referred to as the Contract.

AIA DOCUMENT A311 • PERFORMANCE BOND AND LABOR AND MATERIAL PAYMENT BOND • AIA ®
FEBRUARY 1970 ED. • THE AMERICAN INSTITUTE OF ARCHITECTS, 1735 N.Y. AVE., N.W., WASHINGTON, D. C. 20006   **1**

Figure 5.B4

PERFORMANCE BOND

NOW, THEREFORE, THE CONDITION OF THIS OBLIGATION is such that, if Contractor shall promptly and faithfully perform said Contract, then this obligation shall be null and void; otherwise it shall remain in full force and effect.

The Surety hereby waives notice of any alteration or extension of time made by the Owner.

Whenever Contractor shall be, and declared by Owner to be in default under the Contract, the Owner having performed Owner's obligations thereunder, the Surety may promptly remedy the default, or shall promptly

1) Complete the Contract in accordance with its terms and conditions, or

2) Obtain a bid or bids for completing the Contract in accordance with its terms and conditions, and upon determination by Surety of the lowest responsible bidder, or, if the Owner elects, upon determination by the Owner and the Surety jointly of the lowest responsible bidder, arrange for a contract between such bidder and Owner, and make available as Work progresses (even though there should be a default or a succession of

defaults under the contract or contracts of completion arranged under this paragraph) sufficient funds to pay the cost of completion less the balance of the contract price; but not exceeding, including other costs and damages for which the Surety may be liable hereunder, the amount set forth in the first paragraph hereof. The term "balance of the contract price," as used in this paragraph, shall mean the total amount payable by Owner to Contractor under the Contract and any amendments thereto, less the amount properly paid by Owner to Contractor.

Any suit under this bond must be instituted before the expiration of two (2) years from the date on which final payment under the Contract falls due.

No right of action shall accrue on this bond to or for the use of any person or corporation other than the Owner named herein or the heirs, executors, administrators or successors of the Owner.

Signed and sealed this _____ day of _____ 19____

_____ ⎰ _____ (Principal) _____ (Seal)
(Witness)   ⎱ _____
                             (Title)

_____ ⎰ _____ (Surety) _____ (Seal)
(Witness)   ⎱ _____
                             (Title)

AIA DOCUMENT A311 • PERFORMANCE BOND AND LABOR AND MATERIAL PAYMENT BOND • AIA ®
FEBRUARY 1970 ED. • THE AMERICAN INSTITUTE OF ARCHITECTS, 1735 N.Y. AVE., N.W., WASHINGTON, D. C. 20006

2

Figure 5.B5

161

THE AMERICAN INSTITUTE OF ARCHITECTS

AIA Document A311

Labor and Material Payment Bond

THIS BOND IS ISSUED SIMULTANEOUSLY WITH PERFORMANCE BOND IN FAVOR OF THE OWNER CONDITIONED ON THE FULL AND FAITHFUL PERFORMANCE OF THE CONTRACT

KNOW ALL MEN BY THESE PRESENTS: that

(Here insert full name and address or legal title of Contractor)

as Principal, hereinafter called Principal, and,

(Here insert full name and address or legal title of Surety)

as Surety, hereinafter called Surety, are held and firmly bound unto

(Here insert full name and address or legal title of Owner)

as Obligee, hereinafter called Owner, for the use and benefit of claimants as hereinbelow defined, in the

amount of

(Here insert a sum equal to at least one-half of the contract price)   Dollars ($),

for the payment whereof Principal and Surety bind themselves, their heirs, executors, administrators, successors and assigns, jointly and severally, firmly by these presents.

WHEREAS,

Principal has by written agreement dated   19   , entered into a contract with Owner for

(Here insert full name, address and description of project)

in accordance with Drawings and Specifications prepared by

(Here insert full name and address or legal title of Architect)

which contract is by reference made a part hereof, and is hereinafter referred to as the Contract.

AIA DOCUMENT A311 • PERFORMANCE BOND AND LABOR AND MATERIAL PAYMENT BOND • AIA ®
FEBRUARY 1970 ED. • THE AMERICAN INSTITUTE OF ARCHITECTS, 1735 N.Y. AVE., N.W., WASHINGTON, D. C. 20006

3

Figure 5.B6

LABOR AND MATERIAL PAYMENT BOND

NOW, THEREFORE, THE CONDITION OF THIS OBLIGATION is such that, if Principal shall promptly make payment to all claimants as hereinafter defined, for all labor and material used or reasonably required for use in the performance of the Contract, then this obligation shall be void; otherwise it shall remain in full force and effect, subject, however, to the following conditions:

1. A claimant is defined as one having a direct contract with the Principal or with a Subcontractor of the Principal for labor, material, or both, used or reasonably required for use in the performance of the Contract, labor and material being construed to include that part of water, gas, power, light, heat, oil, gasoline, telephone service or rental of equipment directly applicable to the Contract.

2. The above named Principal and Surety hereby jointly and severally agree with the Owner that every claimant as herein defined, who has not been paid in full before the expiration of a period of ninety (90) days after the date on which the last of such claimant's work or labor was done or performed, or materials were furnished by such claimant, may sue on this bond for the use of such claimant, prosecute the suit to final judgment for such sum or sums as may be justly due claimant, and have execution thereon. The Owner shall not be liable for the payment of any costs or expenses of any such suit.

3. No suit or action shall be commenced hereunder by any claimant:

a) Unless claimant, other than one having a direct contract with the Principal, shall have given written notice to any two of the following: the Principal, the Owner, or the Surety above named, within ninety (90) days after such claimant did or performed the last of the work or labor, or furnished the last of the materials for which said claim is made, stating with substantial

accuracy the amount claimed and the name of the party to whom the materials were furnished, or for whom the work or labor was done or performed. Such notice shall be served by mailing the same by registered mail or certified mail, postage prepaid, in an envelope addressed to the Principal, Owner or Surety, at any place where an office is regularly maintained for the transaction of business, or served in any manner in which legal process may be served in the state in which the aforesaid project is located, save that such service need not be made by a public officer.

b) After the expiration of one (1) year following the date on which Principal ceased Work on said Contract, it being understood, however, that if any limitation embodied in this bond is prohibited by any law controlling the construction thereof such limitation shall be deemed to be amended so as to be equal to the minimum period of limitation permitted by such law.

c) Other than in a state court of competent jurisdiction in and for the county or other political subdivision of the state in which the Project, or any part thereof, is situated, or in the United States District Court for the district in which the Project, or any part thereof, is situated, and not elsewhere.

4. The amount of this bond shall be reduced by and to the extent of any payment or payments made in good faith hereunder, inclusive of the payment by Surety of mechanics' liens which may be filed of record against said improvement, whether or not claim for the amount of such lien be presented under and against this bond.

Signed and sealed this   day of   19

_____
(Witness)

{
_____ (Principal) (Seal)

_____ (Title)

_____
(Witness)

{
_____ (Surety) (Seal)

_____ (Title)

AIA DOCUMENT A311 • PERFORMANCE BOND AND LABOR AND MATERIAL PAYMENT BOND • AIA ®
FEBRUARY 1970 ED. • THE AMERICAN INSTITUTE OF ARCHITECTS, 1735 N.Y. AVE., N.W., WASHINGTON, D. C. 20006

4

Figure 5.B7

STANDARD FORM 25-A JUNE 1964 EDITION GENERAL SERVICES ADMINISTRATION FED. PROC. REG. (41 CFR) 1-16.801	**PAYMENT BOND** *(See Instructions on reverse)*	25-203	DATE BOND EXECUTED *(Must be same or later than date of contract)*

PRINCIPAL *(Legal name and business address)*	TYPE OF ORGANIZATION *("X" one)*
	☐ INDIVIDUAL ☐ PARTNERSHIP ☐ JOINT VENTURE ☐ CORPORATION STATE OF INCORPORATION

SURETY(IES) *(Name(s) and business address(es))*	PENAL SUM OF BOND			
	MILLION(S)	THOUSAND(S)	HUNDRED(S)	CENT(S)
	CONTRACT DATE	CONTRACT NO.		

KNOW ALL MEN BY THESE PRESENTS, That we, the Principal and Surety(ies) hereto, are firmly bound to the United States of America (hereinafter called the Government) in the above penal sum for the payment of which we bind ourselves, our heirs, executors, administrators, and successors, jointly and severally: *Provided,* That, where the Sureties are corporations acting as co-sureties, we, the Sureties, bind ourselves in such sum "jointly and severally" as well as "severally" only for the purpose of allowing a joint action or actions against any or all of us, and for all other purposes each Surety binds itself, jointly and severally with the Principal, for the payment of such sum only as is set forth opposite the name of such Surety, but if no limit of liability is indicated, the limit of liability shall be the full amount of the penal sum.

THE CONDITION OF THIS OBLIGATION IS SUCH, that whereas the Principal entered into the contract identified above;

NOW, THEREFORE, if the Principal shall promptly make payment to all persons supplying labor and material in the prosecution of the work provided for in said contract, and any and all duly authorized modifications of said contract that may hereafter be made, notice of which modifications to the Surety(ies) being hereby waived, then the above obligation shall be void and of no effect.

IN WITNESS WHEREOF, the Principal and Surety(ies) have executed this payment bond and have affixed their seals on the date set forth above.

	PRINCIPAL		
Signature(s)	1. (Seal)	2. (Seal)	Corporate Seal
Name(s) & Title(s) (Typed)	1.	2.	

	INDIVIDUAL SURETY(IES)		
Signature(s)	1. (Seal)	2.	(Seal)
Name(s) (Typed)	1.	2.	

	CORPORATE SURETY(IES)				
	Name & Address		STATE OF INC.	LIABILITY LIMIT	
SURETY A	Signature(s)	1.	2.		Corporate Seal
	Name(s) & Title(s) (Typed)	1.	2.		

Figure 5.B8

PERFORMANCE BOND

(See Instructions on reverse)

DATE BOND EXECUTED *(Must be same or later than date of contract)*

PRINCIPAL *(Legal name and business address)*

TYPE OF ORGANIZATION *("X" one)*

☐ INDIVIDUAL ☐ PARTNERSHIP

☐ JOINT VENTURE ☐ CORPORATION

STATE OF INCORPORATION

SURETY(IES) *(Name(s) and business address(es))*

PENAL SUM OF BOND

MILLION(S)	THOUSAND(S)	HUNDRED(S)	CENT(S)

CONTRACT DATE | CONTRACT NO

KNOW ALL MEN BY THESE PRESENTS, That we, the Principal and Surety(ies) hereto, are firmly bound to the United States of America (hereinafter called the Government) in the above penal sum for the payment of which we bind ourselves, our heirs, executors, administrators, and successors, jointly and severally: *Provided,* That, where the Sureties are corporations acting as co-sureties, we, the Sureties, bind ourselves in such sum "jointly and severally" as well as "severally" only for the purpose of allowing a joint action or actions against any or all of us, and for all other purposes each Surety binds itself, jointly and severally with the Principal, for the payment of such sum only as is set forth opposite the name of such Surety, but if no limit of liability is indicated, the limit of liability shall be the full amount of the penal sum.

THE CONDITION OF THIS OBLIGATION IS SUCH, that whereas the Principal entered into the contract identified above;

NOW, THEREFORE, if the Principal shall:

(a) Perform and fulfill all the undertakings, covenants, terms, conditions, and agreements of said contract during the original term of said contract and any extensions thereof that may be granted by the Government, with or without notice to the Surety(ies), and during the life of any guaranty required under the contract, and shall also perform and fulfill all the undertakings, covenants, terms, conditions, and agreements of any and all duly authorized modifications of said contract that may hereafter be made, notice of which modifications to the Surety(ies) being hereby waived; and

(b) If the said contract is subject to the Miller Act, as amended (40 U.S.C. 270a–270e), pay to the Government the full amount of the taxes imposed by the Government which are collected, deducted, or withheld from wages paid by the Principal in carrying out the construction contract with respect to which this bond is furnished; then the above obligation shall be void and of no effect.

IN WITNESS WHEREOF, the Principal and Surety(ies) have executed this performance bond and have affixed their seals on the date set forth above.

PRINCIPAL			
Signature(s)	1. (Seal)	2. (Seal)	Corporate Seal
Name(s) & Title(s) (Typed)	1.	2.	

INDIVIDUAL SURETY(IES)			
Signature(s)	1. (Seal)	2. (Seal)	(Seal)
Name(s) (Typed)	1.	2.	

CORPORATE SURETY(IES)				
SURETY A	Name & Address		STATE OF INC	LIABILITY LIMIT
	Signature(s)	1.	2.	Corporate Seal
	Name(s) & Title(s) (Typed)	1.	2.	

25-105

Figure 5.B9

Appendix C: Bidder's Statement of Experience and Ability

Figure 5.C1 is a sample form used by some sponsors prior to accepting a bid and awarding a contract. This procedure may be waived at the sponsor's discretion. It is usually required only of a first-time bidder to a public agency, and thereafter remains on file. The sponsor might require an updating from a bidder who wishes to bid a project much larger than or different from any previously bid. The sponsor might waive the requirement of a statement for well-established and well-known bidders.

Statement of Bidder's Qualifications

1. Name license(s) by number(s) and classification(s) held by your company relevant to this project _____
   _____
   _____

2. Attach current financial statement and/or letters of credit ___
   _____

3. List completed construction contracts of a type similar to this project _____

Name of Project	Sponsor	Date Completed

4. Names of principals or officers of your company:

Name	Title

5. List major items of equipment owned by your company:

Description	Year Mfgd.

Figure 5.C1

Appendix D: Contract Forms for Sponsors and Prime Contractors

Figures 5.D1 and 5.D2 are the two sides of a federal (Navy) contract form. Figures 5.D3, 5.D4, and 5.D5 are pages from the AIA's contract form. Articles between 3.2 and 21 are deliberately omitted for brevity and clarity. Most of those articles are an integral part of typical specs and are automatically included in a contract agreement.

STANDARD FORM 23
JANUARY 1961 EDITION
GENERAL SERVICES ADMINISTRATION
FED. PROC. REG. (41 CFR) 1-16.401

CONSTRUCTION CONTRACT
(See instructions on reverse)

CONTRACT NO

DATE OF CONTRACT

NAME AND ADDRESS OF CONTRACTOR

CHECK APPROPRIATE BOX

☐ Individual
☐ Partnership
☐ Joint Venture
☐ Corporation, incorporated in the
State of _____.

DEPARTMENT OR AGENCY

CONTRACT FOR *(Work to be performed)*

PLACE

CONTRACT PRICE *(Express in words and figures)*

ADMINISTRATIVE DATA *(Optional)*

The United States of America (hereinafter called the Government), represented by the Contracting Officer executing this contract, and the individual, partnership, joint venture, or corporation named above (hereinafter called the Contractor), mutually agree to perform this contract in strict accordance with the General Provisions (Standard Form 23-A), Labor Standards Provisions Applicable to Contracts in Excess of $2,000 (Standard Form 19-A), and the following designated specifications, schedules, drawings, and conditions:

WORK SHALL BE STARTED

WORK SHALL BE COMPLETED

23-103

Figure 5.D1

Alterations. The following alterations were made in this contract before it was signed by the parties hereto:

In witness whereof, the parties hereto have executed this contract as of the date entered on the first page hereof.

THE UNITED STATES OF AMERICA   CONTRACTOR

By _____   _____
                                                              (Name of Contractor)

_____   By _____
          (Official title)   *(Signature)*

                                                         _____
                                                                        (Title)

INSTRUCTIONS

1. The full name and business address of the Contractor must be inserted in the space provided on the face of the form. The Contractor shall sign in the space provided above with his usual signature and typewrite or print his name under the signature.

2. An officer of a corporation, a member of a partnership, or an agent signing for the Contractor shall place his signature and title after the word "By" under the name of the Contractor. A contract executed by an attorney or agent on behalf of the Contractor shall be accompanied by two authenticated copies of his power of attorney or other evidence of his authority to act on behalf of the Contractor.

U. S. GOVERNMENT PRINTING OFFICE 1960 OF—572728—44

Figure 5.D2

168

THE AMERICAN INSTITUTE OF ARCHITECTS

AIA Document A107

Abbreviated Form of Agreement Between Owner and Contractor

For CONSTRUCTION PROJECTS OF LIMITED SCOPE where the Basis of Payment is a STIPULATED SUM

1978 EDITION

THIS DOCUMENT HAS IMPORTANT LEGAL CONSEQUENCES; CONSULTATION WITH AN ATTORNEY IS ENCOURAGED WITH RESPECT TO ITS COMPLETION OR MODIFICATION

This document includes abbreviated General Conditions and should not be used with other General Conditions. It has been approved and endorsed by The Associated General Contractors of America.

AGREEMENT

made as of the   day of   in the year of Nineteen
Hundred and

SAMPLE

BETWEEN the Owner:

and the Contractor:

the Project:

the Architect:

The Owner and the Contractor agree as set forth below.

AIA DOCUMENT A107 • ABBREVIATED OWNER-CONTRACTOR AGREEMENT • EIGHTH EDITION • APRIL 1978 • AIA®
© 1978 • THE AMERICAN INSTITUTE OF ARCHITECTS, 1735 NEW YORK AVENUE, N.W., WASHINGTON, D.C. 20006   **A107-1978 1**

Figure 5.D3

ARTICLE 1
THE WORK

1.1 The Contractor shall perform all the Work required by the Contract Documents for

(Here insert the caption descriptive of the Work as used on other Contract Documents.)

ARTICLE 2
TIME OF COMMENCEMENT AND SUBSTANTIAL COMPLETION

2.1 The Work to be performed under this Contract shall be commenced

and, subject to authorized adjustments, Substantial Completion shall be achieved not later than

(Here insert any special provisions for liquidated damages relating to failure to complete on time.)

ARTICLE 3
CONTRACT SUM

3.1 The Owner shall pay the Contractor in current funds for the performance of the Work, subject to additions and deductions by Change Order as provided in the Contract Documents, the Contract Sum of

3.2 The Contract Sum is determined as follows:

(State here the base bid or other lump sum amount, accepted alternates, and unit prices, as applicable.)

Figure 5.D4

ARTICLE 21
OTHER CONDITIONS OR PROVISIONS

This Agreement entered into as of the day and year first written above.

OWNER   CONTRACTOR

_____   _____

_____   _____

AIA DOCUMENT A107 • ABBREVIATED OWNER-CONTRACTOR AGREEMENT • EIGHTH EDITION • APRIL 1978 • AIA®
© 1978 • THE AMERICAN INSTITUTE OF ARCHITECTS, 1735 NEW YORK AVENUE, N.W., WASHINGTON, D.C. 20006   **A107-1978 8**

Figure 5.D5

Appendix E: Telephone Quotation Forms

Figure 5.E1 is a form designed especially for recording sub-bids received by telephone. It is important that *all* data be received and recorded for accurate and fair comparison of bids, in order to avoid time wasted calling back and to avoid possible future disputes. Figure 5.E2 is a form for recording either telephone or person-to-person quotations of materials, equipment, or supplies when no on-site subcontract work is involved.

MEANSCO FORM 140	TELEPHONE QUOTATION		DATE		

TELEPHONE QUOTATION

MEANSCO FORM 140

DATE _____

FIRM QUOTING _____ BY _____ TITLE _____

ADDRESS _____ PHONE _____
(Area Code)

PROJECT _____

LOCATION _____ ESTIMATE NO. _____

ITEM QUOTED _____ RECEIVED BY _____

WORK INCLUDED	AMOUNT OF QUOTATION
DELIVERY TOTAL BID	

DOES QUOTATION INCLUDE THE FOLLOWING: IF ☐ NO IS CHECKED, DETERMINE THE FOLLOWING:

STATE & LOCAL SALES TAXES	☐ YES	☐ NO	MATERIAL VALUE	
DELIVERY TO THE JOB SITE	☐ YES	☐ NO	WEIGHT	
COMPLETE ERECTION	☐ YES	☐ NO	QUANTITY	
COMPLETE SECTION AS PER SPECIFICATIONS	☐ YES	☐ NO	DESCRIBE BELOW	

EXCLUSIONS AND QUALIFICATIONS

ADDENDA ACKNOWLEDGEMENT	TOTAL ADJUSTMENT
	ADJUSTED TOTAL

R.S.MEANS CO.,INC. KINGSTON,MA. 02364

Figure 5.E1

PRICE DATA ON:

VERBAL QUOTATION
R.S. MEANS CO., INC.

Date _____

For Use With:

Job No. _____

Information From:

Company _____

Project _____

Contact _____

Location _____

Telephone _____

ITEM DESCRIPTION	QUANTITY	UNIT	PRICE	PRICE DATA & COMMENTS
			$	
			$	
			$	
			$	
			$	
			$	
			$	
			$	
			$	
			$	

Special Comments _____

Delivery Data: _____ Contact Cooperative? Yes ☐ No ☐

C.S.I.
Code No. _____ Estimator _____

Figure 5.E2

Appendix F: Bid and Estimate Summary Sheets

Figures 5.F1 and 5.F2 are the two sides of a convenient summary sheet that also serves as a check list and is particularly suitable for preliminary estimates and general negotiation work. Figure 5.F3 is a form that serves the same purpose as Figs. 5.F1 and 5.F2, but acts more as a summary and listing of sub-bids or budget figures. (See Fig. 1.7a for a design of a bid spread sheet for tabulating all the sub-bids, as well as for summarizing.)

ESTIMATE SUMMARY

MEANSCO FORM F110

PROJECT			TOTAL AREA		SHEET NO.	
LOCATION			TOTAL VOLUME		ESTIMATE NO.	
ARCHITECT			COST PER S.F.		DATE	
OWNER			COST PER C.F.		NO. OF STORIES	
QUANTITIES BY:		PRICES BY:		EXTENSIONS BY:		CHECKED BY:

NO.	DESCRIPTION	MATERIAL	LABOR	SUBCONTRACT	TOTAL	ADJUSTMENT
2.0	**SITE WORK**					
	SITE PREPARATION, DEMOLITION					
	EARTHWORK					
	CAISSONS & PILING					
	DRAINAGE & UTILITIES					
	SEWAGE TREATMENT					
	PAVING & SURFACING					
	SITE IMPROVEMENT					
	LANDSCAPING					
3.0	**CONCRETE**					
	FORMWORK					
	REINFORCING STEEL & MESH					
	FOUNDATIONS					
	SUPERSTRUCTURE					
	FLOORS & FINISH					
	PRECAST CONCRETE					
	CEMENTITIOUS DECKS					
4.0	**MASONRY**					
	MORTAR & REINFORCING					
	BRICK					
	BLOCK					
	STONEWORK					
5.0	**METALS**					
	STRUCTURAL STEEL					
	OPEN WEB JOISTS					
	DECKS					
	MISCELLANEOUS					
	ORNAMENTAL					
	FASTENERS, ROUGH HARDWARE					
6.0	**CARPENTRY**					
	ROUGH					
	FINISH					
	ARCHITECTURAL WOODWORK					
	LAMINATED CONSTRUCTION					
7.0	**MOISTURE & THERMAL PROTECTION**					
	WATER & DAMPPROOFING					
	INSULATION & FIREPROOFING					
	ROOFING					
	SIDING					
	FLASHING & SHEET METAL					
	ROOF ACCESSORIES					
8.0	**DOORS, WINDOWS, GLASS**					
	DOORS & FRAMES					
	WINDOWS					
	HARDWARE & WEATHER STRIPPING					
	GLASS & GLAZING					
	CURTAIN WALL & ENTRANCES					

R.S. MEANS CO., INC. KINGSTON, MASS. 02364

Figure 5.F1

NO.	DESCRIPTION	MATERIAL	LABOR	SUBCONTRACT	TOTAL	ADJUSTMENT
	TOTAL FROM FRONT PAGE					
9.0	**FINISHES**					
	METAL STUD & SUPPORT					
	LATH, PLASTER & STUCCO					
	DRYWALL					
	TILE, TERRAZZO, etc.					
	ACOUSTICAL TREATMENT					
	FLOOR COVERING					
	PAINTING					
	WALL COVERING					
10.0	**SPECIALTIES**					
	BATHROOM ACCESSORIES					
	CHUTES					
	LOCKERS					
	PARTITIONS					
	SIGNS & BUTTETIN BOARDS					
11.0	**EQUIPMENT**					
	APPLIANCES					
	DOCK					
	KITCHEN					
12.0	**FURNISHINGS**					
	BLINDS					
	SEATING					
13.0	**SPECIAL CONSTRUCTION**					
	INTEGRATED CEILINGS					
	PEDESTAL FLOORS					
	PREFAB, ROOMS & BLDGS.					
14.0	**CONVEYING SYSTEMS**					
	DUMBWAITER					
	ELEVATORS					
	ESCALATORS, MOVING RAMPS					
	PNEUMATIC TUBE SYSTEM					
15.0	**MECHANICAL**					
	PIPE & FITTINGS					
	PLUMBING FIXTURES & APPLIANCES					
	FIRE PROTECTION					
	HEATING					
	AIR CONDITIONING & VENTILATING					
16.0	**ELECTRICAL**					
	RACEWAYS					
	CONDUCTORS & GROUNDING					
	BOXES & WIRING DEVICES					
	STARTERS, BOARDS & SWITCHES					
	TRANSFORMERS & BUS DUCT					
	LIGHTING					
	SPECIAL SYSTEMS					
	TOTAL DIRECT COSTS					
	CONTRACTORS OVERHEAD					
	INSURANCE, TAXES, BONDS					
	EQUIPMENT & TOOLS					
	DESIGN, ENGINEERING & FIELD SUPERVISION					
	PROFIT & CONTINGENCIES					
	TOTAL BID					

Figure 5.F2

CONDENSED ESTIMATE SUMMARY

MEANSCO
FORM 115

PROJECT		TOTAL AREA	SHEET NO.
LOCATION		TOTAL VOLUME	ESTIMATE NO.
ARCHITECT		COST PER S.F.	DATE
OWNER		COST PER C.F.	NO. OF STORIES
QUANTITIES BY	PRICES BY	EXTENSIONS BY	CHECKED BY

NO.	DESCRIPTION	MATERIAL	LABOR	SUBCONTRACT	TOTAL	ADJUSTMENT
	SITE WORK					
	Excavation					
	CONCRETE					
	MASONRY					
	METALS					
	CARPENTRY					
	MOISTURE PROTECTION					
	DOORS, WINDOWS, GLASS					
	FINISHES					
	SPECIALTIES					
	EQUIPMENT					
	FURNISHINGS					
	SPECIAL CONSTRUCTION					
	CONVEYING SYSTEMS					
	MECHANICAL					
	Plumbing					
	Heating, Ventilating, Air Conditioning					
	ELECTRICAL					
	TOTAL DIRECT COSTS					
	CONTRACTORS OVERHEAD					
	Performance Bond					
	Profit & Contingencies					
	TOTAL BID					

R.S. MEANS CO., INC. KINGSTON, MASS. 02364

Figure 5.F3

Appendix G: Bar Charts

Figure 5.G1 is a convenient form for constructing a progress schedule, as demonstrated in Figs. 2.9c and 3.6a in the text. These progress schedules may be prepared in a brief manner to estimate the construction time of a project, or they may be drawn with greater care and detail to serve as an authoritative guide to field management and contract administration. Figure 5.G2 is a form suitable for scheduling projects designed and estimated using the systems method. Readers interested in this method are referred to the current annual edition of *Means Systems Costs*, published by R.S. Means Co., Inc.

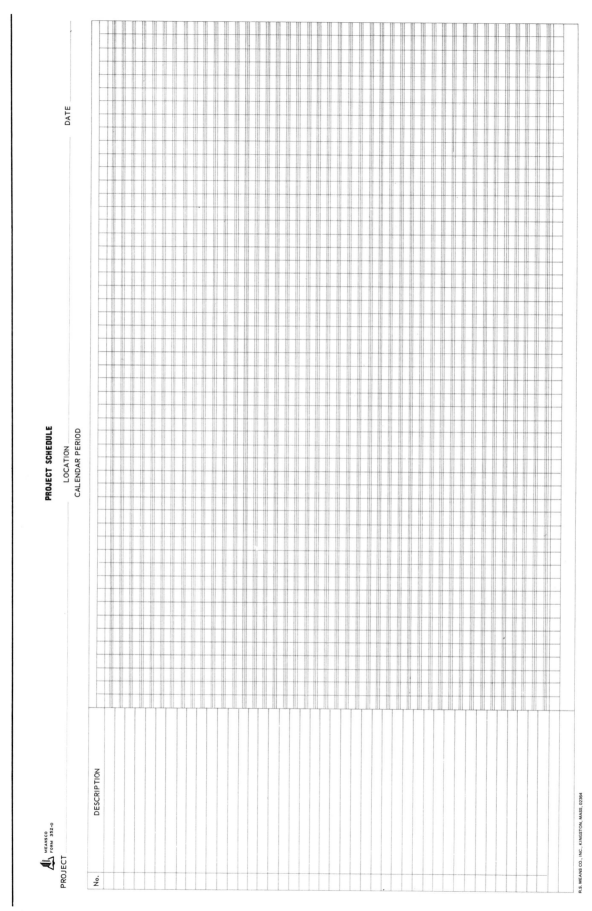

Figure 5.G1

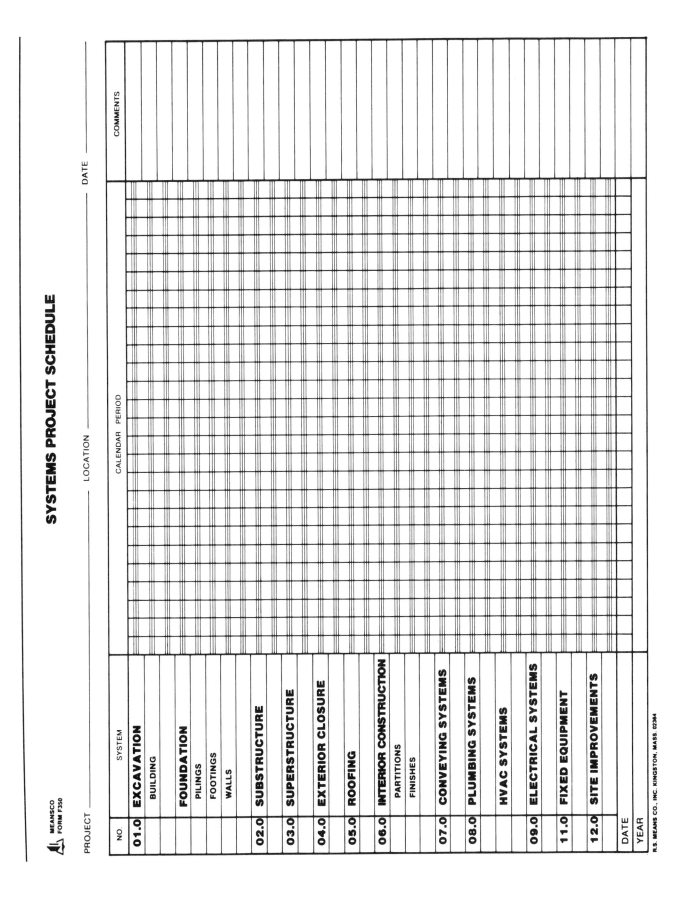

Figure 5.G2

181

Appendix H: Certificate of Insurance

Figure 5.H1 is the AIA's form for the certification of insurance coverage that the sponsor requires of the bidder, usually before construction work is permitted to proceed. A similar certification is usually required of each subcontractor by the prime contractor. As a rule, a subcontract may be cancelled if a sub fails to deliver proof of insurance coverage.

CERTIFICATE OF INSURANCE

AIA DOCUMENT G705

This certificate is issued as a matter of information only and confers no rights upon the addressee. It does not amend, extend or alter the coverage afforded by the policies listed below.

Name and Address of Insured

Covering (Project Name and Location)

Addressee:
(Owner)

COMPANIES AFFORDING COVERAGE

A	
B	
C	
D	
E	
F	

This is to certify that the following described policies, subject to their terms, conditions and exclusions, have been issued to the above named insured and are in force at this time.

SAMPLE

TYPE OF INSURANCE	CO. CODE	POLICY NUMBER	EXPIRATION DATE	LIMITS OF LIABILITY IN THOUSANDS	EACH OCCURRENCE	AGGREGATE
1. (a) Workers' Compensation				Statutory		
(b) Employer's Liability					$	Each Accident
2. Comprehensive General Liability including: □ Premises - Operations □ Independent Contractors				Bodily Injury	$	$
□ Products and Completed Operations				Property Damage	$	$
□ Broad Form Property Damage □ Contractual Liability □ Explosion and Collapse Hazard				Bodily Injury and Property Damage Combined	$	$
□ Underground Hazard □ Personal Injury with Employment Exclusion Deleted				*Applies to Products and Completed Operations Hazard		$ (Personal Injury)
3. Comprehensive Automobile Liability □ Owned				Bodily Injury (Each Person)	$	
□ Hired				Bodily Injury (Each Accident)	$	
□ Non-Owned				Property Damage	$	
				Bodily Injury and Property Damage Combined	$	
4. Excess Liability □ Umbrella Form □ Other than Umbrella				Bodily Injury and Property Damage Combined	$	$
5. Other (Specify)						

1. Products and Completed Operations coverage will be maintained for a minimum period of □ 1 □ 2 year(s) after final payment.

2. Has each of the above listed policies been endorsed to reflect the company's obligation to notify the addressee in the event of cancellation or non-renewal? □ Yes □ No

CERTIFICATION

I hereby certify that I am an authorized representative of each of the insurance companies listed above, and that the coverages afforded under the policies listed above will not be cancelled or allowed to expire unless thirty (30) days written notice has been given to the addressee of this certificate.

Name of Issuing Agency

Signature of Authorized Representative

Address

Date of Issue

AIA DOCUMENT G705 • CERTIFICATE OF INSURANCE • NOVEMBER 1978 EDITION • AIA® • © 1978
THE AMERICAN INSTITUTE OF ARCHITECTS, 1735 NEW YORK AVENUE, N.W., WASHINGTON, D.C. 20006

G705—1978

Figure 5.H1

Appendix I: Construction Cost Data

A bidder, even with the ample feedback of cost records from actual projects, often refers to cost data books for confirmation and for unusual construction items. Figure 5.I1 is a sample page from *Building Construction Cost Data*, published by R.S. Means Co., Inc.

3.1	Formwork	CREW	DAILY OUTPUT	UNIT	BARE COSTS			TOTAL INCL O&P
					MAT.	INST.	TOTAL	
25 410	6' cap diameter	C-1	10	Ea.	16.50	62	78.50	105
415	7' cap diameter	"	9		18.10	68	86.10	120
450	For second and succeeding months, deduct			▼	50%			
460								
500 ㉜	Plywood, 8" x 8" columns, 1 use	C-1	165	S.F.C.A.	1.45	3.73	5.18	6.95
505	2 use		195		.86	3.16	4.02	5.45
510 ㉝	3 use		210		.66	2.93	3.59	4.92
515	4 use		215		.56	2.86	3.42	4.72
550	12" x 12" plywood columns, 1 use		180		1.36	3.42	4.78	6.40
555	2 use		210		.79	2.93	3.72	5.05
560	3 use		220		.60	2.80	3.40	4.67
565	4 use		225		.51	2.74	3.25	4.48
600	16" x 16" plywood columns, 1 use		185		1.39	3.33	4.72	6.30
605	2 use		215		.77	2.86	3.63	4.95
610	3 use		230		.58	2.68	3.26	4.47
615	4 use		235		.48	2.62	3.10	4.28
650	24" x 24" plywood columns, 1 use		190		1.25	3.36	4.61	6.20
655	2 use		216		.69	2.85	3.54	4.84
660	3 use		230		.50	2.68	3.18	4.38
665	4 use		238		.41	2.59	3	4.15
700	36" x 36" plywood columns, 1 use		200		1.34	3.08	4.42	5.90
705	2 use		230		.77	2.68	3.45	4.68
710	3 use		245		.58	2.51	3.09	4.24
715	4 use		250		.48	2.46	2.94	4.05
750	Steel framed plywood, 4 use per mo., rent, 8" x 8"		290		.56	2.12	2.68	3.66
755	10" x 10"		300		.44	2.05	2.49	3.42
760	12" x 12"		310		.37	1.99	2.36	3.25
765	16" x 16"		335		.35	1.84	2.19	3.02
770	20" x 20"		350		.31	1.76	2.07	2.86
775	24" x 24"		365		.26	1.69	1.95	2.70
30-001	FORMS IN PLACE, CULVERT 5' to 8' square or rectangular, 1 use		170		1.43	3.62	5.05	6.75
005	2 use		180		.85	3.42	4.27	5.85
010 ㉝	3 use		190		.66	3.24	3.90	5.35
015	4 use	▼	200	▼	.56	3.08	3.64	5
35-001	FORMS IN PLACE, ELEVATED SLABS							
005	See also corrugated form deck, division 5.2-30-610							
100	Flat plate to 15' high, 1 use	C-2	470	S.F.	1.28	2.03	3.31	4.31
105	2 use		520		.75	1.83	2.58	3.45
110	3 use		545		.57	1.75	2.32	3.13
115	4 use		560		.49	1.70	2.19	2.98
150	15' to 20' high ceilings, 4 use		495		.54	1.92	2.46	3.35
160	21' to 35' high ceilings, 4 use		450		.66	2.12	2.78	3.76
200	Flat slab with drop panels, to 15' high, 1 use		449		1.61	2.12	3.73	4.81
205	2 use		509		.99	1.87	2.86	3.77
210	3 use		532		.78	1.79	2.57	3.42
215	4 use		544		.68	1.75	2.43	3.26
225	15' to 20' high ceilings, 4 use		480		.85	1.98	2.83	3.78
235	21' to 35' high ceilings, 4 use		435		1.02	2.19	3.21	4.26
300	Floor slab hung from steel beams, 1 use		485		1.26	1.96	3.22	4.20
305	2 use		535		.73	1.78	2.51	3.35
310	3 use		550		.54	1.73	2.27	3.08
315	4 use		565		.45	1.68	2.13	2.91
350 ㊱	Floor slab, with 20" metal pans, 1 use		415		2.32	2.29	4.61	5.85
355	2 use		445		1.32	2.14	3.46	4.52
360	3 use		475		.99	2	2.99	3.96
365	4 use		500		.82	1.90	2.72	3.63
370	Floor slab with 30" metal pans, 1 use		418		2.25	2.28	4.53	5.75
372	2 use		455		1.40	2.09	3.49	4.54
374	3 use		470		1.09	2.03	3.12	4.10
376	4 use	▼	480	▼	.95	1.98	2.93	3.89

For expanded coverage of these items see Means' *Concrete & Masonry Cost Data 1985*

69

Figure 5.11

185

Appendix J: Payroll Taxes and Fringe Benefits

It is convenient to estimate labor costs at the base pay level and, in one lump sum, add all taxes, fringe benefits, insurance, and so forth. The ratio changes periodically, so the bidder needs a method of adjusting the latest percentage for use in the bidding of projects. Figure 5.J1 is an example of the "payroll burden" that has been itemized, summed up, and converted into percentages applicable to the prime contractor's three main labor classifications: carpenters, masons, and laborers. The figures shown are for this example only, and are not to be used in estimating and bidding real projects. The figures change from year to year and from state to state.

Payroll Taxes, Insurances and Fringe Benefits			
	Carpenter	Mason	Laborer
Base Pay			
Basis of estimate	$19.94	$19.00	$16.60
Union Benefits			
Supplementary dues	.10	.20	.10
Health & welfare	1.11	1.25	.87
Pension	1.75	2.05	2.57
Apprentice	.07	.07	.13
Industrial advancement	.05	.05	.05
Insurances			
Worker's Compensation	2.14	1.66	1.07
S.U.I. (4.9% of base)	.98	.93	.81
F.I.C.A. (6.13% of base)	1.22	1.16	1.02
F.U.I. (0.7% of base)	.14	.13	.12
General Liability (2.0% of base)	.40	.38	.33
Gross Pay	$27.90	$26.88	$23.67
Fringe Benefit			
(% increase over payroll)	39.90%	41.50%	42.60%

Figure 5.J1

Appendix K: Labor Crew-Hour Costs

It is usually more accurate to use a crew-hour formula for estimating labor costs, rather than the pay scales of individual trades. Unit costs derived from actual field cost records are the average of crew wages. Figure 5.K1 is a sample page of crew wages from *Building Construction Cost Data*, published by R.S. Means Co., Inc. Figure 5.K2 is a convenient table, kept current, for finding at a glance the crew-hour costs of various combinations of carpenters and laborers.

CREWS

Crew No.	Bare Costs		Incl. Subs O & P		Cost Per Man-hour	
Crew C-1	Hr.	Daily	Hr.	Daily	Bare Costs	Incl. O&P
3 Carpenters	$19.60	$470.40	$28.30	$679.20	} $18.57	$26.82
1 Building Laborer	15.50	124.00	22.40	179.20		
Power Tools		21.00		23.10	} .65	.72
32 M.H., Daily Totals		$615.40		$881.50	$19.22	$27.54

Crew No.	Bare Costs		Incl. Subs O & P		Cost Per Man-hour	
Crew C-2	Hr.	Daily	Hr.	Daily	Bare Costs	Incl. O&P
1 Carpenter Foreman (out)	$21.60	$172.80	$31.20	$249.60	} $19.25	$27.80
4 Carpenters	19.60	627.20	28.30	905.60		
1 Building Laborer	15.50	124.00	22.40	179.20		
Power Tools		28.00		30.80	} .58	.64
48 M.H., Daily Totals		$952.00		$1365.20	$19.83	$28.44

Crew No.	Bare Costs		Incl. Subs O & P		Cost Per Man-hour	
Crew C-3	Hr.	Daily	Hr.	Daily	Bare Costs	Incl. O&P
1 Rodman Foreman	$23.30	$186.40	$35.80	$286.40	} $19.81	$29.89
4 Rodmen (reinf.)	21.30	681.60	32.75	1048.00		
1 Equip. Oper. (light)	19.05	152.40	27.55	220.40		
2 Building Laborers	15.50	248.00	22.40	358.40		
Stressing Equipment		31.80		35.00		
Grouting Equipment		51.90		57.05	} 1.30	1.43
64 M.H., Daily Totals		$1352.10		$2005.25	$21.11	$31.32

Crew No.	Bare Costs		Incl. Subs O & P		Cost Per Man-hour	
Crew C-4	Hr.	Daily	Hr.	Daily	Bare Costs	Incl. O&P
1 Rodman Foreman	$23.30	$186.40	$35.80	$286.40	} $21.80	$33.51
3 Rodmen (reinf.)	21.30	511.20	32.75	786.00		
Stressing Equipment		31.80		35.00	} .99	1.09
32 M.H., Daily Totals		$729.40		$1107.40	$22.79	$34.60

Crew No.	Bare Costs		Incl. Subs O & P		Cost Per Man-hour	
Crew C-5	Hr.	Daily	Hr.	Daily	Bare Costs	Incl. O&P
1 Rodman Foreman	$23.30	$186.40	$35.80	$286.40	} $20.89	$31.63
4 Rodmen (reinf.)	21.30	681.60	32.75	1048.00		
1 Equip. Oper. (crane)	20.65	165.20	29.90	239.20		
1 Equip. Oper. Oiler	17.10	136.80	24.75	198.00		
1 Hyd. Crane, 25 Ton		384.00		422.40	} 6.85	7.54
56 M.H., Daily Totals		$1554.00		$2194.00	$27.74	$39.17

Crew No.	Bare Costs		Incl. Subs O & P		Cost Per Man-hour	
Crew C-6	Hr.	Daily	Hr.	Daily	Bare Costs	Incl. O&P
1 Labor Foreman (outside)	$17.50	$140.00	$25.25	$202.00	} $16.38	$23.54
4 Building Laborers	15.50	496.00	22.40	716.80		
1 Cement Finisher	18.80	150.40	26.40	211.20		
2 Gas Engine Vibrators		53.00		58.30	} 1.10	1.21
48 M.H., Daily Totals		$839.40		$1188.30	$17.48	$24.75

Crew No.	Bare Costs		Incl. Subs O & P		Cost Per Man-hour	
Crew C-7	Hr.	Daily	Hr.	Daily	Bare Costs	Incl. O&P
1 Labor Foreman (outside)	$17.50	$140.00	$25.25	$202.00	} $16.75	$24.11
5 Building Laborers	15.50	620.00	22.40	896.00		
1 Cement Finisher	18.80	150.40	26.40	211.20		
1 Equip. Oper. (med.)	20.20	161.60	29.25	234.00		
2 Gas Engine Vibrators		53.00		58.30		
1 Concrete Bucket, 1 C.Y.		14.95		16.45		
1 Hyd. Crane, 55 Ton		526.80		579.50	9.29	10.22
64 M.H., Daily Totals		$1666.75		$2197.45	$26.04	$34.33

Crew No.	Bare Costs		Incl. Subs O & P		Cost Per Man-hour	
Crew C-8	Hr.	Daily	Hr.	Daily	Bare Costs	Incl. O&P
1 Labor Foreman (outside)	$17.50	$140.00	$25.25	$202.00	} $17.40	$24.92
3 Building Laborers	15.50	372.00	22.40	537.60		
2 Cement Finishers	18.80	300.80	26.40	422.40		
1 Equip. Oper. (med.)	20.20	161.60	29.25	234.00		
1 Concrete Pump (small)		498.00		547.80	} 8.89	9.78
56 M.H., Daily Totals		$1472.40		$1943.80	$26.29	$34.70

Crew No.	Bare Costs		Incl. Subs O & P		Cost Per Man-hour	
Crew C-9	Hr.	Daily	Hr.	Daily	Bare Costs	Incl. O&P
1 Cement Finisher	$18.80	$150.40	$26.40	$211.20	$18.80	$26.40
1 Gas Finishing Mach.		27.10		29.80	3.38	3.72
8 M.H., Daily Totals		$177.50		$241.00	$22.18	$30.12

Crew No.	Bare Costs		Incl. Subs O & P		Cost Per Man-hour	
Crew C-10	Hr.	Daily	Hr.	Daily	Bare Costs	Incl. O&P
1 Building Laborer	$15.50	$124.00	$22.40	$179.20	} $17.70	$25.06
2 Cement Finishers	18.80	300.80	26.40	422.40		
2 Gas Finishing Mach.		54.20		59.60	} 2.25	2.48
24 M.H., Daily Totals		$479.00		$661.20	$19.95	$27.54

Crew No.	Bare Costs		Incl. Subs O & P		Cost Per Man-hour	
Crew C-11	Hr.	Daily	Hr.	Daily	Bare Costs	Incl. O&P
1 Struc. Steel Foreman	$23.30	$186.40	$36.65	$293.20	} $20.98	$32.47
6 Struc. Steel Workers	21.30	1022.40	33.50	1608.00		
1 Equip. Oper. (crane)	20.65	165.20	29.90	239.20		
1 Equip. Oper. Oiler	17.10	136.80	24.75	198.00		
1 Truck Crane, 150 Ton		1022.00		1124.20	} 14.19	15.61
72 M.H., Daily Totals		$2532.80		$3462.60	$35.17	$48.08

Crew No.	Bare Costs		Incl. Subs O & P		Cost Per Man-hour	
Crew C-12	Hr.	Daily	Hr.	Daily	Bare Costs	Incl. O&P
1 Carpenter Foreman (out)	$21.60	$172.80	$31.20	$249.60	} $19.42	$28.06
3 Carpenters	19.60	470.40	28.30	679.20		
1 Building Laborer	15.50	124.00	22.40	179.20		
1 Equip. Oper. (crane)	20.65	165.20	29.90	239.20		
1 Hyd. Crane, 12 Ton		234.60		258.05	} 4.88	5.37
48 M.H., Daily Totals		$1167.00		$1605.25	$24.30	$33.43

Crew No.	Bare Costs		Incl. Subs O & P		Cost Per Man-hour	
Crew C-13	Hr.	Daily	Hr.	Daily	Bare Costs	Incl. O&P
1 Struc. Steel Worker	$21.30	$170.40	$33.50	$268.00	} $20.73	$31.76
1 Welder	21.30	170.40	33.50	268.00		
1 Carpenter	19.60	156.80	28.30	226.40		
1 Gas Welding Machine		56.40		62.05	} 2.35	2.58
24 M.H., Daily Totals		$554.00		$824.45	$23.08	$34.34

Crew No.	Bare Costs		Incl. Subs O & P		Cost Per Man-hour	
Crew C-14	Hr.	Daily	Hr.	Daily	Bare Costs	Incl. O&P
1 Carpenter Foreman	$21.60	$172.80	$31.20	$249.60	} $19.00	$27.81
5 Carpenters	19.60	784.00	28.30	1132.00		
4 Building Laborers	15.50	496.00	22.40	716.80		
4 Rodmen (reinf.)	21.30	681.60	32.75	1048.00		
2 Cement Finishers	18.80	300.80	26.40	422.40		
1 Equip. Oper. (crane	20.65	165.20	29.90	239.20		
1 Equip. Oper. Oiler	17.10	136.80	24.75	198.00		
1 Crane, 80 Ton, & Tools		836.00		919.60		
Power Tools		21.00		23.10		
2 Gas Finishing Mach.		54.20		59.60	6.32	6.96
144 M.H., Daily Totals		$3648.40		$5008.30	$25.32	$34.77

Figure 5.K1

Crew-Hour Cost for Carpenters and Laborers ($)

		Laborers (Number of)							
Carpenters (Number of)	**1**	**2**	**3**	**4**	**5**	**6**	**7**	**8**	**9**
1	36.54	53.14	69.74	86.34	102.94	119.54	136.14	152.74	169.34
2	56.48	73.08	89.68	106.28	122.88	139.48	156.08	172.68	189.28
3	76.42	93.02	109.62	126.22	142.82	159.42	176.02	192.62	209.22
4	96.36	112.96	129.56	146.16	162.76	179.36	195.96	212.56	229.16
5	116.30	132.90	149.50	166.10	182.70	199.30	215.90	232.50	249.10
6	136.24	152.84	169.44	186.04	202.64	219.24	235.84	252.44	269.04
7	156.18	172.78	189.38	205.98	222.58	239.18	255.78	272.38	288.98
8	176.12	192.72	209.32	225.92	242.52	259.12	275.72	292.32	308.92
9	196.06	212.66	229.26	245.86	262.46	279.06	295.66	312.26	328.86
10	216.00	232.60	249.20	265.80	282.40	299.00	315.60	332.20	348.80

Basis: Carpenter pay, $19.94/hr; Laborer pay, $16.60/hr.

Notes: (1) For each nonworking carpenter foreman, add $21.19 to crew wage.
(2) For each working carpenter foreman, add $1.25 to crew wage.
(3) For each nonworking labor foreman, add $17.35 to crew wage.
(4) For each working labor foreman, add 75¢ to crew wage.

Example: Four carpenters and five laborers $162.76
Plus one working carpenter foreman + 1.25
(**Total**) $164.01/hr.

Figure 5.K2

188

Appendix L: Typical Labor Production and Unit Costs

A record of average labor costs for the type of work items the bidder's own company undertakes repeatedly is valuable for a rapid review of estimates. Estimated unit prices, or direct quotations of unit prices from subs, that fall above or below the range limitations in the bidder's records are not necessarily incorrect or unjustified, but may need inspection and verification. Figure 5.L1 contains examples of such average values. A list such as this may provide the bidder a quick reference check for the cost range of items of borderline familiarity.

Typical Labor Production and Unit Costs					
	Unit Cost		One Man* Hourly Production		
Layout footings	.11 —	.16	122.00 —	184.00	lf
" slabs	.027—	.033	604.00 —	738.00	sf
" walks	.045—	.055	362.00 —	443.00	sf
" curbs	.077—	.10	199.00 —	259.00	lf
Cleanup structures	.12 —	.17	98.00 —	138.00	sf
" site work	.05 —	.07	237.00 —	332.00	sf
Demo concrete slabs 4"	.18 —	.24	69.00 —	92.00	sf
" mass concrete	32.00 —	48.00	.35 —	.52	cy
Place gravel fill 4"	11.00 —	15.00	1.10 —	1.50	cy
Excavate, hand	24.00 —	34.00	.48 —	.70	cy
Fine grade for slabs	.06 —	.08	208.00 —	277.00	sf
Backfill trenches	6.40 —	9.20	1.80 —	2.60	cy
Form footings w/sides	2.16 —	2.88	6.90 —	9.23	sf
" slab edges 4"	1.53 —	2.04	9.80 —	13.00	lf
" foundation walls	2.97 —	3.63	5.20 —	6.40	sf
" walls to 8' high	2.47 —	3.00	6.3 —	7.7	sf
" columns	3.40 —	4.60	4.00 —	5.6	sf
" suspended slabs 6"	2.25 —	2.88	6.60 —	8.50	sf
" beams	3.57 —	4.83	3.90 —	5.30	sf
" stairs	5.85 —	7.48	2.5 —	3.30	sf
Concrete placing	5.00 —	7.00	2.60 —	3.60	cy
" point/patch	.125—	.17	106.00 —	144.00	sf
" set screeds	.065—	.12	158.00 —	292.00	sf
" finish, trowel	.22 —	.28	64.00 —	82.00	sf
" rub & grind	.26 —	.66	27.00 —	69.00	sf
Carpentry, stud walls	273.00 —	370.00	.05 —	.07	Mbf
" floor framing	321.00 —	435.00	.045—	.06	Mbf
" roof framing	304.00 —	412.00	.04 —	.065	Mbf
" ceiling framing	335.00 —	453.00	.042—	.057	Mbf
" Plywood sheathing	.24 —	.34	56.00 —	79.00	sf
Hang doors	20.00 —	40.00	1.00 —	2.00	ea.

*Crew production converted to average per man.

Figure 5.L1

Appendix M: Equipment Production and Rental Rates

Figure 5.M1 is a sample list of equipment types, rental rates, and average productions which, when kept current, serves as a reference for reviewing estimates. Figure 5.M2 is a sample page from *Building Construction Cost Data*, published by R.S. Means Co., Inc., showing representative equipment types, productions, and unit prices.

Description		Capacity	Un-Operated	Operated	* Production
Dragline		½ cy		$52	30 cy/hr
		¾ cy		65	40 cy/hr
		1 cy		70	45 cy/hr
		1-½ cy		100	75 cy/hr
		2 cy		145	115 cy/hr
Grader, small		hp		53	1500 sf/hr
medium		hp		64	2000 sf/hr
large		hp		70	3000 sf/hr
Scraper, self prop.		10 cy		82	120 cy/hr
		12 cy		110	144 cy/hr
		14 cy		130	168 cy/hr
		24 cy		190	288 cy/hr
Dozer		65 hp		52	40 cy/hr
	(D-3)	105 hp		60	60 cy/hr
	(D-4)	140 hp		70	80 cy/hr
	(D-5)	180 hp		80	100 cy/hr
	(D-8)	270 hp		117	160 cy/hr
		385 hp		143	200 cy/hr
	(D-9)	400 hp		160	250 cy/hr
Hydro crane		15 ton		100	15 ton
		18 ton		103	18 ton
		25 ton		106	25 ton
		30 ton		112	30 ton
		45 ton		120	45 ton
		65 ton		145	65 ton
		75 ton		170	75 ton
Sheepfoot compactor		4' x 4'	$ 10		
Loader, small		½ cy		45	20 cy/hr
medium		1 cy		58	50 cy/hr
large		2 cy		70	100 cy/hr
Compactor, small hand oper.			7		
medium walk behind			10		
large ride on			15	40	
Trencher, 6" x 24" deep			20	40	20 cy/hr
8" x 30" deep			30	52	50 cy/hr
84" deep			45	72	100 cy/hr
Forklift, small			18	45	
medium			23	50	
large			28	55	
Generator, small		2.5 kw	4		
medium		5.0 kw	7		
large		10.0 kw	9		

Figure 5.M1

Description	Capacity	Un-Operated	Operated	* Production
Welding equip, oxy-acetyl		$ 7		
arcwelder		9		
Trucks, Tool truck w/winch			$11	
Flat bed	to 2 ton		9	
Heavy duty	pickup		8	
Dump,	8 cy-2 axle		40	8 cy/ld
	10 cy-3 axle		55	10 cy/ld
	15 cy-5 axle (end)		60	15 cy/ld
	20 cy-5 axle (bottom)		65	20 cy/ld
Stake	16 ft		63	
Water	2 axle		43	1000 gal
	3 axle		52	2500 gal
	6000 gal tanker		60	6000 gal
	8000 gal tanker		65	8000 gal
Tractor	2 axle		45	
	3 axle		50	
Trailers,	40' flatbed	7		
	double bottom	9		
Air compressor	100 cfm	9		
w/hose,	150 cfm	10		
	250 cfm	15		
	600 cfm	25		
	750 cfm	30		
	1000 cfm	37		
Backhoe,	Under ½ cy		52	20 cy/hr
	½ cy		59	30 cy/hr
	⅝ cy		63	40 cy/hr
	¾ cy		65	45 cy/hr
	1 cy		70	60 cy/hr
	1-¼ cy		80	75 cy/hr
	1-½ cy		95	90 cy/hr
	2 cy		125	130 cy/hr
Gradall, G-660	⅝		95	60 cy/hr
G-680	1 cy		110	100 cy/hr
G-1000	1-½ cy		125	150 cy/hr
Clamshell,	½ cy		60	35 cy/hr
	¾ cy		70	45 cy/hr
	1 cy		78	50 cy/hr
	1-½ cy		110	80 cy/hr
	2 cy		150	120 cy/hr

* These production rates are given only for a reference base, and they represent average soil and other conditions.

Figure 5.M1 (cont.)

2.3	Earthwork	CREW	DAILY OUTPUT	UNIT	BARE COSTS			TOTAL INCL O&P
					MAT.	INST.	TOTAL	
070	9" deep	B-14	7,200	S.F.	.18	.13	.31	.38
080	12" deep	"	6,000	"	.24	.16	.40	.48
100	Alternate pricing method, 3" deep		90	C.Y.	6.50	10.45	16.95	22
110	6" deep		160		6.50	5.90	12.40	15.30
120	9" deep		200		6.50	4.70	11.20	13.70
130	12" deep		220		6.50	4.28	10.78	13.10
150	For fill under exterior paving, see division 2.6-07							

2

		CREW	DAILY OUTPUT	UNIT	BARE COSTS			
					EQUIP.	LABOR	TOTAL	
22-001	**GRADING** Site excav. & fill, not incl. mobilization, demobilization or							
002	compaction. Includes 1/4 push dozer per scraper.							
010	Dozer 300 ft. haul, 75 H.P. = 20 C.Y./hr.	B-10L	160	C.Y.	1.24	1.40	2.64	3.39
020	300 H.P., 70 C.Y./hr.	B-10M	560		1.60	.40	2.00	2.34
040	Scraper, towed, 7 C.Y. 300' haul, 55 C.Y./hr.	B-33A	440		2.76	.60	3.36	3.90
050	1000' haul, 25 C.Y./hr.	"	200		6.05	1.32	7.37	8.60
070	10 C.Y. 300' haul, 85 C.Y./hr.	B-33B	680		1.83	.39	2.22	2.57
080	1000' haul, 50 C.Y./hr.	"	400		3.11	.66	3.77	4.37
100	Self-propelled scraper, 15 C.Y., 1000' haul, 95 C.Y./hr.	B-33D	760		1.56	.35	1.91	2.22
110	2000' haul, 70 C.Y./hr.	"	560		2.12	.47	2.59	3.02
130	25 C.Y. 1000' haul, 200 C.Y./hr.	B-33E	1,600		.84	.17	1.01	1.16
140	2000' haul, 160 C.Y./hr.	"	1,280		1.05	.21	1.26	1.45
160	For dozer with ripper, 200 H.P., add, minimum	B-11A	1,980		.31	.14	.45	.55
170	Add, maximum	"	990		.62	.29	.91	1.10
180	300 H.P., add, minimum	B-10M	3,670		.24	.06	.30	.36
190	Add, maximum	"	1,840		.49	.12	.61	.71
210	Fine grade, 3 passes with motor grader	B-11L	1,600	S.Y.	.26	.18	.44	.55
220	With grader plus rolling	B-32	1,600		.37	.20	.57	.70
240	Hand grading, finish	1 Clab	75			1.65	1.65	2.39L
250	Rough		130			.95	.95	1.38L
252	Alternate pricing method, finish		675	S.F.		.18	.18	.27L
254	Rough		1,200	"		.10	.10	.15L

		CREW	DAILY OUTPUT	UNIT	BARE COSTS			
					MAT.	INST.	TOTAL	
25-001	**GROUTING, CHEMICAL** Soil stabilization, phenolic resin,							
002	medium gradation stone, minimum	B-61	10.50	C.Y.	105	88	193	235
010	Average		5.90		130	155	285	355
020	Maximum		3		140	310	450	570
28-001	**GROUTING, PRESSURE** Cement and sand, 1:1 mix, minimum		124	Bag	6	7.50	13.50	16.70
010	Maximum		51	"	6.85	18.20	25.05	32
020	Cement and sand, 1:1 mix, minimum		120	C.F.	4	7.75	11.75	14.85
030	Maximum		51		4.75	18.20	22.95	30
040	Cement grout, minimum (1 bag = 1 C.F.)		137		5.30	6.80	12.10	14.95
050	Maximum		57		5.90	16.30	22.20	28
070	Alternate pricing method: (Add for materials)							
071	5 man crew and equipment	B-61	1	Day		930	930	1,250

		CREW	DAILY OUTPUT	UNIT	BARE COSTS			
					EQUIP.	LABOR	TOTAL	
30-001	**HAULING** Earth 6 C.Y. dump truck 1/4 mile round trip, 5.0 loads/hr.	B-34A	240	C.Y.	.92	.54	1.46	1.78
003	1/2 mile round trip, 4.1 loads/hr.		197		1.12	.66	1.78	2.17
004	1 mile round trip, 3.3 loads/hr.		160		1.37	.81	2.18	2.67
010	2 mile round trip, 2.6 loads/hr.		125		1.76	1.04	2.80	3.42
015	3 mile round trip, 2.1 loads/hr.		100		2.20	1.30	3.50	4.27
020	4 mile round trip, 1.8 loads/hr.		85		2.59	1.52	4.11	5.05
030	⑯							
031	12 C.Y. dump truck, 1/4 mile round trip, 3.7 loads/hr	B-34B	356		.78	.36	1.14	1.38
032	1/2 mile round trip, 3.2 loads/hr.		308		.91	.42	1.33	1.60
033	1 mile round trip, 2.7 loads/hr.		260		1.07	.50	1.57	1.90
040	2 mile round trip, 2.2 loads/hr.		210		1.33	.62	1.95	2.35
045	3 mile round trip, 1.9 loads/hr.		180		1.55	.72	2.27	2.74

For expanded coverage of these items see *Means' Site Work Cost Data 1985*

37

Figure 5.M2

192

Appendix N: Typical Material Prices

The bidder may find it convenient to keep a current list of average costs of the most commonly used materials. Figure 5.N1 is an example of such a list. For greater variety and for particular localities in the United States, the reader is referred to *Building Construction Cost Data*, published by R.S. Means Co., Inc. Typical pages of this book are shown in Figs. 5.N2 and 5.N3.

Piping

PVC Class 150	4"	....	3.30/lf
	6"	....	5.00/lf
Copper 'K'	1"	....	3.00/lf
	1½"	....	3.70/lf
	2"	....	6.00/lf
'L'	1"	....	2.50/lf
	1½"	....	3.30/lf
	2"	....	5.50/lf

Plastic Sheeting, Polyethylene

.004"	....	.017/sf
.006"	....	.025/sf
.008"	....	.033/sf
.010"	....	.037/sf

Plywood & Paneling

Plywood DF CDX	¼"	....	275.00/Msf
	⅜"	....	297.00/Msf
	½"	....	396.00/Msf
	⅝"	....	440.00/Msf
	¾"	....	550.00/Msf
Plyform	⅝"	....	480.00/Msf
	¾"	....	590.00/Msf
ACX	½"	....	520.00/Msf
Particle board	½"	....	.32/sf
	⅝"	....	.42/sf
	¾"	....	.49/sf
Simulated hardwood	¼"	....	.37/sf
Real wood veneer	¼"	....	.65/sf
Hardboard, medium	¼"	....	.25/sf

Roofing

90# roll mineral surface	....	.14/sf
15# asphalt saturated felt	....	.045/sf
Corrugated fiberglass	....	.26/sf
Asphalt shingles 235#	....	.33/sf
Cedar shakes (medium)	....	.88/sf

Sheet Metal

Gutter GI	....	.32/lf
Downspout	....	.44/lf
Gutter els for downspouts	....	1.50/ea
corners	....	1.30/ea
drop inlets	....	1.70/ea
straps	....	.75/ea
Struc. steel sheet 20 gallons	....	1.32/sf
Alum. sheet .063" thick	....	1.20/sf
Alum. corr. roofing .032" thick	....	.15/sf

Figure 5.N1

Steel

Structural shapes	.41/lb
Reinforcing steel bars	.27/lb

Doors

SC good quality entrance door	80.00/ea
SC flush hardwood veneer, 3'-0" x 6'-8" x 1¾" thick	50.00/ea
Fir paint grade 3'-0" x 6'-8" x 1¾" thick	43.00/ea
HC flush Fir paint grade 3'-0" x 6'-8" x ⅜" thick	36.00/ea
HC flush hardboard 3'-0" x 6'-8" x ⅜" thick	30.00/ea

Fencing

Western Red Cedar, rough sawn	500.00/Mbf
split rail — post and rails complete	1.50/lf
rough Redwood, posts, rails & boards	700.00/Mbf

Fiberboard

½"	.12/sf

Gypsum board

½"	.14/sf
⅝"	.18/sf

Insulation

Mineralwool, loose, 40# bag	6.00/bag
Mineralwool, batts 3" thick	.14/sf
Fiberglass, foil faced R-19	.32/sf
R-11	.22/sf

Lumber

Douglas Fir Construction/Standard 2 x 2	396.00/Mbf
2 x 3	374.00/Mbf
2 x 4	363.00/Mbf
2 x 6	352.00/Mbf
2 x 8	370.00/Mbf
2 x 10	396.00/Mbf
2 x 12	400.00/Mbf
Redwood All-heart S4S	979.00/Mbf
Common rough sawn	495.00/Mbf
Common S4S	539.00/Mbf
Pine or clear DF KD	825.00/Mbf

Nails

Common or box, bright	.40/lb
Galvanized	.47/lb

Paint

Latex enamel, interior, semi-gloss	8.80/gal
flat	7.70/gal
Vinyl latex house paint	13.20/gal
Vinyl wood stain	5.50/pt
Acrylic stain	4.40/pt
Olympic stain	13.50/gal
Epoxy rust-stopping primer	19.80/gal
Water seal, Thompson	11.50/gal

Figure 5.N1 (cont.)

Piping
Subdrainage-

asb. cement perf.	4″	. . . .	1.70/lf
	6″	. . . .	2.75/lf
asb. cement unperf.	4″	. . . .	1.00/lf
	6″	. . . .	1.90/lf
porous concrete	4″	. . . .	1.35/lf
	6″	. . . .	1.85/lf
vit. clay perforated	4″	. . . .	1.60/lf
	6″	. . . .	2.55/lf
plastic, solid or perf.	3″	. . . .	.52/lf
	4″	. . . .	.75/lf

Figure 5.N1 (cont.)

㊷ Concrete Material Net Prices (Div. 3.3) p. 78 to 80

Costs below are C.Y. of concrete delivered; per ton of bulk cement; per bag cement delivered T.L.L.; per ton for stone and sand aggregates loaded at plant (no trucking included) and per 4 C.F. bag for perlite or vermiculite aggregate delivered T.L.L.

City	Ready Mix Concrete Regular Weight		Cement T.L. lots		Aggregates per ton			Vermiculite or Perlite 4 C.F. Bag
			Bulk	Bags	Crushed Stone		Sand	
	3000 psi	5000 psi	per Ton	per Bag	1-1/2"	3/4"		
Atlanta	$39.50	$45.65	$60.50	$4.70	$6.90	$6.95	$6.80	$4.60
Baltimore	47.40	52.95	59.00	4.65	5.50	5.60	5.20	4.55
Boston	45.20	50.65	60.00	4.60	6.25	6.25	5.75	4.50
Buffalo	48.50	54.35	63.50	4.75	5.75	6.00	5.00	5.20
Chicago	46.20	51.75	61.00	4.70	5.50	5.80	5.50	4.50
Cincinnati	42.25	47.90	60.00	4.90	5.25	5.40	5.25	5.20
Cleveland	43.20	49.00	62.50	4.95	7.20	7.50	7.00	4.80
Columbus	46.50	52.80	68.50	5.20	5.80	6.00	5.20	5.10
Dallas	47.50	53.25	63.00	4.80	7.10	7.35	6.40	4.50
Denver	52.30	59.65	78.00	5.55	6.70	6.95	6.10	4.65
Detroit	45.25	50.70	59.50	4.75	5.60	5.80	5.00	4.90
Houston	47.20	51.30	61.50	4.80	8.20	8.50	7.20	4.50
Indianapolis	46.50	52.40	62.50	4.95	6.50	6.90	6.00	5.20
Kansas City	45.20	50.20	68.00	5.25	7.25	7.30	6.25	5.10
Los Angeles	45.00	51.60	72.00	5.35	6.90	7.20	6.30	6.50
Memphis	45.20	50.80	59.50	4.95	6.30	6.50	5.50	5.25
Milwaukee	45.40	51.15	65.00	4.85	6.10	6.50	5.30	5.40
Minneapolis	46.20	52.95	72.00	5.50	7.55	7.60	6.50	5.75
Nashville	45.20	50.65	58.00	4.75	7.00	7.30	6.20	5.20
New Orleans	47.50	53.05	61.00	4.80	8.10	8.30	7.10	5.30
New York City	62.50	68.25	61.50	5.00	9.00	9.20	8.20	4.70
Philadelphia	42.00	47.20	59.00	4.60	8.20	8.40	8.30	4.50
Phoenix	44.20	51.25	76.00	5.75	6.50	7.00	6.00	5.10
Pittsburgh	45.60	51.45	62.00	4.75	9.20	9.40	8.50	4.80
St. Louis	42.10	47.20	55.50	4.50	7.60	8.00	6.50	5.00
San Antonio	43.20	48.85	60.00	4.60	6.90	7.40	5.50	4.70
San Diego	45.50	52.25	72.00	5.50	8.90	9.20	8.20	4.80
San Francisco	47.20	54.15	76.50	5.70	9.25	9.50	9.10	4.65
Seattle	46.50	53.90	79.50	6.00	8.10	8.50	8.00	5.75
Washington, D.C.	48.50	54.25	61.00	4.90	9.40	9.70	8.65	5.30
Average	$46.15	$52.05	$64.60	$5.00	$7.15	$7.40	$6.55	$5.00

㊸ Ready Mix Material Prices (Div. 3.3) p. 80

Table below lists national average prices per C.Y. of concrete. Prices in the key cities for different strengths can be closely estimated by factoring against the 3000 psi or 5000 psi price from ㊷ above or from Div. 19, City Cost Indexes, cast-in-place concrete material factor.

Strength in psi	Design Mix Nominal Mix	Bags per C.Y.	Heavy Weight Regular	High Early	Light Weight 110# per C.F.	All Light Weight	Admixtures and Special Items Add to Each C.Y. of Concrete for the Following Items:	
2,000	1:3:5	4.5	$43.00	$46.60	$56.00	$66.00	Calcium chloride, 1%	$1.00 per C.Y.
2,500	1:2½:4½	5	44.60	48.60	57.60	67.60	" " 2%	2.00 per C.Y.
3,000	1:2:4	5.5	46.15	50.55	59.15	69.15	Lampblack	2.60 per lb.
3,500	1:2:3½	6	47.70	52.50	60.70	70.70	Water reducing agent	.25 per bag
3,750	1:2:3¼	6.3	48.60	53.65	62.00	72.00	Set retarder	.25
4,000	1:2:3	6.5	49.25	54.45	62.65	72.65	High early cement	.80
4,500	1:2:2½	7	51.10	56.70	64.50	74.50	White cement	8.75
5,000	1:1½:2½	7.5	52.05	58.05	65.40	75.40	Pump aid	1.50 per C.Y.
	1:1:2	8	53.55	59.95		Perlite 1:6= $63.00	Winter concrete	2.50 per C.Y.
	1:4 topping	7.5	52.10	58.10				
	1:3 topping	8.5	55.15	61.95				
	1:2 topping	11	62.80	71.60				

373

Figure 5.N2

196

CIRCLE REFERENCE NUMBERS

⑧⑥ Thirty City Lumber Prices (Jan. 1st, 1985) (Div. 6.1) p. 123 to 129

Prices for boards are for #2 or better or sterling, whichever is in best supply. Dimension lumber is "Standard or Better" either Southern Yellow Pine (S.Y.P.), Spruce-Pine-Fir (S.P.F.), Hem-Fir (H.F.) or Douglas Fir (D.F.). The species of lumber used in a geographic area is listed by city. Rough Sawn lumber is Douglas Fir, Hem-Fir, or a variety of hardwood, sheathing or lagging grade. Plyform is 3/4" BB oil sealed fir or S.Y.P. whichever

prevails locally, 5/8" CDX is S.Y.P. or Fir.

For 10 MBF lots add 5%; for retail add 10% to prices.

These are prices at the time of publication and should be checked against the current market price. Relative differences between cities will stay approximately constant.

City	Species	Carload Lots per M.B.F.								Carload Lots per M.S.F.	
		S4S					Rough Sawn Lumber				
		Dimensions			Boards		3"x12"	6"x12"	12"x12"	3/4 Ext. Plyform	5/8" Thick CDX
		2"x4"	2"x6"	2"x10"	1"x6"	1"x12"					
Atlanta	S.Y.P.	$290	$305	$350	$745	$870	$430	$460	$460	$625	$345
Baltimore	S.P.F.	295	315	345	725	925	390	415	420	650	510
Boston	S.P.F.	290	305	340	745	950	460	495	490	700	450
Buffalo	S.P.F.	330	350	380	750	955	450	485	480	690	450
Chicago	S.P.F.	345	365	395	750	930	440	475	470	690	425
Cincinnati	S.Y.P.	320	335	380	750	895	440	480	480	650	345
Cleveland	S.P.F.	300	320	345	735	935	455	490	490	700	450
Columbus	S.P.F.	315	335	360	730	920	450	490	480	700	440
Dallas	S.Y.P.	330	350	390	795	920	450	480	475	625	330
Denver	H.F.	310	300	320	720	915	465	495	495	740	440
Detroit	S.P.F.	295	315	350	730	920	470	500	495	700	445
Houston	S.Y.P.	330	350	390	790	925	455	485	475	620	330
Indianapolis	S.P.F.	310	330	360	750	950	455	480	475	700	440
Kansas City	D.F.	375	365	415	720	910	455	495	490	750	425
Los Angeles	D.F.	330	320	375	700	870	435	465	465	700	400
Memphis	S.Y.P.	320	340	380	740	870	460	490	490	625	350
Milwaukee	S.P.F.	285	305	335	730	910	445	470	470	695	440
Minneapolis	S.P.F.	280	300	330	735	930	430	470	460	680	430
Nashville	S.Y.P.	330	350	390	745	880	470	500	495	630	360
New Orleans	S.Y.P.	300	315	360	760	890	440	475	470	630	330
New York City	H.F.	340	325	350	670	950	490	525	520	710	445
Philadelphia	H.F.	325	310	340	750	925	410	450	460	700	445
Phoenix	S.Y.P.	350	370	410	795	925	470	500	495	650	340
Pittsburgh	S.P.F.	300	320	350	745	920	490	525	525	705	440
St. Louis	S.Y.P.	330	350	390	745	880	430	450	460	750	350
San Antonio	S.Y.P.	340	360	400	780	960	460	490	495	630	330
San Diego	D.F.	325	315	365	700	880	455	480	480	705	400
San Francisco	D.F.	320	310	360	680	870	430	470	470	690	405
Seattle	D.F.	285	275	325	655	840	415	450	450	675	380
Washington, D.C.	H.F.	320	305	330	730	930	375	415	415	655	440
Average		$315	$325	$365	$735	$910	$445	$480	$475	$680	$405

To convert square feet of surface to board feet, 4% waste included

S4S Size	Multiply S.F. by	T & G size	Multiply S.F. by	Flooring Size	Multiply S.F. by
1 x 4	1.18	1 x 4	1.27	25/32" x 2-1/4"	1.37
1 x 6	1.13	1 x 6	1.18	25/32" x 3-1/4"	1.29
1 x 8	1.11	1 x 8	1.14	15/32" x 1-1/2"	1.54
1 x 10	1.09	2 x 6	2.36	1" x 3"	1.28
				1" x 4"	1.24

6

399

Figure 5.N3

Appendix O: Labor Cost Function

With all the unit cost references data available, the bidder still must make adjustments based on judgment of the unique conditions that exist in a project. Figure 5.O1 illustrates a kind of formula and function leading to unit pricing decisions. Various cost increasing factors are added algebraically to various cost decreasing factors, and the net amount raises or lowers the average unit cost. Note that on the cost decreasing side, all factors are generally positive. On the cost increasing side, the factors are generally negative. Quality is an exception, acting inversely.

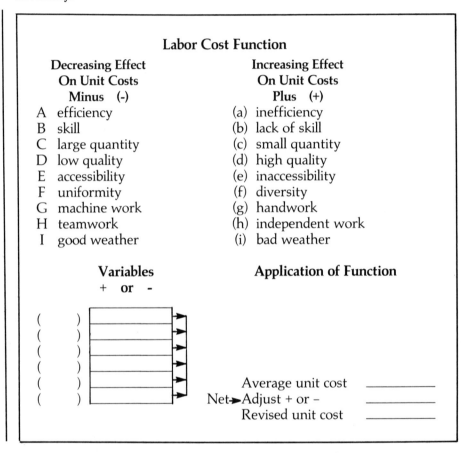

Figure 5.O1

Appendix P: Jobsite Analysis Sheet

In the text, Fig. 2.11a is an example of a jobsite analysis check sheet. Figures 5.P1 and 5.P2 are the two sides of a more detailed form available from R.S. Means Co., Inc. Although the bidder should investigate all sites personally, it is possible that, with a form such as this and a camera, another person may make preliminary investigations.

JOB SITE ANALYSIS

Date _____

Project | Bid Date

Location		Nearest Town
Architect	Engineer	Owner
Access, Highway	Surface	Capacity
Railroad Siding	Freight Station	Bus Station
Airport	Motels/Hotels	Hospital
Post Office	Communications	Police
Distance & Travel Time to Site		Dock Facilities

Water Source	Amount Available	Quality
Distance from Site	Pipe/Pump Req'd?	Tanks Req'd?
Owner	Price (MG)	Treatment necessary?
Natural Water Availability		Amount

Power Availability	Location	Transformer
Distance	Amount Available	
Voltage Phase	Cycle	KWH or HP Rate

Temporary Roads	Length & Widths
Bridges/Culverts	Number & Size
Drainage Problems	
Clearing Problems	
Grading Problems	
Fill Availability	Distance
Mobilization Time	Cost
Maintenance Method	Cost
Camps or Housing	Size of Work Force
Sewage Treatment	
Material Storage Area	Office & Shed Area

Labor Source	Union Affiliation
Common Labor Supply	Skilled Labor Supply
Local Wage Rates	Fringe Benefits
Travel Time	Per Diem

Taxes, Sales	Facilities	Equipment
Hauling	Transportation	Property
Other		

Material Availability: Aggregates		Cement
Ready Mix Concrete		
Reinforcing Steel	Structural Steel	
Brick & Block	Lumber & Plywood	
Building Supplies	Equipment Repair & Parts	

Demolition: Type		Number
Size		Equip. Req'd.
Dump Site	Distance	Dump Fees
Permits		

R.S. MEANS CO., INC. KINGSTON, MASS. 02364

Figure 5.P1

Clearing: Area   Timber   Diameter   Species

Brush Area   Burn on Site   Disposal Area

Saleable Timber   Useable Timber   Haul

Equipment Required

Weather: Mean Temperatures

Highs   Lows

Working Season Duration   Bad Weather Allowance

Winter Construction

Average Rainfall   Wet Season   Dry Season

Stream or Tide Conditions

Flood Potential

Job Drainage Considerations

Haul Road Problems

Long Range Weather

Soils: Job Borings Adequate?   Test Pits

Additional Borings Needed   Location   Extent

Visible Rock

U.S. Soil & Agriculture Maps

Bureau of Mines Geological Data

County/State Agriculture Agent

Tests Required

Ground Water

Construction Plant Required

Alternate Method

Equipment Available

Rental Equipment   Location

Miscellaneous: Contractor Interest

Sub Contractor Interest

Material Fabricator Availability

Possible Job Delays

Political Situation

Construction Money Availability

Unusual Conditions

Summary

Figure 5.P2

Appendix Q: Subcontract Forms

In the text, Figs. 4.4a and 4.4b show the face sheets of the AIA's *Standard Form Subcontract*. The reverse sides of those sheets contain itemized subcontract provisions important to both the prime and subcontractors. The reverse sides are shown in Figs. 5.Q1 and 5.Q2 of this appendix. This subcontract form is shown only as an example. Many contractors have their own custom-designed forms that contain their preferred selections and priorities for general provisions.

GENERAL SUBCONTRACT PROVISIONS

A. INSURANCE – SUBCONTRACTOR shall at all times carry on all operations hereunder. Workers' Compensation Insurance covering all of its employees, Public Liability and Property Damage Insurance and Automotive Public Liability and Property Damage Insurance, including liability coverage for (a) all operations, (b) subcontract work, (c) contractual obligations, (d) product or completed operations, (e) all owned vehicles, (f) non-owned vehicles, in forms, amounts and underwritten by insurance companies satisfactory to CONTRACTOR. Before SUBCONTRACTOR performs any work at, or prepares or delivers materials to, the site of construction, SUBCONTRACTOR shall furnish certificates of insurance evidencing the foregoing insurance coverages and such certificates shall provide that the insurance is in force and will not be cancelled without ten days written notice to CONTRACTOR. SUBCONTRACTOR shall maintain all of the foregoing insurance coverages in force until the work under this Agreement is fully completed. The requirement for carrying the foregoing insurance shall not derogate from the provisions for indemnification of CONTRACTOR by SUBCONTRACTOR under paragraph B of this Agreement.

B. GENERAL INDEMNITY – All work covered by this Agreement done at the site of construction or in preparing or delivering materials or equipment, or any or all of them, to the site shall be at the risk of SUBCONTRACTOR exclusively. SUBCONTRACTOR shall, with respect to all work which is covered by or incidental to this subcontract, indemnify and hold CONTRACTOR harmless from and against all of the following:

1. Any claim, liability, loss, damage, cost, expenses, including reasonable attorneys' fees, awards, fines or judgments arising by reason of the death or bodily injury to persons, injury to property, design defects (if design originated by SUBCONTRACTOR), or other loss, damage or expense, including any of the same resulting from CONTRACTOR'S alleged or actual negligent act or omission, regardless of whether such act or omission is active or passive; and

2. Any and all claims, liability, loss, damage, costs, including reasonable attorneys' fees, awards, fines or judgments arising by reason of any obligation or indemnity which CONTRACTOR has to OWNER.

It is expressly acknowledged and agreed that each of the foregoing indemnities is independent, and that both shall be given effect. However, SUBCONTRACTOR shall not be obligated under this Agreement to indemnify CONTRACTOR with respect to the sole negligence or willful misconduct of CONTRACTOR, his agents or servants or subcontractors who are directly responsible to CONTRACTOR, excluding SUBCONTRACTOR herein.

C. BONDING OF SUBCONTRACTOR – Concurrently with the execution of this Agreement, or at any time during its performance, SUBCONTRACTOR shall, if required by CONTRACTOR, execute a Labor and Material Bond and Faithful Performance Bond, in an amount equal to 100% of the Contract Price in Section 3. Said bonds shall be executed by a corporate surety acceptable to CONTRACTOR and shall be in a form satisfactory to CONTRACTOR. CONTRACTOR shall pay the premium on said bonds unless otherwise provided herein or in the Contract Documents.

D. TIME – Time is the essence of this Agreement. It shall be SUBCONTRACTOR'S obligation to conform to CONTRACTOR'S progress schedule, subject to CONTRACTOR'S modification, which is incorporated herein by this reference and made a part hereof. SUBCONTRACTOR shall prepare and obtain approval as required by the Contract Documents for all shop drawings, details, samples, and do all other things necessary and incidental to the prosecution of his work in conformance with the said progress schedule. He shall coordinate the work covered by this Agreement with that of all other contractors, subcontractors, and of the CONTRACTOR in a manner that will facilitate the efficient completion of the entire work. CONTRACTOR shall have complete control of the premises on which the work is to be performed and shall have the right to decide the time or order in which the various portions of the work shall be installed or the priority of the work of other subcontractors, and, in general, all matters representing the timely and orderly conduct of the work of SUBCONTRACTOR on the premises.

Should SUBCONTRACTOR be delayed in the prosecution or completion of the work by the act, neglect or default of OWNER, of ARCHITECT, or of CONTRACTOR, or should SUBCONTRACTOR be delayed waiting for materials, if required by this CONTRACT to be furnished by OWNER or CONTRACTOR, or by damage caused by fire or other casualty for which SUBCONTRACTOR is not responsible, or by the combined action of the workmen, in no wise caused by, or resulting from default or collusion on the part of SUBCONTRACTOR, or in the event of a lockout by CONTRACTOR, then the time herein fixed for the completion of the work shall be extended the number of days that SUBCONTRACTOR has thus been delayed, but no allowance or extension shall be made unless a claim therefor is presented in writing to the CONTRACTOR within 48 hours of the commencement of such delay, and under no circumstances shall the time of completion be extended to a date which will prevent CONTRACTOR from completing the entire project within the time that OWNER allows CONTRACTOR for such completion.

No claims for additional compensation or damages for delays, whether in the furnishing of material by CONTRACTOR, or delays by other subcontractors or OWNER, will be allowed by the CONTRACTOR, and said extension of time for the completion shall be the sole remedy of SUBCONTRACTOR; provided, however, that in the event, and in such event only, that CONTRACTOR obtains additional compensation from OWNER on account of such delays, SUBCONTRACTOR shall be entitled to such portion of the additional compensation so received by CONTRACTOR from OWNER as is equitable under all of the circumstances. Nothing herein contained shall require CONTRACTOR to make any claim against OWNER for such delays, and it is specifically agreed that the failure of CONTRACTOR to prosecute any such claim against OWNER shall not entitle SUBCONTRACTOR to any claim for damages against CONTRACTOR.

E. CHANGES IN THE WORK – SUBCONTRACTOR hereby agrees to make any and all changes, furnish the materials and perform the work that CONTRACTOR may require, without nullifying this Agreement, at a reasonable addition to, or reduction from, the Contract Price stated herein, and pro rata to the same. SUBCONTRACTOR shall adhere strictly to the plans and specifications unless a change therefrom is authorized in writing. Under no conditions shall SUBCONTRACTOR make any changes, either as additions or deductions, without the written order of the CONTRACTOR and CONTRACTOR shall not pay any extra charges made by the SUBCONTRACTOR that have not been agreed upon in writing by CONTRACTOR; and, in no event, shall CONTRACTOR make payment for any such extra charges unless and until the CONTRACTOR itself receives payment from OWNER. SUBCONTRACTOR shall submit immediately to the CONTRACTOR written copies of his firm's cost or credit proposal for changes in the work. Disputed work shall be performed as ordered in writing by the CONTRACTOR and the proper cost or credit breakdowns therefor shall be submitted without delay by SUBCONTRACTOR to CONTRACTOR.

SUBCONTRACTOR shall give notice of claim relating to any work for which extra compensation is asserted within 30 days after such work is performed or SUBCONTRACTOR shall be deemed to have abandoned any claim therefor.

If the SUBCONTRACTOR initiates a substitution, deviation or change in the work which affects the scope of the work or the expense of other trades, SUBCONTRACTOR shall be liable for the expense thereof.

No change, alteration or modification in or deviations from this Agreement or the plans or specifications, whether made in the manner herein provided or not, shall release or exonerate, in whole or in part any surety on any bond given in connection with this Agreement and neither OWNER nor CONTRACTOR shall be under any obligation to notify the surety or sureties of any such change.

F. DAMAGES CAUSED BY DELAYS – Should SUBCONTRACTOR default in the proper performance of his work, thereby causing delay to the prime contract work, he shall be liable for any and all loss and damages, including liquidated damages sustained by CONTRACTOR as a result thereof. SUBCONTRACTOR shall not be liable under this paragraph if such default be caused by strikes, lockouts, acts of God or other reasons beyond the control of SUBCONTRACTOR, concerning which, however, notice of occurrence of same shall be given in writing immediately by SUBCONTRACTOR to CONTRACTOR.

G. LIENS – SUBCONTRACTOR shall at all times indemnify and save CONTRACTOR and OWNER harmless against all liability for claims and liens for labor performed or materials used or furnished to be used on the job, including any costs and expenses for attorneys' fees and all incidental or consequential damages resulting to CONTRACTOR or OWNER from such claims or liens. Further, in case suit on such claim is brought, SUBCONTRACTOR shall defend said suit at his own cost and expense, and will pay and satisfy any such lien or judgment as may be established by the decision of the court in said suit. SUBCONTRACTOR agrees within ten (10) days after written demand to cause the effect of any suit or lien to be removed from the premises, and in the event SUBCONTRACTOR shall fail so to do, CONTRACTOR is authorized to use whatever means in its discretion it may deem appropriate to cause said lien or suit to be removed or dismissed and the cost thereof, together with reasonable attorney's fees, shall be immediately due and payable to CONTRACTOR by SUBCONTRACTOR. SUBCONTRACTOR may litigate any such lien or suit provided he causes the effect thereof to be removed, promptly in advance, from the premises, and shall further do such things as may be necessary to cause OWNER not to withhold any monies due to CONTRACTOR from OWNER by reason of such liens or suits.

It is understood and agreed that the full and faithful performance of this Agreement on the part of SUBCONTRACTOR (including the payment of any obligations due from SUBCONTRACTOR to CONTRACTOR, and any amounts due to labor or materialmen furnishing labor or material for said work) is a condition precedent to SUBCONTRACTOR'S right to receive payment for the work performed, and any monies paid by CONTRACTOR to SUBCONTRACTOR under the terms of this Agreement shall be impressed with a trust in favor of labor and materialmen furnishing labor and material to SUBCONTRACTOR on the work herein subcontracted.

H. RECOURSE BY CONTRACTOR – In the event that SUBCONTRACTOR at any time refuses or neglects to supply a sufficient number of properly skilled workmen or a sufficient quantity of materials of proper quality, or be adjudicated a bankrupt, or files an arrangement proceeding, or commits any act of insolvency, or makes an assignment for benefit of creditors without CONTRACTOR'S consent, or fails to make prompt payment to his materialmen and laborers, or fails in any respect to properly and diligently prosecute the work covered by this Agreement, or becomes delinquent with respect to contributions or payments required to be made to any Health and Welfare, Pension, Vacation, Apprenticeship or other employee benefit program or trust, or fails to fulfill any of the provisions of Paragraph J of these General Subcontract Provisions by him to be performed, or otherwise fails to perform fully any and all of the agreements herein contained, CONTRACTOR may, at his option: (1) after giving forty-eight (48) hours written notice to SUBCONTRACTOR, provide any such labor and materials as may be necessary and deduct the cost thereof from any money then due or thereafter to become due to the SUBCONTRACTOR under this Agreement; or (2) terminate SUBCONTRACTOR'S right to proceed with the work and, in that event, CONTRACTOR shall have the right to enter upon the premises of the project and take possession, for the purpose of completing the work included under this Agreement, of all materials, tools, and appliances of SUBCONTRACTOR, and may employ any other person or persons to finish the work and provide the materials therefor. In case of such termination of SUBCONTRACTOR'S right to proceed with the work, said SUBCONTRACTOR shall not be entitled to receive any further payment under this Agreement until the work undertaken by CONTRACTOR in his prime contract is completely finished. At that time, if the unpaid balance of the amount to be paid under this Agreement exceeds the expenses incurred by CONTRACTOR in finishing SUBCONTRACTOR'S work, such excess shall be paid by CONTRACTOR to SUBCONTRACTOR; but, if such expense shall exceed such unpaid balance, then SUBCONTRACTOR shall promptly pay to CONTRACTOR the amount by which such expense exceeds such unpaid balance. The expense referred to in the last sentence shall include expenses incurred by CONTRACTOR for furnishing materials, for finishing the work, for attorneys' fees, and any damages sustained by CONTRACTOR by reason of SUBCONTRACTOR'S default, plus a markup of 15% General Overhead and 10% Profit on any and all of such expenses; and CONTRACTOR shall have a lien upon all materials, tools and appliances taken possession of, as aforesaid, to secure the payment thereof. The notice referred to in this paragraph will be sufficient and complete when mailed to SUBCONTRACTOR at his address shown in this Agreement.

CONTRACTOR may withhold, or on account of subsequently discovered evidence, nullify the whole or a part of any payment under SECTION 4 to such extent as may be necessary to protect CONTRACTOR from loss, including costs and attorney's fees, on account of (1) defective work not remedied; (2) claims filed or reasonable evidence indicating probable filing of claim; (3) failure of SUBCONTRACTOR to make payments properly to his subcontractors or for material, labor, or for fringe benefits; (4) a reasonable doubt that this Agreement can be completed for the balance then unpaid; (5) damage to another subcontractor.

When the above grounds are removed, such amounts as are then due and owing shall be paid or credited to SUBCONTRACTOR.

I. TERMINATION OF AGREEMENT – In the event the prime contract is terminated prior to its completion, SUBCONTRACTOR shall be entitled only to payment for the work actually completed by it at the pro rata of the price herein set forth unless CONTRACTOR itself receives additional compensation or damages on account of such termination; in which event, SUBCONTRACTOR shall be entitled to such proportion of the additional compensation or damages actually received as is equitable under all of the circumstances. Nothing herein contained shall require CONTRACTOR to make any claim against OWNER for such additional compensation or damages in the event of termination before completion, and it is specifically agreed that the failure of CONTRACTOR to prosecute any such claim against OWNER shall not entitle SUBCONTRACTOR to any claim for additional compensation or damages against CONTRACTOR.

Notwithstanding the preceding paragraph, CONTRACTOR reserves the absolute right to terminate this Agreement. In the event of termination without cause, SUBCONTRACTOR shall be entitled to payment only as follows:

1. Cost of the work actually completed in conformity with this Agreement; plus
2. Other costs actually incurred by SUBCONTRACTOR; plus
3. 15% of costs referred to in Paragraph 1 above, for overhead and profit.

There shall be deducted from such sums as provided in this paragraph the amount of any payments made to SUBCONTRACTOR prior to the date of termination of this Agreement. SUBCONTRACTOR shall not be entitled to any claim, or claim of lien, against CONTRACTOR or against OWNER for any additional compensation or damages in the event of such termination and payment.

In the event this Agreement is terminated for cause, SUBCONTRACTOR shall not be entitled to receive any further payment until the work undertaken by CONTRACTOR in his prime contract is completely finished. At that time, if the amounts earned but not paid SUBCONTRACTOR before said termination exceed the expenses incurred by CONTRACTOR in finishing SUBCONTRACTOR'S work, any excess shall be paid by CONTRACTOR TO SUBCONTRACTOR; but, if such expense shall exceed the said amount earned and unpaid, SUBCONTRACTOR shall promply pay to CONTRACTOR the amount by which the expense exceeds said sum. The expense incurred by CONTRACTOR, as just referred to, shall include CONTRACTOR'S expense for furnishing materials, for finishing the work, for attorney's fees, and any damages incurred by CONTRACTOR by reason of SUBCONTRACTOR'S default.

CONTRACTOR may terminate this Agreement in the event that SUBCONTRACTOR, or any of his subcontractors, is listed by the Administrative Office of the various Employee Fringe Benefit Trusts, including, but not limited to, Health and Welfare, Pension, Vacation, or Apprenticeship Trusts, as being delinquent in payment or payments to any such trust, regardless of the project in connection with which the delinquency or delinquencies occurred. With respect to any and all payments to be made by CONTRACTOR to said SUBCONTRACTOR under this Agreement, CONTRACTOR at his option may issue joint checks payable to SUBCONTRACTOR and any of the Employee Fringe Benefit Trusts referred to herein to the extent necessary to assure that payments required from SUBCONTRACTOR or any of his subcontractors with respect to work performed under this Agreement are paid.

Figure 5.Q1

GENERAL SUBCONTRACT PROVISIONS

J. LABOR RELATIONS – Employment of labor by SUBCONTRACTOR shall be effected under conditions which are satisfactory to CONTRACTOR. SUBCONTRACTOR shall keep a representative at the job site during all times when SUBCONTRACTOR'S work is in progress, and such representative shall be authorized to represent SUBCONTRACTOR as to all phases of the work. Prior to commencement of the work, SUBCONTRACTOR shall notify CONTRACTOR who SUBCONTRACTOR'S representative is to be, and in the event of any change of representative SUBCONTRACTOR shall notify CONTRACTOR who the new representative is to be prior to such change becoming effective.

SUBCONTRACTOR acknowledges that CONTRACTOR has entered into labor agreements covering work at his construction job sites with the following labor unions:

____

____

SUBCONTRACTOR agrees to comply with all of the terms and conditions of those labor agreements including trust fund payments into the respective trust funds set forth in the respective labor agreements, referred to above insofar as SUBCONTRACTOR may lawfully do so, and in particular agrees to comply with the terms and provisions of said agreements setting forth the jurisdiction and the scope of work claimed by each of such crafts and the procedure contained therein for resolution of jurisdictional disputes. In the absence of any such procedure, or if such procedure fails to promptly resolve the jurisdictional dispute, SUBCONTRACTOR agrees, at his own cost and expense, upon request of CONTRACTOR, to take any and all lawful steps to secure a binding and final determination of said jurisdictional dispute by the National Labor Relations Board.

Should there be picketing on the CONTRACTOR'S job site, and the CONTRACTOR establishes a reserved gate for the SUBCONTRACTOR'S purposes, it shall be the obligation of the SUBCONTRACTOR to continue the proper performance of his work without interruption or delay.

SUBCONTRACTOR further promises and agrees that he will bind and require all of his subcontractors and their subcontractors performing job site work of the type covered by any of the labor agreements specified above to agree to all of the foregoing promises and undertakings, to the same effect as herein provided with respect to him.

SUBCONTRACTOR will indemnify and hold harmless CONTRACTOR from and against any liability, loss, damage, cost, claims, awards, judgments, fines, expenses, including litigation expenses, reasonable attorneys' fees and any other costs which may be incurred by the CONTRACTOR resulting from SUBCONTRACTOR'S failure to fulfill the covenant set forth in this paragraph.

(If the project is located in the eleven Southern Counties, excepting San Diego County, the provisions of Rider No. 1 attached hereto shall be a part of this Agreement.)

K. LAYOUT RESPONSIBILITY – CONTRACTOR shall establish principal axis lines and levels whereupon SUBCONTRACTOR shall lay out and shall be strictly responsible for the accuracy of his work, for the coordination of his work with others, and for any loss or damage to other contractors engaged in work on the site by reason of failure of SUBCONTRACTOR to set out or perform his work correctly or to coordinate his work with the work of others. SUBCONTRACTOR shall exercise prudence in laying out and performing the subcontract work so that the actual final conditions and details shall result in perfect alignment of finished surfaces.

L. WORKMANSHIP – Every part of the work herein described shall be executed in strict accordance with the Contract Documents in the most sound, workmanlike, and substantial manner. All workmanship shall be of the best of its several kinds, and all materials used in the work herein described shall be furnished in ample quantities to facilitate the proper and expeditious execution of the work, and shall be new and the best of their respective kinds, except such materials as may be expressly provided in the Contract Documents to be otherwise.

M. PROVISIONS FOR INSPECTION – SUBCONTRACTOR shall at all times furnish to CONTRACTOR and its representatives safe and ample facilities for inspecting materials at the site of construction, shops, factories or any place of business of SUBCONTRACTOR and its subcontractors and materialmen where materials under this Agreement may be in course of preparation, process, manufacture or treatment. SUBCONTRACTOR shall furnish to CONTRACTOR as often as required by CONTRACTOR, full reports of the progress of the work at any place where materials under this Agreement may be in the course of preparation or manufacture. Such reports shall show the progress of such preparation and manufacture in such details as may be required by CONTRACTOR, including, but not limited to, any plans, drawings or diagrams in the course of preparation.

N. MATERIALS AND WORK FURNISHED BY OTHERS – In the event the scope of work includes installation of materials or equipment furnished by others or work to be performed in areas to be constructed or prepared by others, it shall be the responsibility of SUBCONTRACTOR to examine and accept, at the time of delivery or first access, the items or areas so provided and thereupon handle, store and install the items or so protect such areas with such skill and care as to insure a satisfactory completion of the work. Use of such items or commencement of work by SUBCONTRACTOR in such areas shall be deemed to constitute acceptance thereof by SUBCONTRACTOR. Loss or damage due to acts of SUBCONTRACTOR shall be charged to the account of SUBCONTRACTOR and deducted from monies otherwise due under this Agreement.

O. PROTECTION OF WORK – SUBCONTRACTOR shall effectually secure and protect the work done hereunder and assume full responsibility for the condition thereof until final acceptance by ARCHITECT, OWNER and CONTRACTOR. SUBCONTRACTOR further agrees to provide such protection as is necessary to protect the work and the workmen of the CONTRACTOR, OWNER and other subcontractors from his operations.

SUBCONTRACTOR shall be liable for any loss or damage to any work in place or to any equipment and materials on the job site caused by him or his agents, employees or guests.

P. USE OF CONTRACTOR'S EQUIPMENT – In the event SUBCONTRACTOR shall use CONTRACTOR'S equipment, materials, labor, supplies or facilities SUBCONTRACTOR shall reimburse CONTRACTOR at a predetermined rate, unless otherwise stated herein. Further, SUBCONTRACTOR assumes all responsibility for, and shall hold CONTRACTOR harmless from any claims, actions, demands, damages, liabilities, or expenses, including attorneys' fees, resulting from the use of such equipment, materials, labor, supplies, or facilities by SUBCONTRACTOR or his agents, employees, or permittees. In the event that CONTRACTOR'S employees are used by SUBCONTRACTOR, SUBCONTRACTOR shall have full responsibility for all acts or omissions of CONTRACTOR'S employees with regard to such operation. SUBCONTRACTOR accepts any and all of CONTRACTOR'S equipment, materials, labor, supplies, or facilities as furnished.

Q. CLEAN-UP – At all times during the course of construction, SUBCONTRACTOR shall perform his work so as to maintain the site in a clean, safe and orderly condition. Upon completion of the work under this Agreement, SUBCONTRACTOR shall remove from the site all temporary structures, debris and waste incident to his operation and clean all surfaces, fixtures, equipment, etc. relative to the performance of this Agreement. CONTRACTOR may order SUBCONTRACTOR to clean up his areas at any time CONTRACTOR deems such action necessary. If SUBCONTRACTOR fails to perform a clean-up function within two days after notification from CONTRACTOR to do so, CONTRACTOR may proceed with that function as he judges necessary and in the manner he may deem expedient, and the cost thereof shall be charged to SUBCONTRACTOR and deducted from monies due under this Agreement. In the event CONTRACTOR is unable to determine which SUBCONTRACTOR is responsible for the clean-up of any debris, etc., CONTRACTOR may apportion the cost of such clean-up in such manner as he may determine to be equitable.

R. GUARANTEE – SUBCONTRACTOR guarantees all materials and workmanship and agrees to replace at his sole cost and expense, and to the satisfaction of CONTRACTOR, any and all materials adjudged defective or improperly installed as well as guarantee the OWNER and CONTRACTOR against liability, loss or damage arising from said installation during a period of one year from completion and acceptance of the work covered by the prime contract. If, however the period of guarantee is stipulated in excess of one year by the Contract Documents, SUBCONTRACTOR shall be bound during the longer period stipulated.

S. INDEMNIFICATION FROM PATENT RIGHTS -- SUBCONTRACTOR shall indemnify and hold CONTRACTOR harmless against any claim, suit or action, or any alleged violation or infringement of patent rights which may be made against CONTRACTOR by reason of the use in connection with or as a part of the performance of the work or the furnishing of the materials hereunder of anything which is now or may hereafter be covered by patent, copyright or trademark, and also against all expense, including attorneys' fees, which CONTRACTOR may incur in defending or adjusting any such claim, suit or action.

T. ASSIGNMENT OF CONTRACT – SUBCONTRACTOR shall not, without written consent of CONTRACTOR, assign, transfer, nor sublet any portion or part of the work required by this Agreement nor assign any payments hereunder to others. CONTRACTOR may assign or transfer the whole or part of this Agreement, and his rights hereunder to any corporation, individual, or partnership.

U. INDEPENDENT CONTRACTOR – SUBCONTRACTOR is an independent contractor and shall, at his sole cost and expense, and without increase in the Contract Price, comply with all laws, rules, ordinances, and regulations of all governing bodies having jurisdiction over the work; obtain all necessary permits and licenses therefor; pay all manufacturers' taxes, sales taxes, use taxes, processing taxes, and all federal and state taxes, insurance and contributions for Social Security and Unemployment which are measured by wages, salaries, or other remunerations paid to SUBCONTRACTOR'S employees, whether levied under existing or subsequently enacted laws, rules, or regulations. SUBCONTRACTOR, upon request, shall furnish evidence satisfactory to CONTRACTOR that any or all of the foregoing obligations have been fulfilled.

V. EXCUSE – Any act or omission of CONTRACTOR which SUBCONTRACTOR might claim as an excuse for his own failure to perform shall be deemed waived by SUBCONTRACTOR unless he shall notify CONTRACTOR of his intention to assert such excuse within ten days after the occurrence of any such act or omission. SUBCONTRACTOR waives any right it might have to assert the provisions of California Civil Code Section 1654 against CONTRACTOR.

W. ATTORNEYS' FEES – In the event either CONTRACTOR or SUBCONTRACTOR institutes suit in court against the other party, or against the surety of such party, in connection with any dispute or matter arising under this Agreement, the party which prevails in that suit shall be entitled to recover from the other its attorneys fees in reasonable amount, which shall be determined by the court and included in the judgment in said suit.

X. DISPUTE RESOLUTION - ARBITRATION –

(a) CONTRACTOR and SUBCONTRACTOR shall not be obligated to resolve disputes arising under this Subcontract by arbitration, unless (i) the prime contract has an arbitration provisions; and (ii) a particular dispute between CONTRACTOR and SUBCONTRACTOR involves issues of fact or law which the CONTRACTOR is required to arbitrate under the terms of the prime contract. In the event that arbitration is required under the terms of this provision, the same arbitrator(s) utilized to resolve the dispute between the OWNER and CONTRACTOR shall be utilized to resolve the dispute under this provision.

(b) In the event that the CONTRACTOR and OWNER or others arbitrate matters relating to this Subcontract, the SUBCONTRACTOR shall be required, at the request of the CONTRACTOR, to prepare and present the CONTRACTOR'S case, at SUBCONTRACTOR'S expense, to the extent the proceedings relate to this Subcontract.

(c) Should the CONTRACTOR enter into arbitration with the OWNER or others with regard to issues relating to this Agreement, the SUBCONTRACTOR shall be bound by the result of the arbitration to the same degree as the CONTRACTOR.

Y. SAFETY AND EQUAL EMPLOYMENT OPPORTUNITY VIOLATIONS - SUBCONTRACTOR'S INDEMNITY – SUBCONTRACTOR shall, at its expense, conform to the basic safety policy of the CONTRACTOR, and comply with all specific safety requirements promulgated by any governmental authority, including, without limitation, Safety Act of 1969, the California Labor Code, including Sections 6300 through 6604, and 7100 through 7332, inclusive, and all successors and amendments thereto, and all standards and regulations which have been or shall be promulgated by the parties or agencies which administer said Acts.

SUBCONTRACTOR shall, at his own expense, conform to the equal employment opportunity policies of the CONTRACTOR, and, in addition, shall comply with all equal employment opportunity requirements promulgated by any governmental authority, including, without limitation, the requirements of the Civil Rights Act of 1964, 42 United States Code, Section 1983, Executive Orders 11246, 11375 and 11478, the California Fair Employment Practices Act, the California Plan, any other applicable statute or ordinences, plans or programs, inclusive, and all successors and amendments thereto, and all plans, programs, standards and regulations which have been or shall be promulgated or approved by the parties or agencies which administer said Acts or Orders (hereinafter collectively referred to as EEO laws).

SUBCONTRACTOR shall have and exercise full responsibility for compliance hereunder by itself, its agents, employees, materialmen, and subcontractors with respect to its portion of the work on this Project; and shall directly receive, respond to, defend and be responsible for any citation, assessment, fine or penalty by reason of SUBCONTRACTOR'S failure or failure of SUBCONTRACTOR'S agents, employees, materialmen and subcontractors to so comply. SUBCONTRACTOR shall indemnify and hold harmless CONTRACTOR from and against any liability, loss, damage, cost, claims, awards, judgments, fines, expenses, including litigation expenses, reasonable attorneys' fees, claims or liability for harm to persons or property, expenses incurred pursuant to or attendant to any hearing or meeting and any other applicable cost which may be incurred by CONTRACTOR resulting from SUBCONTRACTOR'S failure to fulfill the covenants set forth in this paragraph.

In the event SUBCONTRACTOR fails to eomply: (1) with any citation issued by the Secretary of Labor, any order issued by the Occupational Safety and Health Review Commission or any order issued by the Division of Industrial Safety of the State of California or of any other body responsible for the administration and/or enforcement of any statute, regulation or ordinance relating to occupational health and safety within the period specified in any such citation or order; (2) with any of the aforementioned EEO laws, or any judgment, order or award issued by the Office of Federal Contract Compliance, United States Department of Labor, or any other federal, state or local agency or any court of law, or any other body responsible for the administration and/or enforcement of any EEO laws, within the period specified in any such laws, judgment, order or award, CONTRACTOR may, in his discretion, exercise the rights and remedies provided him under the terms of this SUBCONTRACT, including but not limited to, the rights and remedies provided in Paragraph H, Recourse by Contractor.

Figure 5.Q2

Appendix R: Parameter Cost System

Before estimates are available, an approximate total project cost may be "guesstimated" roughly by comparing the projection to completed projects of similar type and physical dimensions. Figure 5.R1 is a sample page from the square foot and cubic foot section of *Building Construction Cost Data*, published by R.S. Means Co., Inc., showing the parameter pricing method.

17.1 S.F., C.F. and % of Total Costs	UNIT	UNIT COSTS			% OF TOTAL		
		1/4	MEDIAN	3/4	1/4	MEDIAN	3/4
48 900 Per rental unit, total cost	Unit	38,800	45,500	50,200			
950 Total: Mechanical & Electrical	"	7,680	9,630	11,300			
50-001 HOUSING Public (low-rise)	S.F.	33.10	45.15	62.30			
002 Total project costs	C.F.	2.77	3.62	4.54			
010 Sitework	S.F.	4.78	6.45	10.30	9%	11.70%	16.40%
180 Equipment		.95	1.69	2.54	2.20%	3.20%	4.20%
272 Plumbing		2.41	3.24	4.26	7.10%	9.50%	11.60%
273 Heating, ventilating, air conditioning		1.10	2.27	2.64	4.20%	5.10%	6.40%
290 Electrical		2.11	3.04	4.27	5%	6.50%	8.20%
310 Total: Mechanical & Electrical	↓	5.95	8.90	12.15	15.70%	19.20%	22.20%
900 Per apartment, total cost	Apt.	36,760	41,420	51,540			
950 Total: Mechanical & Electrical	"	6,110	8,470	10,520			
51-001 ICE SKATING RINKS	S.F.	31.10	43.45	71.30			
002 Total project costs	C.F.	1.80	2.25	2.65			
272 Plumbing	S.F.	.94	1.38	2.12	3.10%	3.20%	4.60%
290 Electrical		2.45	3.24	4.46	5.70%	7%	10.10%
310 Total: Mechanical & Electrical	↓	4.45	6.30	9.50	12.40%	16.40%	25.90%
52-001 JAILS	S.F.	101	113	128			
002 Total project costs	C.F.	7.40	9.25	11.60			
180 Equipment	S.F.	3.86	10.15	17	3.80%	8.90%	14.80%
272 Plumbing		5.85	10.10	12.10	7%	8.90%	12%
277 Heating, ventilating, air conditioning		5.85	8.35	13.65	6.30%	8%	10.40%
290 Electrical		8.55	11.35	13.45	7.80%	9.80%	12.40%
310 Total: Mechanical & Electrical	↓	22.10	31.75	40.60	22.20%	28.80%	35.30%
53-001 LIBRARIES	S.F.	55.95	68.90	87.10			
002 Total project costs	C.F.	3.93	4.70	5.90			
050 Masonry	S.F.	3.13	5.60	9.35	4%	6.70%	9%
114 Roofing		2.03	2.55	3.65	1.90%	3.30%	3.50%
158 Painting		1.07	1.52	1.88	.90%	1.90%	2.10%
180 Equipment		.68	1.73	3.41	1.40%	2.70%	4.80%
272 Plumbing		2.33	3.20	4.29	3.60%	4.50%	5.80%
277 Heating, ventilating, air conditioning		5.70	8.05	10.50	8.70%	11%	13.20%
290 Electrical		5.80	7.05	9.25	8.40%	10.90%	12.10%
310 Total: Mechanical & Electrical		12.10	16.95	24	19.40%	24.50%	29.60%
55-001 MEDICAL CLINICS	↓	54.20	66.65	82.50			
002 Total project costs	C.F.	4.02	5.25	7			
180 Equipment	S.F.	1.43	2.80	4.59	1.90%	4.30%	6.80%
272 Plumbing		3.74	5.15	7.10	6.10%	8.40%	10.20%
277 Heating, ventilating, air conditioning		4.55	5.90	8.55	6.70%	9%	11.70%
290 Electrical		5.10	6.55	8.60	8.10%	10%	12%
310 Total: Mechanical & Electrical	↓	11.85	15.10	21.05	19%	24.20%	30.10%
350 See also division 11.1-37							
57-001 MEDICAL OFFICES	S.F.	50.85	62.85	75.75			
002 Total project costs	C.F.	3.85	5.10	6.75			
180 Equipment	S.F.	1.73	3.37	4.73	3.40%	5.90%	7.10%
272 Plumbing		3.15	4.59	6.26	5.70%	7%	9.40%
277 Heating, ventilating, air conditioning		3.61	5.40	6.85	6.50%	8%	10.40%
290 Electrical		4.34	6.15	8.05	7.90%	9.80%	11.80%
310 Total: Mechanical & Electrical	↓	9.85	14	18.60	17.20%	22.80%	27.70%
59-001 MOTELS	S.F.	46.85	48.70	71.80			
002 Total project costs	C.F.	2.87	5.40	6.60			
272 Plumbing	S.F.	2.17	3.93	6.70	3.80%	8.90%	12.60%
277 Heating, ventilating, air conditioning		1.71	2.94	3.13	4.10%	6.20%	8.20%
290 Electrical		2.56	4.63	6.95	4.70%	9.50%	10.90%
310 Total: Mechanical & Electrical	↓	8.15	13.70	16	17.30%	27.70%	33.30%
900 Per rental unit, total cost	Unit	13,170	22,120	31,480			
950 Total: Mechanical & Electrical	"	3,655	4,900	5,380			

17

332

For expanded coverage of these items see *Means' Square Foot Costs 1985*

Figure 5.R1

Appendix S: Miscellaneous Forms

Figure 5.S1 is a convenient form letter of transmittal for any project documents or materials. Figure 5.S2 is a general-purpose estimating sheet for making cost studies, such as for change orders and alternative systems of construction. Section 2.15 of the text presented a check list for general conditions cost items and an example of a price out. Figures 5.S3 and 5.S4 of the appendix are the two sides of a form that serves the dual purpose of check list and price out.

LETTER OF TRANSMITTAL

MEANSCO
FORM 200

FROM:

DATE
PROJECT
LOCATION
ATTENTION
RE:

TO:

GENTLEMEN:

WE ARE SENDING YOU ☐ HEREWITH ☐ DELIVERED BY HAND ☐ UNDER SEPARATE COVER

VIA_____THE FOLLOWING ITEMS:

☐ PLANS ☐ PRINTS ☐ SHOP DRAWINGS ☐ SAMPLES ☐ SPECIFICATIONS

☐ ESTIMATES ☐ COPY OF LETTER ☐ _____

COPIES	DATE OR NO.	DESCRIPTION

THESE ARE TRANSMITTED AS INDICATED BELOW

☐ FOR YOUR USE ☐ APPROVED AS NOTED ☐ RETURN ____CORRECTED PRINTS

☐ FOR APPROVAL ☐ APPROVED FOR CONSTRUCTION ☐ SUBMIT ____COPIES FOR ____

☐ AS REQUESTED ☐ RETURNED FOR CORRECTIONS ☐ RESUBMIT____COPIES FOR ____

☐ FOR REVIEW AND COMMENT ☐ RETURNED AFTER LOAN TO US ☐ FOR BIDS DUE ____

☐ _____

REMARKS:

IF ENCLOSURES ARE NOT AS INDICATED,
PLEASE NOTIFY US AT ONCE.

SIGNED: _____

R.S. MEANS CO., INC. KINGSTON, MA 02364

Figure 5.S1

COST ANALYSIS

MEANSCO
FORM 150-L

PROJECT									SHEET NO.				
LOCATION									ESTIMATE NO.				
ARCHITECT			OWNER						DATE				
QUANTITIES BY		PRICES BY			EXTENSIONS BY			CHECKED BY					

DESCRIPTION	QUANTITY	UNIT	MATERIAL		LABOR		TOTAL COST	
			UNIT	TOTAL	UNIT	TOTAL	UNIT	TOTAL

R.S. MEANS CO., INC. KINGSTON, MASS. 02364

Figure 5.S2

PROJECT OVERHEAD SUMMARY

MEANSCO FORM 112

PROJECT						SHEET NO.		
LOCATION						ESTIMATE NO.		
ARCHITECT			OWNER			DATE		
QUANTITIES BY		PRICES BY		EXTENSIONS BY		CHECKED BY		

DESCRIPTION	QUANTITY	UNIT	MATERIAL		LABOR		TOTAL COST	
			UNIT	TOTAL	UNIT	TOTAL	UNIT	TOTAL
Job Organization: Superintendent								
Accounting and bookkeeping								
Timekeeper and material clerk								
Clerical								
Shop								
Safety, watchman and first aid								
Engineering: Layout								
Quantities								
Inspection								
Shop drawings								
Drafting & extra prints								
Testing: Soil								
Materials								
Structural								
Supplies: Office								
Shop								
Utilities: Light and power								
Water								
Heating								
Equipment: Rental								
Light trucks								
Freight and hauling								
Loading, unloading, erecting, etc.								
Maintenance								
Travel Expense								
Main office personnel								
Freight and Express								
Demurrage								
Hauling, misc.								
Advertising								
Signs and Barricades								
Temporary fences								
Temporary stairs, ladders & floors								
Photos								
Page total								

R.S. MEANS CO., INC. KINGSTON, MASS. 02364

Figure 5.S3

DESCRIPTION	QUANTITY	UNIT	MATERIAL		LABOR		TOTAL COST	
			UNIT	TOTAL	UNIT	TOTAL	UNIT	TOTAL
Total Brought Forward								
Legal								
Medical and Hospitalization								
Field Offices								
Office furniture and equipment								
Telephones								
Heat and Light								
Temporary toilets								
Storage areas and sheds								
Permits: Building								
Misc.								
Insurance								
Bonds								
Interest								
Taxes								
Cutting and Patching & Punch list								
Winter Protection								
Temporary heat								
Snow plowing								
Thawing materials								
Temporary Roads								
Repairs to adjacent property								
Pumping								
Scaffolding								
Small Tools								
Clean up								
Contingencies								
Main Office Expense								
Special Items								
Total: Transfer to Meansco Form 110 or 115								

Figure 5.S4

Appendix T: Bidding Room Arrangement

Most bidding room arrangements are improvised; they are not originally designed by bidders. As a rule, bidders adapt themselves to the facilities offered them. In this section an efficient arrangement is described. Figure 5.T1 illustrates a functional layout designed for a small team who make bidding a full time profession. These are the main features.

1. The spread sheet (see Sec. 2.12, The Bid Spread Sheet), which is the hub of activity, is on a standing-height island table that has free access to three sides. No stools interfere with traffic. Only the spread sheet, a calculator, and a phone reserved for out-going calls are on the bid table.
2. The fourth side of the table is available only to the bid receivers. They are seated at semi-insulated phone booths and, because of their proximity can receive, record on a special form (see Appendix E), and place bids on the bid table without standing or walking. They can thus easily communicate with the bidder and all other members of the team.
3. A separate standing-height table within arm's reach of the bid table supports the drawings and specs for the necessary continuous reference.
4. A separate table with file slots, or pigeon holes, provides immediate organization of the sub-bids, segregated by trades for quick reference and comparison.

The bidding team makeup is not greatly altered by the size (in dollars) of the project. The number of people depends on the complexity of the project and on the alternative bid items, the number of trades, the volume of sub-bids to analyze, and the quantity of computations to be made. Two examples are given in Fig. 5.T2 to show reason for differing personnel requirements.

Figure 5.T1

	Example 1	Example 2
Type of construction	Warehouse	Science lab
Size of project	4,000,000	7,000,000
Number of sub trades	15	40
Complexity of detail	simple	complex
Number of bid items	1	6
Team makeup (min. number of people)	4	7

Figure 5.T3 is an action diagram of the procedure used in bidding a typical complex project requiring a seven-person team. Using the sub-bid quotation form (Appendix E), the bid receivers at position I write down the phoned-in sub-bids and place them in baskets within reach of the bidder, position II, who analyzes, compares, and records them on the spread sheet. The bidder then eventually selects the "best" in each trade.

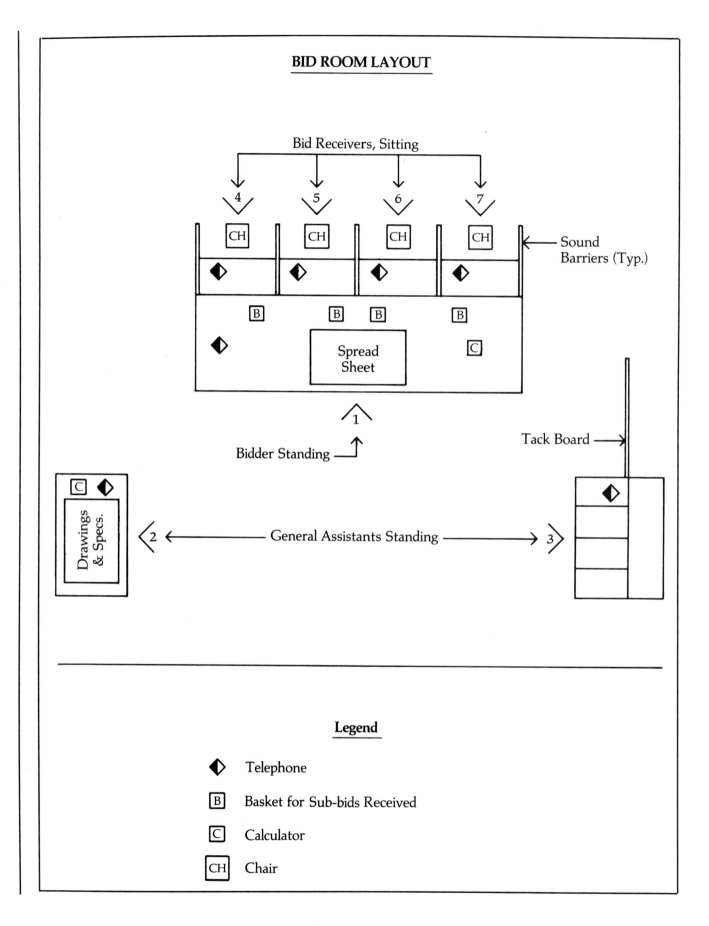

BID ROOM LAYOUT

Bid Receivers, Sitting

Sound Barriers (Typ.)

Spread Sheet

Bidder Standing

Tack Board

Drawings & Specs.

General Assistants Standing

Legend

◆ Telephone

B Basket for Sub-bids Received

C Calculator

CH Chair

Figure 5.T2

An assistant, position III, files the quotation sheets for convenient reference and assists the bidder in the analysis of the numerous minor trades. A phone is available to ask subs specific questions.

An assistant, position IV, analyzes and compares the more complicated sub-bids, such as structural steel, mechanical, and electrical, and then prepares budget figures for reasons explained in Sec. 2.14, Budgets, Plug-in-Figures, and Allowances. A phone is available for out-going research calls.

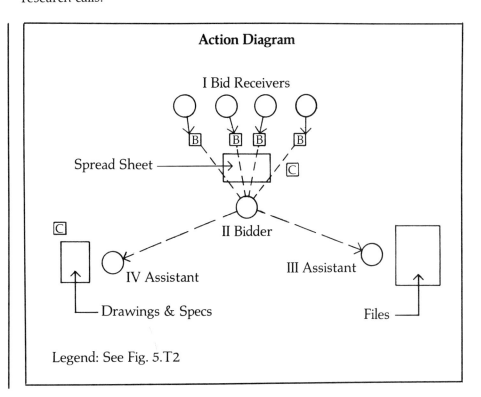

Figure 5.T3

Appendix U: Glossary and Abbreviations

Many expressions in the construction industry are idiomatic and cannot be found in most dictionaries. The most commonly used idioms as well as ordinary and technical terms are listed below in alphabetical order.

A

Activity Any portion of construction work, regardless of size; for instance, window cleaning, installing door frames, or the entire electrical trade.

A&E The designing architect or engineer. The term applies even if there is only one or the other. (See also *Sponsor*.)

Addendum A written change made by the A&E to the drawings and specs *prior* to bidding.

Allowance A money amount allotted to an item in lieu of an estimated amount.

Arithmetic (See *Math*.)

B

Back-up figures The detailed calculations that produce unit prices.

Ballpark figure A rough estimate.

Bare cost The total estimated cost of a project before the bidder's markup for overhead and profit.

Bid A formal offering to do construction work for a monetary consideration.

Bidder A construction company offering a bid; the person in charge of the company's bidding procedure.

Bid assembly The compiling of all estimates, prices, and sub-bids to produce a bid.

Bid package All drawings, specifications, documents, estimates, paperwork bid forms, and bid bonds relevant to a construction project. A contract is based on the bid package.

Bid results The display of all the bids on a project.

Break down (verb) To separate a project into parts.

Breakdown (noun) The actual list of parts of a project.

Brokered project A project completely sublet.

Budget A rough estimate of a subtrade.

Buy a job Accept a construction contract at bare cost or below.

C

Calcs Engineer's formal mathematical analysis of loads.

Calculate (verb) To do mathematical work; to seek a numerical value.

Calculation (noun) The product or result of math work.

Category One of the divisions of the breakdown, smaller than a trade.

Change order A formal change to the drawings and/or specs *after* the bidding.

Company The construction organization represented by the bidder.

Complimentary bid A bid intentionally high.

Computation (noun) Same as calculation, but more formal.

Compute (verb) Same as calculate, but more formal.

Contingency A percentage to be added for unknown or unexpected costs.

Cost Total expenditure in dollars proved *after* the completion of a project.

Coverage Dependable estimates or firm bids for portions of a construction project.

Craft Synonymous with trade, but implies a trade of above average skill.

Cut Reduce a cost item.

D

Demo Short for "demolition."

Drawings All of the sheets of illustrations that graphically portray the sponsor's concept of the project. (See also *Plans*.)

E

Educated guess The guess of an experienced person. (Also called a "guesstimate.")

Element The smallest division of a breakdown.

Estimate (both verb and noun) A time/cost prediction; the act of preparing an estimate; the estimate itself.

Extension The product of a quantity multiplied by a unit price; the completion of a mathematical equation.

Extra Work added to a project after the contract is let.

F

Field Two meanings: (1) occupation such as a trade, profession, or specialty; (2) the actual construction site.

Figures Numbers, digits, or symbols for quantities or cost values.

Figuring Calculating, computing, or working with numbers.

Firm Price Promise to do work for a guaranteed price.

Fringe benefits An employment benefit given in addition to regular wages or salary. These benefits may be paid directly to the employee or may be paid by the employer to various agencies on behalf of the employees.

G

Grade Three meanings: (1) the elevation of the earth; (2) (verb) to move earth; (3) slope (usually in degrees).

H

Hashing over Discussing, debating, and revising estimates.

Hungry In need of work.

I

Item A subdivision of the breakdown, smaller than a category, but larger than an element.

J

Job Two meanings: (1) same as construction project; (2) any work.

Jobsite Within the property lines of a construction project.

L

Labor Any work performed by an employee.

Left on the table The dollar difference between the low bid and the next bid above.

Legitimate Ethical and legal.

Let or sublet Issue a contract for a portion of the project.

Line item Any item on a price out sheet and all of the quantities, unit prices, and extensions

Loaded Two meanings: (1) having no need for new work; (2) an item priced high.

Loose estimate One allowing for contingencies; a "safe" or high estimate.

Lump sum An item or category priced as a whole rather than broken down into its elements.

M

Material A quantity of one kind, such as lumber.

Materials A quantity composed of several kinds, such as forming materials.

Math Mathematics, calculating, computing, figuring, arithmetic.

Markup A contractor's overhead and profit.

Main divisions Two meanings: (1) general contractor's work; (2) each subcontractor's work.

N

Neat Idiom for exact dimensions; i.e., excavation to width of footing.

Negotiating Arriving at an agreement by bargaining.

O

Overhead The costs to conduct business, not direct job costs; included in bidder's markup.

Overrun (1) The amount by which an item costs more than estimated. (2) The amount a quantity increases over the estimated quantity.

Owner The person (or institution) who initiates the project, furnishes the concept, the land, and the funds, and holds title of ownership. (See also *Sponsor.*)

P

Pickup The amount by which an estimate for an item is higher than the actual cost; savings; underrun.

Plans Drawings in *plan* view. A portion of a total set of drawings. (See *Drawings.*)

Plug-in A temporary figure in an estimate price out sheet to be used until a more dependable one is obtained.

Precon Contraction for "preconstruction meeting."

Preliminary estimate A rough estimate made in an early stage of the design work, or prior to receipt of firm bids.

Prices Quotations; dollar values used in an estimate before actual costs are proved.

Price out (verb) The activity of applying dollar values to the items in a take-off.

Price-out (noun) The final estimate sheet showing all the dollar values.

Prime bid A bid for the *total* project; general contractor's bid rather than a subcontractor's bid.

Procure To obtain or receive, as a construction contract.

Production Quantity of work performed, usually related to a time period, such as square feet per hour (sf/hr).

Project A construction job, planned or under way, but not completed.

Prorate Distribute proportionately; divide by ratio.

Q

Quantities Measured amounts of building materials.

Quantity survey Same as take-off, but more formal. (See *Take-off.*)

Quote (verb) To make an offer at a guaranteed price.

Quotation (noun) The price as quoted.

R

Range The difference between prices, costs, estimates, and bids.

Rebar Short for "reinforcing steel."

Rough estimate An estimate made without detailed investigation.

S

Sharp pencil A great effort to be competitive through accuracy in estimating.

Slack The amount allowed for contingency in an estimate. (See *Loose estimate.*)

Specs Contraction of "specifications."

Sponsor Any person or institution representing the owner. (See *Owner.*)

Spread Same as range; the difference between prices or bids.

Spread sheet Large, wide sheet with many columns that is used to tabulate all estimates and sub-bids when putting a bid together. (See *Bid Assembly.*)

Sub Contraction of "subcontractor."

Sub-bid A bid offered by a subcontractor.

Sublet Issue a contract to a subcontractor.

Submit the bid Deliver a bid to a sponsor. (See *Tender.*)

Successful bid A bid that is accepted by a sponsor for award of contract; a low bid (assuming that there will be an award of contract).

Super Contraction of "superintendent."

T

Take off (verb) The activity of determining quantities from drawings and specifications. (See *Quantity survey.*)

Take-off (noun) The actual quantity lists.

Tender A formal offer of a bid. (See *Submit the bid.*)

Tight Opposite of loose; an estimate that does not allow for contingencies and that has no slack.

Trade A subdivision of a breakdown, composed of workmen specializing in a particular skill.

U

Underrun (1) Opposite of overrun; same as pickup; the amount that an actual cost is less than the estimate. (2) Decrease in estimated quantity

Unit costs The actual costs of items or materials when work has been completed.

Unit prices The estimated or quoted prices given prior to the start of construction. (These prices are yet to be "proved.")

W

Work Physical exertion toward some construction objective; the actual accomplishment of a construction objective.

Workman One who performs the work of any trade. (See *Work*.)

Work capacity The greatest volume in number and/or size of construction projects that a contractor can manage efficiently without increasing the overhead costs.

Work sheet The paper on which the calculations supporting the final estimate are recorded.

Abbreviations

Because designers, spec writers, and others vary somewhat in their abbreviations, each customarily provides an individual list as a part of the sponsor's bid package. The following list is typical of the abbreviations used in the construction industry. Periods were deliberately omitted except in cases where they are needed for clarity.

A

ab	anchor bolt
a.c.	asphaltic concrete
a/c	air conditioning
A&E	architect & engineer
al	aluminum
alt	alternative
appr.	approximate
arch.	architect

B

bbl	barrel
bd	board
bldg	building
blk	block
blkg	blocking
bm	beam
b.m.	bench mark

C

cal	calendar
carp	carpenter
cb	concrete block
cf	cubic foot (feet)
cfm	cubic ft/min
chr	crew-hour
ci	cast iron
c. in.	cubic in

cip	cast-in-place
cir	circle
circum	circumference
cl	center line
clr	clear
col	column
conc	concrete
const	construction
cont	continuous
contr	contractor
cov'g	covering
ctr	center
CWT	hundred weight
cy	cubic yard

D

deg	degree
demo	demolition
det	detail
DF	Douglas Fir
diam	diameter
dim	dimension
disp	disposal
dp	deep
dr	door
drg	drawing

E

ea.	each
elec	electrical
elev	elevation
engr	engineer
equip	equipment
etc.	et cetera
excav	excavation
exist'g	existing
exp	expansion
ext	exterior

F

fb	fringe benefits
fin	finish
flr	floor
foun.	foundation
ft	foot
ftg	footing

G

ga	gauge
gal	gallon
galv	galvanize
gen	general
grd	grade
gyp	gypsum

H

hdwe	hardware
horiz	horizontal
hp	horsepower
hr	hour
ht	height
hyd	hydraulic

I

id	inside diameter
in.	inch
ins	insurance
insul	insulation
int	interior
irrig	irrigation

J

jst	joist
jt	joint

L

lab	labor
lam	laminated

(continued)

lb	pound
ld	load
lf	linear foot
lg	long
lin	linear
L.S.	lump sum
lt	light

M

mach	machine
max	maximum
mb	machine bolt
Mbf	thousand board feet
meas	measure
mech	mechanical
membr	membrane
met	metal
mhr	man-hour
min	minute
min'm	minimum
misc	miscellaneous
mat'l	material

N

nic	not in contract
No.	number
nts	not to scale

O

oc	on center
od	outside diameter
opp	opposite

P

PC	Portland cement
perim	perimeter
plbg	plumbing
plt	plate
prec	precast
prestr	prestressed
ptg	painting
pt'n	partition

R

r	radius
ref	reference
reinf	reinforcing
req'd	required
Rwd	Redwood

S

Sec.	Section
sec	second
sf	square foot
sht	sheet
sim	similar
s. in.	square inch
specs	specifications
std	standard
stl	steel
struc	structural
sym	symmetrical

T

temp	temperature
thk	thick
tot	total
typ	typical

U

uon	unless otherwise noted

W

wdw	window
wp	waterproof
ws	waterstop
wt	weight

Y

yd	yard
yr	year
&	and
%	percent

INDEX